Operating Systems Foundations

with Linux on the Raspberry Pi

Operating Systems Foundations

with Linux on the Raspberry Pi

TEXTBOOK

Wim Vanderbauwhede

Jeremy Singer

arm Education Media

Contents

2. A Practical view of the Linux System

4. Process management

5. Process scheduling

6. Memory management

7. Concurrency and parallelism

8. Input/output

9. Persistent storage

10. Networking

11. Advanced topics

Foreword

In 1983, when I started modeling a RISC processor using a simulator written in BBC Basic on a BBC Microcomputer, I could hardly have conceived that there would be billions of Arm (then short for 'Acorn RISC Machine') processors all over the world within a few decades.

I expect Linus Torvalds has similar feelings, when he thinks back to the early days, crafting a prototype operating system for his i386 PC. Now Linux runs on a vast array of devices, from smartwatches to supercomputers. I am delighted that an increasing proportion of these devices are built around Arm processor cores.

In a more recent tale of runaway success, the Raspberry Pi single-board computer has far exceeded its designers' initial expectations. The Raspberry Pi Foundation thought they might sell one thousand units, 'maybe 10 thousand in our wildest dreams.' With sales figures now around 20 million, the Raspberry Pi is firmly established as Britain's best-selling computer.

This textbook aims to bring these three technologies together—Arm, Linux, and Raspberry Pi. The authors' ambitious goal is to 'make Operating Systems fun again.' As a professor in one of the UK's largest university Computer Science departments, I am well aware that modern students demand engaging learning materials. Dusty 900-page textbooks with occasional black and white illustrations are not well received. Today's learners require interactive content, gaining understanding through practical experience and intuitive analogies. My observation applies to students in traditional higher education, as well as those pursuing blended and fully online education. I am confident this innovative textbook will meet the needs of the next generation of Computer Science students.

While the modern systems software stack has become large and complex, the fundamental principles are unchanging. Operating Systems must trade-off abstraction for efficiency. In this respect, Linux on Arm is particularly instructive. The authors do an excellent job of presenting Operating Systems concepts, with direct links to concrete examples of these concepts in Linux on the Raspberry Pi. Please don't just read this textbook – buy a Pi and try out the practical exercises as you go.

Was it Plutarch who said, 'The mind is not a vessel to be filled but a fire to be kindled'? We could translate this into the Operating Systems domain as follows: 'Learning isn't just reading source code; it's bootstrapping machines.' I hope that you enjoy all these activities, as you explore Operating Systems with Linux on Arm using your Raspberry Pi.

Steve Furber CBE FRS FREng
ICL Professor of Computer Engineering
The University of Manchester, UK
February 2019

Disclaimer

The design examples and related software files included in this book are created for educational purposes and are not validated to the same quality level as Arm IP products. Arm Education Media and the author do not make any warranties of these designs.

Note

When we developed the material for this textbook, we worked with Raspberry Pi 3B boards. However, all our practical exercises should work on other generations and variants of Raspberry Pi devices, including the more recent Raspberry Pi 4.

Preface

Introduction

Modern computer devices are fabulously complicated both in terms of the processor hardware and the software they run.

At the heart of any modern computer device sits the operating system. And if the device is a smartphone, IoT node, datacentre server or supercomputer, then the operating system is very likely to be Linux: about half of consumer devices run Linux; the vast majority of smartphones worldwide (86%) run Android, which is built on the Linux kernel. Of the top one million web servers, 98% run Linux. Finally, the top 500 fastest supercomputers in the world all run Linux.

On the hardware side, Arm has a 95% market share in smartphone and tablet processors as well as being used in the majority of Internet of Things (IoT) devices such as webcams, wireless routers, etc. and embedded devices in general.

Since its creation by Linus Torvalds in 1991, the efforts of thousands of people, most of them volunteers, have turned Linux into a state-of-the-art, flexible and powerful operating system, suitable for any system from tiny IoT devices to the most powerful supercomputers.

Meanwhile, in roughly the same period, the Arm processor range has expanded to cover an equally wide gamut of systems and devices, including the remarkably successful Raspberry Pi.

So if you want to learn about Operating Systems but keep a practical, real-world focus, then this book is an ideal starting point. This book will help you answer questions such as:

- What is a file, and why is the file concept so important in Linux?

- What is scheduling and how can knowledge of Linux scheduling help you create a high-throughput video processor or a mission-critical real-time system?

- What are POSIX threads, and how can the Linux kernel assist you in making your multithreaded applications faster and more responsive?

- How does the Linux kernel support networking, and how do you create network clients and servers?

- How does the Arm hardware assist the Linux kernel in managing memory and how does understanding memory management make you a better programmer?

The aim of this book is to provide a practical introduction to the foundations of modern operating systems, with a particular focus on GNU/Linux and the Arm platform. Our unique perspective is that we explain operating systems theory and concepts but ground them in practical use through illustrative examples of their implementation in GNU/Linux, as well as making the connection with the Arm hardware supporting the OS functionality.

Is this book suitable for you?

This book does not require prior knowledge of operating systems, but some familiarity with command-line operations in a GNU/Linux system is expected. We discuss technical details of operating systems, and we use source code to illustrate many concepts. Therefore, you need to know C and Python, and you need to be familiar with basic data structures such as arrays, queues, stacks and trees.

This textbook is ideal for a one-semester course introducing the concepts and principles underlying modern operating systems. It complements the Arm online courses in *Real-Time Operating Systems Design and Programming*, and *Embedded Linux*.

Online additional material

The companion web site of the book (www.dcs.gla.ac.uk/operating-system-foundations) contains:

▦ Source code for all original code snippets listed in the book;

▦ Answers to questions and exercises;

▦ Lab materials;

▦ Additional content;

▦ Additional teaching materials;

▦ Further reading.

Target platform

This textbook focuses on the Raspberry Pi 3, an Arm Cortex-A53 platform running Linux. We use the Raspbian GNU/Linux distribution. However, the book does not specifically depend on this platform and distribution, except for the exercises.

If you don't own a Raspberry Pi 3, you can use the QEMU emulator which supports the Raspberry Pi 3.

Software development environment

The code examples in this book are either in C or Python 3. We assume that the reader has access to a Linux system with an installation of Python, a C compiler, the *make* build tool and the git version control tool.

Structure

The structure of this textbook is based on our many years of teaching operating systems courses at undergraduate and masters level, taking into account the feedback provided by the reviewers of the text. The content of the text is closely aligned to the Computing Curricula 2001 Computing Science report recommendations for teaching Operating Systems, published by the Joint Task Force of the IEEE Computing Society and the Association for Computing Machinery (ACM).

The book is organized into eleven chapters.

Chapters 1 and 2 provide alternate introductory views to operating systems.

Chapter 1 *A memory-centric system model* presents a top-down view. In this chapter, we introduce a number of abstract models for processor-based systems. We use Python code to describe the models and only use simple data structures and functions. The purpose is to help the student understand that in a processor-based system, *all* actions fundamentally reduce to operations on *addresses*. The models are gradually being refined as the chapter advances, and by the end, the model integrates the basic operating system functionality into a runnable Python-based processor model.

Chapter 2 *A practical view of the Linux system* approaches the Linux system from a practical perspective: what actually happens when we boot and run the system, how does it work and what is required to make it work. We first introduce the essential concepts and techniques that the student needs to know in order to understand the overall system, and then we discuss the system itself. The aim of this part is to help the student answer questions such as "what happens when the system boots?" or "how does Linux support graphics?". This is not a how-to guide, but rather, provides the student with the background knowledge behind how-to guides.

In Chapter 3 *Hardware architecture*, we discuss the hardware on which the operating system runs, the hardware support for operating systems (dedicated registers, MMU, DMA, interrupt architecture, relevant details about the bus/NoC architecture, ...), the memory subsystem (caches, TLB), high-level language support, boot subsystem and boot sequence. The purpose is to provide the student with a useable mental model for the hardware system and to explain the need for an operating system and how the hardware supports the OS. In particular, we study the Linux view on the hardware system.

The next seven chapters form the core of the book, each of these introduces a core Operating System concept.

In Chapter 4, *Process management*, we introduce the process abstraction. We outline the state that needs to be encapsulated. We walk through the typical lifecycle of a process from forking to termination. We review the typical operations that will be performed on a process.

Chapter 5 *Process scheduling* discusses how the OS schedules processes on a processor. This includes the rationale for scheduling, the concept of context switching, and an overview of scheduling policies (FCFS, priority, ...) and scheduler architectures (FIFO, multilevel feedback queues, priorities, ...). The Linux scheduler is studied in detail.

While memory itself is remarkably straightforward, OS architects have built lots of abstraction layers on top. Principally, these abstractions serve to improve performance and/or programmability. In Chapter 6 *Memory management*, we review caches (in hardware and software) to improve access speed. We go into detail about virtual memory to improve the management of physical memory resource. We will provide highly graphical descriptions of address translation, paging, page tables, page faults, swapping, etc. We explore standard schemes for page replacement, copy-on-write, etc. We will examine concrete examples in Arm architecture and Linux OS.

In Chapter 7, *Concurrency and parallelism*, we discuss how the OS supports concurrency and how the OS can assist in exploiting hardware parallelism. We define concurrency and parallelism and discuss how they relate to threads and processes. We discuss the key issue of resource sharing, covering locking, semaphores, deadlock and livelock. We look at OS support for concurrent and parallel programming via POSIX threads and present an overview of practical parallel programming techniques such as OpenMP, MPI and OpenCL.

Chapter 8 *Input/output* presents the OS abstraction of an IO device. We review device interfacing, covering topics like Polling, Interrupts and DMA. We will investigate a range of device types, to highlight their diverse features and behavior. We will cover hardware registers, memory mapping and coprocessors. Further, we will examine the ways in which devices are exposed to programmers. We will review the structure of a typical device driver.

Chapter 9 *Persistent storage* focuses on data storage. We outline the range of use cases for file systems. We explain how the raw hardware (block- and sector-based 2d storage, etc.) is abstracted at the OS level. We talk about mapping high-level concepts like files, directories, permissions, etc., down to physical entities. We review allocation, space management, and recovery from failure. We present a case study of a Linux file system. We also discuss Windows-style FAT, since this is how USB bulk storage operates.

Chapter 10 *Networking* introduces networking from an OS perspective: why is networking treated differently from other types of IO, what are the OS requirements to support the OSI stack. We introduce socket programming with a focus of the role the OS plays (e.g. zero-copy buffers, file abstraction, supporting multiple clients, ...).

Finally, Chapter 11 *Advanced topics* discusses a number of concepts that go beyond the material of the previous chapters: The first part of this chapter deals with customisation of Linux for Embedded Systems, Linux on systems without MMU, and datacentre level operating systems. The second part discusses the security of Linux-based systems, focusing on validation and verification of OS components and the analysis of recent security exploits.

We hope that you enjoy both reading our book and doing the exercises – especially if you are trying them on the Raspberry Pi. Please do let us know what you think about our work and how we could improve it by sending your comments to Arm Education Media edumedia@arm.com

Jeremy Singer and **Wim Vanderbauwhede**, 2019

About the Authors

Wim Vanderbauwhede
School of Computing Science, University of Glasgow, UK

Prof. Wim Vanderbauwhede is Professor in Computing Science at the School of Computing Science of the University of Glasgow. He has been teaching and researching operating systems for over a decade. His research focuses on high-level programming, compilation, and architectures for heterogeneous manycore systems and FPGAs, with a special interest in power-efficient computing and scientific High-Performance Computing (HPC). He is the author of the book 'High-Performance Computing Using FPGAs'. He received his Ph.D. in Electrotechnical Engineering with Specialisation in Physics from the University of Gent, Belgium in 1996. Before moving into academic research, Prof. Vanderbauwhede worked as an ASIC Design Engineer and Senior Technology R&D Engineer for Alcatel Microelectronics.

Jeremy Singer
School of Computing Science, University of Glasgow, UK

Dr. Jeremy Singer is a Senior Lecturer in Systems at the School of Computing Science of the University of Glasgow. His main research theme involves programming language runtimes, with particular interests in garbage collection and manycore parallelism. He leads the Federated Raspberry Pi Micro-Infrastructure Testbed (FRµIT) team, investigating next-generation edge compute platforms. He received his Ph.D. from the University of Cambridge Computer Laboratory in 2006. Singer and Vanderbauwhede also collaborated in the design of the FutureLearn 'Functional Programming in Haskell' massive open online course.

Acknowledgements

The authors would like to thank the following people for their help:

- Khaled Benkrid, who made this book possible.

- Ashkan Tousimojarad, who originally suggested the project.

- Melissa Good, Jialin Dou and Michael Shuff who kept us on track and assisted us with the process.

- The reviewers at Arm who provided valuable feedback on our drafts.

- Tony Garnock-Jones, Dejice Jacob, Richard Mortier, Colin Perkins, and other colleagues who commented on early versions of the text.

- Steve Furber, for his kind endorsement of the book.

- Lovisa Sundin, for her help with illustrations.

- Jim Garside, Kristian Hentschel, Simon McIntosh-Smith, Magnus Morton and Michèle Weiland for kindly allowing us to use their photographs.

- The countless volunteers who made the Linux kernel what it is today.

Chapter 1

A Memory-centric
system model

1.1 Overview

In this chapter, we will introduce a number of abstract memory-centric models for processor-based systems. We will use Python code to describe the models and only use simple data structures and functions. The models are abstract in the sense that we do not build the processor system starting from its physical building blocks (transistors, logic gates, etc.), but rather, we model it in a functional way.

The purpose is to help you understand that in a processor-based system, *all* actions fundamentally reduce to operations on *addresses*. This is a very important point: *every observable action in a processor-based system is the result of writing to or reading from an address location.*

In particular, this includes all peripherals of the system, such as the network card, keyboard, and display.

What you will learn
After you have studied the material in this chapter, you will be able to:

1. Discuss the importance of state and the address space in a processor-based system.

2. Create a processor-based system model in a high-level language.

3. Implement basic operating system concepts such as time slicing in machine code.

4. Explain how hardware and software features of a processor-based system are designed to handle I/O, concurrency, and performance.

1.2 Modeling the system

- A microprocessor is driven by a *clock*.

- Our model will describe the *actions* at every tick of the clock using *functions*.

- We will model the system through its *state*, represented as a simple *data structure*.

By "state," we mean information that is persistent, i.e., some form of memory. This is not limited to actual computer memory. For example, if our system controls a robot arm, then the position of the arm is part of the state of the system.

1.2.1 The simplest possible model
We start our system model by stating that the action of the processor modifies the system state:

```Python
systemState = processorAction(systemState)
```

In practice, the system also interacts with the outside world through peripherals such as the keyboard, network interface, etc., generally called "I/O devices", storage devices such as disks, etc. Let's just call these types of actions to modify the state 'non-processor actions'. Adding this to our model, we get:

Listing 1.2.1: System state with non-processor actions *Python*

```
1    systemState = nonProcessorAction(systemState)
2    systemState systemState = processorAction(systemState)
```

In a real system, these actions happen at the same time (we call concurrent actions), so one of the questions (that we will address in detail in Chapters 7, 'Concurrency and parallelism') is how to make sure that the system state does not become undetermined as a result of concurrent actions. But first, let's look in a bit more detail at the system state.

1.2.2 What is this 'system state'?

We say that the processor "modifies the system state", so let's take a closer look at this system state. From the point of view of the processor, the system state is simply a *fixed-size array of unsigned integers*. Nothing more than that. In C syntax, we can express this as shown in Listing 1.2.2:

Listing 1.2.2: System state as C array *C*

```
1    int systemState[STATE_SZ]
```

Which means that manipulation of the system state, and by consequence, anything that happens in a processor-based system boils down to modifying this array.

So, what does this array actually represent? It represents *all of the memory in the system*, not just the actual system memory (DRAM, *Dynamic Random Access Memory*) but including the I/O devices and other peripherals such as disks. In system terms, this is known as the 'physical address space', and we will discuss this in detail in Chapter 6, "Memory management."[1]

In other words, the system state is composed of the states of all the system components, for example for a system with a keyboard **kbd**, network interface card **nic**, solid state disk **ssd**, graphics processing unit **gpu**, and random access memory **ram**:

```
systemState = ramState + kbdState + nicState + ssdState + gpuState          Python
```

Where **ramState**, **kbdState**, **nicState**, etc. are all fixed-size arrays of integers.

However, it could of course equally be:

```
systemState = ssdState + kbdState + nicState + ramState + gpuState          Python
```

The above are two examples of *address space layouts*. The description of the purpose, size, and position of the address regions for memory and peripherals is called the *address map*. As an illustration, the Arm address map for A-class systems [1] is shown in Figure 1.1.

---

[1] As our model focuses on Arm-based systems, we do not discuss port-mapped I/O.

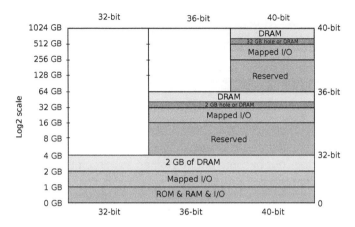

Figure 1.1: Arm 40-bit address map.

Figure 1.1. If the address size is 32 bits, we can address 2^{32} = 4GB of memory. We see from the figure that different regions are reserved for different purposes, e.g., the second GB is memory mapped I/O, and the upper 2 GB are random access memory (DRAM).

1.2.3 Refining non-processor actions

Using the more detailed state from above, we can split the non-processor actions into per-peripheral actions, so that our model becomes:

```python
1    kbdState=kbdAction(kbdState)
2    nicState=nicAction(nicState)
3    ssdState=ssdAction(ssdState)
4    gpuState=gpuAction(gpuState)
5    systemState = ramState+kbdState+nicState+diskState+gpuState
6    systemState = processorAction(systemState)
```

Listing 1.2.3: Model with per-peripheral actions — Python

Each of these actions only affects the state of the peripheral; the rest of the system state remains unaffected.

1.2.4 Interrupt requests

Let's return now to the potential problem of state modified by concurrent actions. The way we just separated the state offers a possible solution. Now we can create a kind of notification mechanism which lets the processor know that an outside action has modified the state[2].

This is exactly what happens in real systems, and the mechanisms used are called *interrupts*. We will discuss this in detail in Chapter 8, 'Input/output', but it is useful to add an interrupt mechanism to our abstract model.

A peripheral can send an *interrupt request* (IRQ) to the processor. We will model the interrupt request as a boolean flag which is returned by every peripheral action together with its state (as a tuple). The processor

---

[2] We could also let the processor check if the state of a peripheral was changed before acting on it. This approach is called polling and will be discussed in Chapter 8, 'Input/output'.

action receives an array of these interrupt requests and uses the array index to identify the peripheral that raised the interrupt ('raising an interrupt' in our model means setting the boolean flag to `True`).

In practice, the mechanism is more complicated because many peripherals can raise multiple different interrupt requests depending on the condition. Typically, a dedicated peripheral called *interrupt controller* is used to manage the interrupts from the various devices.

Note that the interrupt mechanism is purely a notification mechanism: it does not stop the processor from modifying the peripheral state, all it does is notify the processor that the peripheral unilaterally changed its state. So in principle, the peripheral could still be modifying its state at the very same time that the processor is modifying it. In what follows, we simply assume that this cannot happen, i.e., if a peripheral is modifying its state, then the processor can't change it and vice versa. A possible model for this is that the peripheral state change and the interrupt request are happening at the same time and that the processor always needs to process the request before making a state change.

Listing 1.2.4: Model with interrupt requests   *Python*

```python
1    (kbdState,kbdIrq)=kbdAction(kbdState)
2    ...
3
4    irqs=[kbdIrq,...]
5
6    systemState = ramState+kbdState+nicState+diskState+gpuState
7    (systemState,irqs) = processorAction(systemState,irqs)
```

We will see in the next section how the processor handles interrupts.

1.2.5 An important peripheral: the timer

A timer is a peripheral that counts time in terms of the system clock. It can be programmed to 'fire' periodically at given intervals, or after a one-off interval. When a timer 'fires' it raises an interrupt request. The timer is particularly important because it is the principal mechanism used by the operating system to track the progress of time and allows it to schedule tasks.

```python
(timerState, timerIrq)=timerAction(timerState)
```
Python

1.3 Bare-bones processor model

To gain more insight into the way the processor modifies the system state, we will build a simple processor model which models how the processor changes the system state at every clock cycle. The purpose of this model is to make the introduction of the more abstract model in Section 1.4 easier to understand.

1.3.1 What does the processor do?

The processor is a machine to modify the system state. You need to know that ...

- A key feature of a processor is the ability to run arbitrary *programs*.

- A program consists of a series of *instructions*.

■ An instruction determines how the processor interacts with the system through the address space: it can *read* values at given addresses, *compute* new values and addresses, and *write* values to given addresses.

Note that the program is itself part of the system state. The program running on the processor can control which part of the entire program code to access. This is what allows us to create an operating system.

1.3.2 Processor internal state: registers

Although in principle, a processor could directly manipulate the system state, this is not practical because DRAM memory access is quite slow. Therefore, in practice, processors have a dedicated internal state known as the *register file*, an array of words called *registers* which you can consider as a small but very fast memory. The register file is separate from the rest of the system state (it is a 'separate address space'). This means we have to refine our model to separate the register file from the rest of the system state, which we will call `systemState`. We do this using a tuple[3]:

```python
(systemState,irqs,registers) = processorAction(systemState,irqs,registers)     Python
```

For convenience, registers often have names (mnemonics). For example, Figure 1.2 shows the core AArch32 register set of the Arm Cortex-A53 [2].

There are 16 ordinary registers (and five special ones which we have omitted). Registers R0-R12 are the 'General-purpose registers'. Then there are three registers with special names: the Stack Pointer (SP), the Link Register (LR) and the Program Counter (PC).

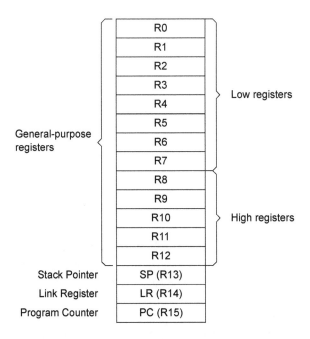

Figure 1.2: Arm Cortex-A53 AArch32 register set.

---

[3] Alternatively, we could make the registers part of the system state similar to the state of the peripherals. Our choice is purely for convenience because it makes it easier to manipulate the registers in the Python code.

1.3.3 Processor instructions

A typical processor can perform a wide range of instructions on memory addresses and/or register values. We will use a simple list-based notation for all instructions. We will use the (uppercase) Arm mnemonics for registers and instructions; in Python, these are simply variables; their definitions can be found in the code repository in file abstract_system_constants.py.

We will assume that all instructions take up to three registers as arguments, for example

```
add_instr = [ADD,R3,R1,R2]                                  Python
```

which means that the result of **ADD** operating on registers **R1** and **R2** is stored in register **R3**.

Apart from computational (arithmetic and logic) instructions we also introduce the instructions **LDR**, e.g.

```
load_instr = [LDR,R1,R2]                                    Python
```

and **STR**, e.g.

```
store_instr=[STR,R1,R2]                                     Python
```

which respectively load the content of a memory address stored in **R2** into register **R1** and store the content of register **R1** at the address location given in **R2**.

We also have **MOV**, which copies data between two registers, e.g.

```
set_instr = [MOV,R1,R2]                                     Python
```

will set the content of **R1** to the content of **R2**.

We have a special non-Arm instruction called **SET**, which takes a register and a value as arguments, e.g.

```
set_instr = [SET,R1,42]                                     Python
```

will set the content of **R1** to **42**.

We also need some instructions to control the flow of the program, such as branches (**B**)

```
goto_instr = [B,R1]                                         Python
```

where **R1** contains the address of the target instruction in the program, and conditional branches (**CBZ**, 'Compare and Branch if Zero')

```
if_instr = [CBZ,R1,R2]                                      Python
```

where register **R1** contains the condition variable (0 or 1) and the program branches to the address in **R2** if **R1**=0 and continues on the next line otherwise. We also have **CBNZ**, 'Compare and Branch if Non-Zero'.

Finally, we have two instructions which take no arguments: **NOP** does nothing, and **WFI** stops the processor until an interrupt occurs.

1.3.4 Assembly language

To write instructions for actual processors, a similar, but more expressive, notation called *assembly language* is used. For example, consider the following program that reads two values from memory, stores them in registers, adds them, and writes the result back:

Listing 1.3.1: Example program   Python

```
1    [
2        [LDR,R1,R4],
3        [LDR,R2,R5],
4        [ADD,R3,R1,R2],
5        [STR,R3,R6]
6    ]
```

In the assembly language for the Arm processor [3], this code would look as follows:

Listing 1.3.2: Example Arm assembly program   Python

```
1    ldr    r1,    r4
2    ldr    r2,    r5
3    add    r3,    r1,    r2
4    str    r3,    r6
```

Assembly languages have many other features, such as a rich set of addressing mechanisms, labeling options, etc. However, for our current purpose, our simple function-based notation is sufficient. For more details, see, e.g., [4].

1.3.5 Arithmetic logic unit

The part of a processor that performs computations is known as the arithmetic logic unit (ALU). We can create a simple ALU in Python as follows:

Listing 1.3.3: ALU model   Python

```
1    from operator import *
2
3    alu = [
4        add,
5        sub,
6        mul,
7        ...
8    ]
```

This is simply an array of functions; more instructions can be added trivially.

1.3.6 Instruction cycle

A processor operates what is known as the instruction cycle or fetch-decode-execute cycle. We can define each of these operations as follows. First, we define **fetchInstruction**. This function fetches an instruction from memory. To determine which instruction to fetch, it uses a dedicated register known as the *program counter*, which has address **PC** in our register file. Then we also need to know where in our memory space, we can find the program code. We use **CODE** to denote the starting address of the program in the system state. After reading the instruction, we increment the program counter, so it points to the next instruction in the program.

Listing 1.3.4: Instruction fetch model · *Python*

```
1   def fetchInstruction(registers,systemState):
2       # get the program counter
3       pctr = registers[PC]
4       # get the corresponding instruction
5       ir = systemState[CODE+pctr]
6       # increment the program counter
7       registers[PC]+=1
8       return ir
```

The instruction is stored in the temporary *instruction register* (ir in our code). The processor now has to decode this instruction, i.e., extract the register addresses and instruction opcode from the instruction word. Remember that the state stores unsigned integers, so an instruction is encoded as an unsigned integer. The details of the implementation can be found in the repository in file abstract_system_cpu_decode.py. For this discussion, the important point is that the function returns a tuple **opcode,args** where **args** is a tuple containing the decoded arguments (registers, addresses or constants). In the code, if an element of a tuple is unused, we used _ as variable name to indicate this.

Listing 1.3.5: Instruction decode model · *Python*

```
1   def decodeInstruction(ir):
2       ...
3       return (opcode,args)
```

Finally, the processor executes the decoded instruction. In our model, we implement instruction using a function. The load instruction (mnemonic **LDR**) is simply an array read operation, store (mnemonic **STR**) is simply an array write operation. The **B** and **CBZ** branching instructions only modify the program counter. By using an array of functions **alu** as discussed above, the ALU execution is very simple too. The complete code can be found in the repository in file abstract_- system_cpu_execute.py.

Listing 1.3.6: Individual instruction execute model · *Python*

```
1   def doLDR(registers,systemState,args):
2       (r1,addr,_)=args
3       registers[r1] = systemState[addr]
4       return (registers,systemState)
5
6   def doSTR(registers,systemState,args)
7       (r1,addr,_)=args
8       systemState[addr]=registers[r1]
9       return (registers,systemState)
```

```
10
11   def doB(registers,args):
12       (_,addr,_)=args
13       registers[PC] = addr
14       return registers
15
16   def doCBZ(registers,args):
17       (r1,addr1,addr2)=args
18       if registers[r1]:
19           registers[PC] = addr1
20       else:
21           registers[PC] = addr2
22       return registers
23
24   def doALU(instr,registers,args):
25       (r1,r2,r3)=args
26       registers[r3] = alu[instr](registers[r1],registers[r2])
27       return registers
```

The **executeInstruction** function simply calls the appropriate handler function via a condition on the instruction:

Listing 1.3.7: Instruction execute model   Python

```
1    def executeInstruction(instr,args,registers,systemState):
2        if instr==LDR:
3            (registers,systemState)=doLDR(registers,systemState,args)
4        elif instr==STR:
5            (registers,systemState)=doSTR(registers,systemState,args)
6        elif ...
7        else:
8            registers = doALU(instr,registers,args)
9        return (registers,systemState)
```

1.3.7 Bare bones processor model
With these definitions, we can build a very simple processor model:

Listing 1.3.8: Simple processor model   Python

```
1    def processorAction(systemState,registers):
2        # fetch the instruction
3        ir = fetchInstruction(registers,systemState)
4        # decode the instruction
5        (instr,args) = decodeInstruction(ir)
6        # execute the instruction
7        (registers,systemState)= executeInstruction(instr,args,registers,systemState)
8        return (systemState,registers)
```

In the source code, we have also provided an **encodeInstruction** in file abstract_system_en- coder.py. We can encode an instruction using this function, assuming the mnemonics have been defined:

Listing 1.3.9: Instruction encoding   *Python*

```
1    # multiply value in R1 with value in R2
2    # store result in R3
3    instr=[MUL,R3,R1,R2]
4
5    iw=encodeInstruction(instr)
```

Now you can run this as follows:

Listing 1.3.10: Running the code   *Python*

```
1    # Set the program counter relative to the location of the code
2    registers[PC]=0
3    # Set the registers
4    registers[R1]=6
5    registers[R2]=7
6
7    # Store the encoded instructions in memory
8    systemState[CODE] = iw
9
10   # Now run this
11   (systemState,registers) = processorAction(systemState,registers)
12
13   # Inspect the result
14   print( registers[R3] )
15   # prints 42
```

You can find the complete Python code for this bare-bones model in the folder bare-bones-model, have a look and try it out. The file to run is bare-bones-model/abstract_- system_model.py.

1.4 Advanced processor model

The bare-bones model is missing a number of features that are essential to support an operating system; in this section, we introduce these features and add them to the model.

1.4.1 Stack support

A stack is a contiguous block of memory that is accessed in LIFO (last in, first out) fashion. Data is added to the top of the stack using a 'push' operation and taken from the top of stack using a 'pop' operation. Stacks are used to store temporary data, and they are commonly used to handle function calls. Most computer architectures include at least a register that is usually reserved for the stack pointer (e.g., as we have seen the Arm processor has a dedicated 'SP' register) as well as 'PUSH' and 'POP' instructions to access the stack. In our model, we will implement the stack as part of the RAM memory, and we define the push and pop instructions as in the Arm instruction set, for example:

Listing 1.4.1: Example stack instructions *Python*

```
1    push_pop=[
2    [PUSH,R1],
3    [POP,R2]
4    ]
```

would push the content of **R1** onto the stack and then pop it into **R2**. The **PUSH** and **POP** instructions are encoded similar to the **LDR** and **STR** memory operations. We extend the **executeInstruction** definition to support the stack with the following functions:

Listing 1.4.2: Push/pop implementation *Python*

```
1    def doPush(registers,systemState,args):
2            sptr = registers[SP]
3            (r1,_,_)=args
4            systemState[sptr]=registers[r1]
5            registers[SP]+=1
6            return (registers,systemState)
7
8    def doPop(registers,systemState,args):
9            sptr = registers[SP]
10           (r1,_,_)=args
11           registers[r1] = systemState[sptr]
12           registers[SP]-=1
13           return (registers,systemState)
```

1.4.2 Subroutine calls

One of the main reasons for having a stack is so that the processor can handle subroutine calls, and in particular, subroutines that call other subroutines or call themselves (recursive call). This is because whenever we call a subroutine, the code in the subroutine will overwrite the register file, so we need to store the registers somewhere before we call a subroutine.

To support this mechanism, most processors have instructions to change the control flow: a first instruction, the call instruction changes the program counter to the location of the subroutine to be called. A second instruction, the return instruction, returns the location after the subroutine call instruction. These instructions can use either the stack or a dedicated register to save the program counter.

In the Arm 32-bit instruction set the call and return instructions are usually implemented using BL and BX; the Arm convention is to store the return address in the link register LR, and we will use the same convention in our model. We extend the executeInstruction definition to support subroutine call and return as follows:

Listing 1.4.3: Call/return implementation *Python*

```
1    def doCall(registers,args):
2            pctr = registers[PC]
3            (_,sraddr,_)=args
4            registers[LR] = pctr
5            registers[PC]=sraddr
```

```
6              return registers
7
8    def doReturn(registers,args):
9              lreg = registers[LR]
10             registers[PC]=lreg
11             return registers
```

1.4.3 Interrupt handling

Now let's extend the processor model to support interrupts. When the processor receives an interrupt request, it must take some specific actions. These actions are simply special small programs called *interrupt handlers* or *interrupt service routines* (ISR). The processor uses a region of the main memory called the *interrupt vector table* (IVT) to link the interrupt requests to interrupt handlers.

How does the processor handle interrupts? On every clock tick (i.e., on every call to **processorAction** in our model), if an interrupt was raised, the processor has to run the corresponding ISR. In our model, this means the processor needs to inspect **irqs**, get the corresponding ISR from the **ivt** (which in our model is a slice of the **systemState** array), and execute it. So in fact, the call to the ISR is a normal subroutine call, but one that does not have a corresponding CALL instruction in the code. Before executing the ISR, the processor typically stores some register values on the stack, e.g., the Arm Cortex-M3 stores R0-R3, R12, PC, and LR [5]. According to the Arm Architecture Procedure Call Standard [6], the called subroutine is responsible for storing R4-R11. In our simple model, we only store the PC, extending it to support the AAPCS is a trivial exercise.

Listing 1.4.4: Interrupt handling   *Python*

```
1    def checkIrqs(registers,ivt,irqs):
2        idx=0
3        for irq in irqs:
4            if irq :
5                # Save the program counter in the link register
6                registers[LR] = registers[PC]
7                # Set program counter to ISR start address
8                registers[PC]=ivt[idx]
9                # Clear the interrupt request
10               irqs[idx]=False
11               break
12           idx+=1
13       return (registers,irqs)
```

1.4.4 Direct memory access

Another important component of a modern processor-based system is support for Direct Memory Access (DMA). This is a mechanism that allows peripherals to transfer data directly into the main memory without going through the processor registers. In Arm systems, the DMA controller unit is typically a peripheral (e.g., the PrimeCell DMA Controller), so we will implement our DMA model as a peripheral as well.

The principle of a DMA transfer is that the CPU initiates the transfer by writing to the DMA unit's registers, then runs other instructions while the transfer is in progress, and finally receives an interrupt from the DMA controller when the transfer is done.

Typically, a DMA transfer is a transfer of a large block of data, which would otherwise keep the processor occupied for a long time. In our simple model, the DMA controller has four registers:

- Source Address Register (DSR)

- Destination Address Register (DDR)

- Counter (DCO)

- Control Register (DCR)

This peripheral is different from the others in our model because it can manipulate the entire system state. In a way, we can view a DMA controller as a special type of processor that only performs memory transfer operations. The model implementation is:

```python
Listing 1.4.5: DMA model                                             Python
1    def dmaAction(systemState):
2        dmaIrq=0
3        # DMA is the start of the address space
4        # DCR values: 1 = do transfer, 0 = idle
5        if systemState[DMA+DCR]!=0:
6            if systemState[DMA+DCO]!=0:
7                ctr = systemState[DMA+DCO]
8                to_addr = systemState[DMA+DDR]+ctr
9                from_addr = systemState[DMA+DSR]+ctr
10               systemState[to_addr] = systemState[from_addr]
11               systemState[DMA+DCO]=-1
12           systemState[DMA+DCR]=0
13           dmaIrq=1
14       return (systemState,dmaIrq)
```

To initiate a memory transfer using the DMA controller, the processor writes the source and destination addresses to DSR and DDR, and the size of the transfer to DCO (the 'counter'). Then the status is set to 1 in the DCR. The DMA controller then starts the transfer and decrements the counter for every word transferred. When the counter reaches zero, an interrupt is raised (count-zero interrupt).

1.4.5 Complete cycle-based processor model
By including this interrupt support, the complete cycle-based processor model now becomes:

```python
Listing 1.4.6: Complete cycle-based processor model                  Python
1    def processorAction(systemState,irqs,registers):
2        ivt = systemState[IVT:IVTsz]
3        # Check for interrupts
4        (registers,irqs)=checkIrqs(registers,ivt,irqs)
5        # Fetch the instruction
6        ir = fetchInstruction(registers,systemState)
7        # Decode the instruction
8        (instr,args) = decodeInstruction(ir)
9        # Execute the instruction
10       (registers,systemState)= executeInstruction(instr,args,registers,systemState)
11       return (systemState,irqs,registers)
```

1.4.6 Caching

In an actual system, accessing DRAM memory requires many clock cycles. To limit the time spent in waiting for memory access, processors have a cache, a small but fast memory. For every memory read operation, first the processor checks if the data is present in the cache, and if so (this is called a 'cache hit') it uses that data rather than accessing the DRAM. Otherwise ('cache miss') it will fetch the data from memory and store it in the cache.

For a single-core processor, memory write operations are treated in the same way. Real-life caches are very complicated and will be discussed in more detail in Chapters 3 'Hardware architecture' and 6 'Memory management'. Here we will create a simple conceptual model of a cache to illustrate the key points.

First of all, as a cache is limited in size, how do we store portions of the DRAM content in it? Like the other memories, we will model the storage part of the cache as an array of fixed size. So if we want to store some data in the cache, we find a free location and copy the data into it. At some point, the data will be removed from the cache, freeing up this location. So we need a data structure, e.g., a stack to keep track of the free locations.

So what happens when the cache is full (so the stack is empty)? We need to free up space by evicting data from the cache. As we will see in Chapter 6 'Memory management', there are several different policies to do this. The simplest one (but certainly not the best one) is to evict data from the most recently used location because all it requires is that we keep track of that single location. When we evict data from the cache, it needs to be written back to the DRAM memory. Conversely, the data that we put into the cache was read from an address location in the DRAM memory. Therefore the cache must not only keep track of the data but also of its original address. In other words, we need a lookup between the address in the DRAM and the corresponding address in the cache. In Python, we can use a *dictionary* for this, a data structure that associates keys with values. A cache which behaves like a dictionary – in that it allows us to store any memory address at any cache location – is called 'fully associative'.

In Python, we can write such a cache model as follows:

```
Listing 1.4.7: Cache model: initialization and helper functions                    Python

1    # Initialise the cache
2    def init_cache():
3    # Cache of size CACHE_SZ
4        cache_storage=[]
5        location_stack_storage=range(0,CACHE_SZ)
6        location_stack_ptr=CACHE_SZ-1
7        last_used_loc = location_stack[location_stack_ptr]
8        location_stack = (location_stack_storage,location_stack_ptr,last_used_loc)
9        address_to_cache_loc={}
10       cache_loc_to_address={}
11       cache_lookup=(address_to_cache_loc,cache_loc_to_address)
12       cache = (cache_storage, address_to_cache_loc,cache_loc_to_address,location_stac
13       return cache
14
15   # Some helper functions
16   def get_next_free_location(location_stack):
17       (location_stack_storage,location_stack_ptr,last_used_loc) = location_stack
18       loc = location_stack_storage[location_stack_ptr]
19       location_stack_ptr-=1
```

```
20      location_stack = (location_stack_storage,location_stack_ptr,last_used_loc)
21      return (location,location_stack)
22
23  def evict_location(location_stack):
24      (location_stack_storage,location_stack_ptr,last_used_loc) = location_stack
25      location_stack_ptr+=1
26      location_stack[location_stack_ptr] = last_used
27      location_stack = (location_stack_storage,location_stack_ptr,last_used_loc)
28      return location_stack
29
30  def cache_is_full(location_stack_ptr):
31      if location_stack_ptr==0
32          return True
33      else
34          return False
```


Listing 1.4.8: Cache model: cache read and write functions   *Python*

```
1   def write_data_to_cache(memory, address, cache):
2       (cache_storage, address_to_cache_loc,cache_loc_to_address, location_stack) = cache
3       (location_stack_storage,location_stack_ptr,last_used_loc) = location_stack
4   # If the cache was full, evict first
5       if cache_is_full(location_stack_ptr):
6           location_stack = evict_location(location_stack)
7           evicted_address = cache_loc_to_address[last_used]
8           memory[evicted_address]=cache_storage[last_used]
9   # Get a free location.
10      (loc,location_stack) = get_next_free_location(location_stack)
11  # Get the DRAM content and write it to the cache storage
12      data = memory[address]
13      cache_storage[loc] = data
14  # Update the lookup table and the last used location
15      address_to_cache_loc[address]=loc
16      cache_loc_to_address[loc] = address
17      last_used=loc
18      location_stack = (location_stack_storage,location_stack_ptr,last_used_loc)
19      cache = (cache_storage,address_to_cache_loc,cache_loc_to_address,location_stack)
20      return (memory,cache)
21
22  def read_data_from_cache(memory,address,cache):
23      (cache_storage, address_to_cache_loc,cache_loc_to_address,location_stack) = cache
24      location_stack = evict_location(location_stack)
25  # If the data is not yet in the cache, fetch it from the DRAM
26  # Note this may result in eviction, which could modify the memory
27      if address not in address_to_cache_loc:
28          (memory, cache) = write_data_to_cache(memory,address,cache):
29  # Get the data from the cache
30      loc = address_to_cache_loc[address]
31      data = cache_storage[loc]
32      cache = (cache_storage, address_to_cache_loc,cache_loc_to_address, location_stack)
33      return (data,memory,cache)
```

The problem with the above model is that for a cache of a given size, we need a location stack and two lookup tables of the same size. This requires a lot of silicon. Therefore, in practice, the cache will not simply fetch the content of a single memory address, but a contiguous block of memory called a *cache line*. For example, the Arm Cortex-A53 has a 64-byte cache line. Assuming that our memory stores 32-bit words, then the size of the location stack and lookup tables is 16x smaller than the actual cache size.

There is another reason for the use of cache lines: when a given address is accessed, subsequent memory accesses are frequently to neighboring addresses. So fetching an entire cache line on a cache miss tends to reduce the number of subsequent cache misses. Adapting our model to use cache lines is straightforward:

Listing 1.4.9: Cache model with cache lines *Python*

```python
# Initialise the cache
def init_cache():
# Cache of size CACHE_SZ, cache line = 64 bytes = 16 words
    cache_storage=[[0]*16]*(CACHE_SZ/16)
    location_stack_storage=range(0,CACHE_SZ/16)
    location_stack_ptr=(CACHE_SZ/16)-1
    last_used_loc = location_stack[location_stack_ptr]
    location_stack = (location_stack_storage,location_stack_ptr,last_used_loc)
    address_to_cache_loc={}
    cache_loc_to_address={}
    cache_lookup=(address_to_cache_loc,cache_loc_to_address)
    cache = (cache_storage,address_to_cache_loc,cache_loc_to_address,location_stack)
    return cache

# The helper functions remain the same

def write_data_to_cache(memory,address,cache):
    (cache_storage, address_to_cache_loc,cache_loc_to_address,location_stack) = cache
    (location_stack_storage,location_stack_ptr,last_used_loc) = location_stack
# If the cache was full, evict first
    if cache_is_full(location_stack_ptr):
        location_stack = evict_location(location_stack)
        evicted_address = cache_loc_to_address[last_used]
        cache_line = cache_storage[last_used]
        for i in range(0,16):
        data = cache_line[i]
            memory[(evicted_address<<4) + i]=data
# Get a free location.
    (loc,location_stack) = get_next_free_location(location_stack)
# Get the DRAM content and write it to the cache storage
    cache_line = []
    for i in range(0,16):
        cache_line.append(memory[((address>>4)<<4)+i]
    cache_storage[loc] = cache_line
# Update the lookup table and the last used location
    address_to_cache_loc[address>>4]=loc
    cache_loc_to_address[loc] = address>>4
    last_used=loc
    location_stack = (location_stack_storage,location_stack_ptr,last_used_loc)
    cache = (cache_storage,address_to_cache_loc,cache_loc_to_address,location_stack)
    return (memory,cache)

def read_data_from_cache(memory,address,cache):
    (cache_storage,address_to_cache_loc,cache_loc_to_address,location_stack) = cache
    location_stack = evict_location(location_stack)
# If the data is not yet in the cache, fetch it from the DRAM
# Note this may result in eviction, which could modify the memory
    if address not in address_to_cache_loc:
        (memory,cache) = write_data_to_cache(memory,address,cache):
# Get the data from the cache
    loc = address_to_cache_loc[address>>4]
    cache_line = cache_storage[loc]
    data = cache_line[addres & 0xF]
    cache = (cache_storage,address_to_cache_loc,cache_loc_to_address,location_stack)
    return (data,memory,cache)
```

The only complication in the cache line-based model is that we need to manipulate the memory address to determine the start of the cache line and the location of the data inside the cache line. Do this using bit shift and bit mask operations: the first 4bits of the address identify the position of the data in the cache line. We don't need to store these bits in the lookup tables of the cache because the cache stores only whole cache lines. In other words, from the perspective of the cache, the memory consists of cache lines rather than individual locations. So we have the following formulas:

```
data_position_in_cache line = address & 0xF
cache_line_address = address >> 4

address = (cache_line_address << 4) + data_position_in_cache line
```

1.4.7 Running a program on the processor

The processor model is complete and can run arbitrary programs. For example, the following program generates the first 10 Fibonacci numbers greater than 1 and writes them to main memory:

Listing 1.4.10: Fibonacci code   Python

```
1    fib_prog=[
2    [SET,R1,1],
3    [SET,R2,1],
4    [SET,R3,0],
5    [SET,R4,10],
6    [SET,R5,1],
7    ('loop',[ADD,R3,R1,R2]),
8    [MOV,R1,R2],
9    [MOV,R2,R3],
10   [SUB,R4,R4,R5],
11   [STR,R3,R4],
12   [CBNZ,R4,'loop'],
13   [WFI]
14   ]
```

Note: the **encodeProgram** function from abstract_model_encoder.py supports strings as labels for instructions as shown above. Similar to Arm assembly language, the instructions CBZ, CBNZ, ADR, BL, and B actually take labels rather than explicit addresses.

To run this program, we need to encode it, load it into memory, and ensure that the program counter points to the start of code in the memory:

Listing 1.4.11: Running a program on the processor   Python

```
1    # Encode the program
2    fib_iws=encodeProgram(fib_prog)
3
4    # Write the program to RAM memory
5    pc=0
6    for iw in fib_iws:
7        ramState[CODE+pc] = iw
8        pc+=1
9
10   # Initialise the processor state
11   registers[PC]=CODE
```

```
12
13   # Run the system for a given number of cycles
14   MAX_NCYCLES=50
15   for ncycles in range(1,MAX_NCYCLES):
16          # Run the peripheral actions
17          (kbdState,kbdIrq)=kbdAction(kbdState)
18          (nicState,nicIrq)=nicAction(nicState)
19          (ssdState,ssdIrq)=ssdAction(ssdState)
20          (gpuState,gpuIrq)=gpuAction(gpuState)
21          (systemState,dmaIrq)=dmaAction(systemState)
22
23          # The RAM does not have any action,
24          # it is just a slice of the full address space
25          ramState=systemState[0:MEMTOP]
26          # Collect the IRQs
27          irqs=[kbdIrq,nicIrq,ssdIrq,gpuIrq,dmaIrq]
28          # Compose the system state
29          systemState = ramState+timerState+kbdState+nicState+ssdState+gpuState+dmaState
30          # Run the processor action
31          (systemState,irqs,registers) = processorAction(systemState,irqs,registers)
32
33   # Print the portion of memory that holds the results
34   print(systemState[0:10])
```

1.4.8 High-level instructions

The model introduced in the previous section is cycle-based, i.e., it models all actions and state changes on a cycle-by-cycle, instruction-by-instruction basis. To simplify the explanations in what follows and to speed up the execution of the model code, we add support for direct execution of high-level Python code using the **HLI** instruction. This allows us to work at a higher level of abstraction, while still preserving the low-level features of the system that are used by the operating system.

The previous model required us to write individual instructions and encode them. The **HLI** instruction allows us to use Python functions that will replace groups of instructions, as follows:

Listing 1.4.12: Multi- instruction action   *Python*

```
1   def multi_instruction_action( systemState,registers ):
2          .... (arbitrary Python code) ...
3          return ( systemState,registers )
4
5   hli_prog = [...,
6   [HLI,multi_instruction_action],
7   ...
8   ]
```

To execute such functions in the processor, we add the **doHLI** function to the **executeInstrucion** code:

Listing 1.4.13: Adapting push for high-level instructions   *Python*

```
1   def doHLI(registers,systemState,args)
2          (hl_instr,_,_)=args
3          (systemState,registers) = hl_instr(systemState,registers)
4          return (registers,systemState)
```

To illustrate the approach, the Fibonacci example from the previous section could become a single HLI instruction:

```
Listing 1.4.14: Fibonacci with high-level instructions                                    Python

1    def fib_hl( systemState,registers ):
2        (r1,r2,r4)=(1,1,10)
3        while r4!=0:
4            r3=r1+r2
5            r1=r2
6            r2=r3
7            r4-=1
8            systemState[r4]=r3
9        registers[1:5]=[r1,r2,r3,r4]
10       return ( systemState,registers )
```

The key point is that the functions manipulate the system state and registers in the same way as the individual instructions did.

1.5 Basic operating system concepts

In this section, we use the abstract system model to introduce a number of fundamental operating system concepts that will be discussed in detail in the following chapters.

1.5.1 Tasks and concurrency

One of the main tasks of an operating system is to support multiple tasks at the same time ('concurrently'). If there is only one processor, it means that the code that implements these tasks must time-share the processor. Let us assume that we have two programs in memory and we want to run them concurrently so that each running program is a single task, Task 1 and Task 2.

We have seen in Section 1.4.7 how we run a program: set the program counter to the starting address, then the fetch-decode-execute cycle will execute each instruction on subsequent clock ticks until the program is finished.

Now we want to run *two programs at the same time*. Therefore, we will need a mechanism to run instructions of each program alternatingly. This mechanism translates to managing the state. As we have seen before, the state of a running program consists in principle of the complete system state. In practice, each program should have its own section of memory, as we don't want one program to modify the memory of another program.

We start, therefore, by assuming that when the program code is loaded into memory, it is part of a region of memory that the program is allowed to use when it is running. We will see in Chapter 6 'Memory management' that this is indeed the case in Linux. As shown in Figure 1.3, this region (called 'user space') contains the program code, the stack for the program and the random-access memory for the program, commonly known as the 'heap'. Typically, each task gets a fixed amount of memory allocated to it, and in the code, this memory is referenced relative to the program counter.

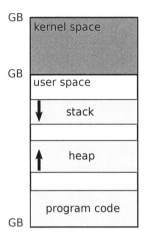

Figure 1.3: Task memory space (Linux).

1.5.2 The register file

However, as we have seen, the processor also has some state, namely the register file. So if we want to run two tasks alternately, we need to ensure that the register file contains the correct state for each task. So conceptually, we can store a snapshot of the register file contents for Task 1, then load the previous snapshot of the register file contents for Task 2.

1.5.3 Time slicing and scheduling

So how can we make two tasks alternate? The code to do this will be the core of our Operating System kernel and is called a 'task scheduler' or scheduler for short. Let's assume we will simply alternate two (or more) tasks for fixed amounts of time (this is called 'round-robin scheduling'). For example, on the Raspberry Pi 3, the Linux real-time scheduler uses an interval (also called 'time slice' or 'quantum') of 10 ms. For comparison, the average duration of an eye blink is 100 ms. Note that at a typical clock speed of 1 GHz, this means a task can execute 10 million (single-cycle) instructions in this time.

The duration of a time slice is controlled by a system timer. As we have seen before, a timer can be configured to fire periodically, so in our case, the system timer will raise an interrupt request every 10 ms. On receiving this request, the processor will execute the corresponding Interrupt Service Routine (ISR). It is this ISR that will take care of the time slicing; in other words, the interrupt service routine is actually our operating system kernel.

In the Python model, the timer peripheral has a register to store the interval and a control register. We can set the timer as follows:

Listing 1.5.1: Timer *Python*

```python
1    # Set timer to periodic with 100-ticks interval
2    set_timer=[
3        [SET,R1,100],
4        [SET,R2,100], # start periodic timer
5        [STR,R1,TIMER],
6        [STR,R2,TIMER+1]
7    ]
```

On running this program, the timer will fire every 100 clock ticks and raise an interrupt request. Let's have a look at the interrupt handler. What should this routine do to achieve time slicing between two tasks? Let's assume Task 1 has been running and we now want to run Task 2.

- First, save the register file for Task 1, we do this by pushing all register contents onto the stack. (If you spot an issue here, well done! We'll get back to this in Section 1.5.4.)

- Then determine which task has to be run next (i.e., Task 2). We can identify each task using a small integer (the 'task identifier') that we store in the memory accessible by the kernel. We load the task identifier for Task 2 into a register and update the memory with the task identifier for the next task (in our case, again Task 1).

- We now move the register file of Task 1 from the stack to kernel memory. In practice, the kernel uses a special data structure, the Task Control Block (TCB), for this purpose.

- Now we can read the register file contents for Task 2 from its TCB. Again, we have to do this via the stack (why?).

- Once this is done, Task 2 will start running from the location indicated by PC and run until the next timer interrupt.

We can express this sequence of actions in high-level Python code for our processor model:

```
Listing 1.5.2: Time slicing model                                          Python

1    def time_slice(systemState,registers ):
2    # Push registers onto the stack
3        for r in range(0,16):
4            systemState[registers[MSP]]]=registers[r]
5    registers[MSP]+=1
6    # Get next task
7        pid1 = systemState[PID] # 0 or 1
8        pid2 = 1-pid1
9        systemState[PID]=pid2
10       tcb1= TCB_OFFSET+pid1*TCB_SZ
11       tcb2= TCB_OFFSET+pid2*TCB_SZ
12   # Pop registers from stack and store to tcb1
13   # We use r0 to show that in actual code we'd need to read into a tempory register
14       for r in range(0,16):
15           r0=systemState[registers[MSP]]
16       systemState[tcb1+r]=r0
17       registers[MSP]-=1
18   # Push registers for Task 2 from tcb2 onto stack
19       for r in range(0,16):
20           r0=systemState[tcb2+r]
21           systemState[registers[MSP]]=r0
22       registers[MSP]+=1
23   # Pop registers for Task 2 from stack
24       for r in range(0,16):
25           registers[r]=systemState[registers[MSP]]
26       registers[MSP]-=1
```

This code is a minimal example of a round-robin scheduler for two tasks.

You can already try and answer these questions by thinking about how you would address these issues.

1.5.4 Privileges

In Section 1.5.3, we hinted at a potential issue with the stack. The problem is that 'pushing onto the stack' means modifying the stack pointer SP. So how can we preserve the stack pointer of the current task? The short answer for the Arm processor is that it has *two* stack pointers, one for user space task stacks (PSP) and one for the kernel stack (MSP). User tasks cannot access the kernel stack pointer; the kernel code can select between the two using the MRS and MSR instruction.

This raises the topic of *privileges*: clearly if the kernel code can access more registers than the user task code, the kernel code is privileged. This is an essential security feature of any operating system because, without privileges, a userspace task code could modify the kernel code or other task code.

We will discuss this in more detail in Chapter 4, 'Process management'. For the moment, it is sufficient to know that in the Arm Cortex-M3 there are two privilege levels[4], 'Unprivileged' and 'Privileged'; in Unprivileged mode the software has limited access to the MSR and MRS instructions which allow access to special registers, and cannot use the CPS instruction which allows us to change the privilege level. For further restrictions, see [2].

1.5.5 Memory management

So far, we have assumed that tasks already reside in memory. In practice, the OS will have to load the program code into memory. To do so, the OS must find a sufficient amount of memory for both the program code and the memory required by the program. It would clearly not be practical if the program were to use absolute memory addresses: this would mean that the compiler (or the programmer) would need to know in advance where the program would reside in memory. This would be very inflexible. Therefore, program code will use relative addressing, e.g., relative to the value of the program counter. The OS will set the PC to the starting address of the code in memory.

However, relative addressing does not solve all problems. The main question is how to allocate space in memory for the processes. Initially, we could of course simply fill up the memory, as shown in Figure 1.4. But what happens with the memory of finished tasks? The OS should, of course, reuse it, but it could only do so if a new task does not use any more memory than one of the finished tasks. Again, this would be very restrictive.

The commonly used solution to this problem is to introduce the concept of a *logical address space*. This is a contiguous address space allocated to a process. The *physical* addresses that correspond to this logical address space do not have to be contiguous. The operating system is responsible for the translation between the logical and physical address spaces. What this involves is explained in detail in Chapter 6, 'Memory management', but you can already think of ways to organize non-contiguous blocks of physical memory of varying size into a logical contiguous space. Apart from address translation, the OS also must ensure that a process cannot access the memory space of another process: this is called *memory protection*. Typically, this involves checking a logical address against the upper and a lower bound of the process logical address space. Because this is a very common

---

[4] In more advanced processors such as the Arm Cortex-A53, there are 4 levels of privilege, called 'Exception Levels' (EL) and numbered EL0-EL3. The userspace tasks run in EL0, the OS kernel in EL1.

operation, there is usually hardware support for it in the form of a Memory Protection Unit (MPU) in low-end processors such as the Cortex-M3 or as part of a more elaborate Memory Management Unit (MMU) in processors such as the Cortex-A53.

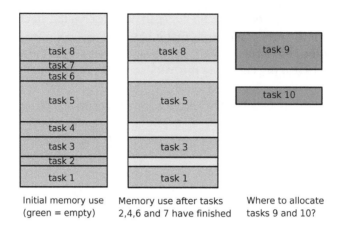

Initial memory use (green = empty)	Memory use after tasks 2,4,6 and 7 have finished	Where to allocate tasks 9 and 10?

Figure 1.4: Problem with contiguous memory allocation.

1.5.6 Translation look-aside buffer (TLB)

The MMU can be implemented as a peripheral as we have done for the DMA unit above, but we will defer this to the in-depth discussion of memory management provided in Chapter 6. However, we want to introduce one particular part of the MMU, a special type of cache called the translation look-aside buffer (TLB). The translation from logical to physical addresses is quite time-consuming, and therefore, the MMU uses the TLB to keep track of recently used translations (Figure 1.5). Unlike the memory cache, which contains the data stored in the memory, the TLB contains the physical address corresponding to a logical address.

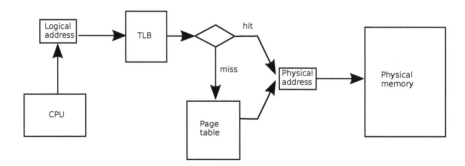

Figure 1.5: Logical to physical address translation with translation look-aside buffer (TLB).

The same considerations which lead us to use cache lines lead to a similar approach to reducing the memory space: we divide both the logical and physical memory into chunks of a fixed size (which we call respectively *pages* and *frames*), and we store the starting addresses of those chunks in the TLB, rather than individual addresses. The position inside the page is calculated in quite the same way as the position in a cache line, using a fixed number of LSBs. Typically, pages in Linux are 4KB; different sizes are possible; see Chapter 3 and Chapter 7. The TLB differs from the cache in that a miss does not result in a fetch from memory but in a lookup of the physical address in what is called the Page Table; also, writes to the TLB only happen on a miss. However, the similarity between the cache and TLB serves allows us to explain the main points of memory management without the need to know anything about how the actual Page Table works.

1.6 Exercises and questions

1.6.1 Task scheduling

1. Create a scheduler for a single task in Python. You can use the above code and the Fibonacci example, or you can write your own code.
2. Extend the **time_slice** function and the memory layout to support a larger number (**NTASKS**) tasks.

1.6.2 TLB model

1. Create a TLB model in Python, starting from the cache model code in Section 1.4.6.
2. Given the concept of logical and physical address spaces and the idea of pages, propose a data structure that allows the OS to allocate non-contiguous blocks of physical memory to a process as a contiguous logical address space. Discuss the pros and cons of your proposed data structure.
3. Assuming 4GB of memory divided into 4KB-size pages, and assuming that the page table lookup is 100x slower than the TLB lookup. What should be the hit rate of the TLB to have an average lookup time of twice the TLB lookup time? What would the TLB size have to be?

1.6.3 Modeling the system

1. In a physical system, all actions in the above model take place in parallel. What effect does this have on the model?
2. Suppose you have to design the peripheral for a keyboard which has no locking keys nor modifier keys. What would be the state and which events would raise interrupts?

1.6.4 Bare-bones processor model

1. The LDR and STR instructions work on memory addresses. In principle, there is nothing that stops two programs from using the same memory addresses, but this is, of course, in general, not desirable. What could we do to avoid this?
2. Can you think of features that our bare bones processor is missing?

1.6.5 Advanced processor model

1. If the processor has multiple cores that can execute tasks in parallel, what would need to change to the processor model?
2. Can you see any issues with the cache if every core would have its own cache? What if they share a single cache?

1.6.6 Basic operating system concepts

The explanation in Section 1.5 omits a lot of detail and raises several questions, which will be answered in the later chapters. For example:

◾ What happens if there are more than 2 running tasks?

◾ How does a user start a task?

- How does the OS load programs from disk into in memory?

- How does the OS ensure that programs can only access their own memory?

- What about sharing of peripherals?

- What happens when a task is finished?

The issues of privileges and memory management are discussed in more detail in Chapters 5 and 6. The model presented so far raises several questions:

- What does it involve to guarantee memory protection? For example, how could the OS know the bounds of the logical address space of each process?

- Is it sufficient to provide memory protection? Should other resources have similar protections? What could be the reason that the default page size on Linux is 4KB? What would happen if it was 10x smaller, or 10x larger?

- Can you think of scenarios where logical memory is not necessary?

References

[1] *Principles of Arm Memory Maps*, Arm Ltd, 10 2012, issue C. [Online].
Available: http://infocenter.arm.com/help/topic/com.arm.doc.den0001c/DEN0001C_principles_of_arm_memory_maps.pdf

[2] *Arm® Cortex®-A53 MPCore Processor – Technical Reference Manual Rev: r0p4*, Arm Ltd, 2 2016, revision: r0p4. [Online].
Available: http://infocenter.arm.com/help/topic/com.arm.doc.ddi0500g/DDI0500G_cortex_a53_trm.pdf

[3] *ARM Compiler toolchain Version 5.03 Assembler Reference*, Arm Ltd, 1 2013. [Online].
Available: http://infocenter.arm.com/help/topic/com.arm.doc.dui0489i/DUI0489I_arm_assembler_reference.pdf

[4] A. G. Dean, *Embedded Systems Fundamentals with Arm Cortex-M based Microcontrollers: A Practical Approach*.
Arm Education Media UK, 2017.

[5] *Cortex™-M3 Devices Generic User Guide*, Arm Ltd, 12 2010. [Online].
Available: http://infocenter.arm.com/help/topic/com.arm.doc.dui0552a/DUI0552A_cortex_m3_dgug.pdf

[6] *Procedure Call Standard for the Arm Architecture ABI r2.10*, Arm Ltd, 2015. [Online].
Available: https://developer.arm.com/docs/ihi0042/latest/procedure-call-standard-for-the-arm-architecture-abi-2018q4-documentation

Chapter 2

A practical view
of the Linux system

2.1 Overview

In this chapter, we approach the Linux system from a practical perspective, as experienced by users of the system, in particular administrators and application programmers rather than kernel or driver programmers. We first introduce the essential concepts and techniques that you need to know in order to understand the overall system, and then we discuss the system itself from different angles: what is the OS role in booting and initializing the system; what OS knowledge does a system administrator and systems programmer need. This chapter is *not* a how-to guide, but rather provides you with the background knowledge behind how-to guides. It also serves as a roadmap for the rest of the book.

What you will learn
After you have studied the material in this chapter, you will be able to:

1. Explain basic operating system concepts: processes, users, files, permissions, and credentials.

2. Analyze the chain of events when booting Linux on the Raspberry Pi.

3. Create a Linux kernel module and build a custom Linux kernel.

4. Discuss the administrator and programmers view on the key operating system concepts covered in the further chapters.

2.2 Basic concepts

To understand what happens when the system boots and initializes, as well as how the OS affects the tasks of system administrator and systems programmer, we need to introduce a number of basic operating system concepts. Most of these apply to any operating system, although the discussion here is specific to Linux on Arm-based systems. The in-depth discussion of these concepts forms the subject of the later chapters, so this section serves as a roadmap for the rest of the book as well.

The original Linux announcement on Usenet (1991). Photo by Krd.

```
From: torvalds@klaava.Helsinki.FI (Linus Benedict Torvalds)
Newsgroups: comp.os.minix
Subject: What would you like to see most in minix?
Summary: small poll for my new operating system
Message-ID: <1991Aug25.205708.9541@klaava.Helsinki.FI>
Date: 25 Aug 91 20:57:08 GMT
Organization: University of Helsinki
Hello everybody out there using minix -
I'm doing a (free) operating system (just a hobby, won't be big and
professional like gnu) for 386(486) AT clones. This has been brewing
since april, and is starting to get ready. I'd like any feedback on
things people like/dislike in minix, as my OS resembles it somewhat
(same physical layout of the file-system (due to practical reasons)
among other things).
I've currently ported bash(1.08) and gcc(1.40), and things seem to work.
This implies that I'll get something practical within a few months, and
I'd like to know what features most people would want. Any suggestions
are welcome, but I won't promise I'll implement them :-)
Linus (torvalds@kruuna.helsinki.fi)
PS. Yes - it's free of any minix code, and it has a multi-threaded fs.
It is NOT protable (uses 386 task switching etc), and it probably never
will support anything other than AT-harddisks, as that's all I have :-(.
```

2.2.1 Operating system hierarchy

The Linux kernel is only one component of the complete operating system. Figure 2.1 illustrates the complete Linux system hierarchy. Interfacing between the kernel and the user space applications is the system call interface, a mechanism to allow user space applications to interact with the kernel and hardware. This interface is used by system tools and libraries, and finally by the user applications. The kernel provides functionality such as scheduling, memory management, networking and file system support, and support for interacting with system hardware via device drivers.

Interfacing between the kernel and the hardware are device drivers and the firmware. In the Linux system, device drivers interact closely with the kernel, but they are not considered part of the kernel because depending on the hardware different drivers will be needed, and they can be added on the fly.

2.2.2 Processes

A *process* is a running program, i.e., the code for the program and all system resources it uses. The concept of a process is used for the separation of code and resources. The OS kernel allocates memory resources and other resources to a process, and these are private to the process, and protected from all other processes. The scheduler allocates time for a process to execute. We also use the term *task*, which is a bit less strictly defined, and usually relates to scheduling: a task is an amount of work to be done by a program. We will also see the concept of *threads*, which are used to indicate multiple concurrent tasks executing within a single process. In other words, the threads of a process share its resources. For a process with a single thread of execution, the terms task and process are often used interchangeably.

When a process is created, the OS kernel assigns it a unique identifier (called process ID or PID for short) and creates a corresponding data structure called the Process Control Block or Task Control Block (in the Linux kernel this data structure is called `task_struct`). This is the main mechanism the kernel uses to manage processes.

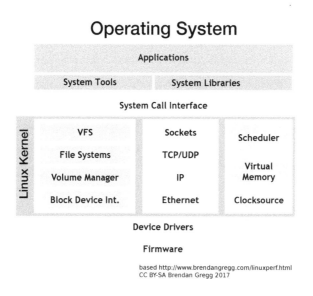

Figure 2.1: Operating System Hierarchy.

2.2.3 User space and kernel space

The terms 'user space' and 'kernel space' are used mainly to indicate process execution with different privileges. As we have seen in Chapter 1, the kernel code can access all hardware and memory in the system, but for user processes, the access is very much restricted. When we use the term 'kernel space,' we mean the memory space accessible by the kernel, which is effectively the complete memory space in the system[1]. By 'user space,' we mean the memory accessible by a user process. Most operating systems support multiple users, and each user can run multiple processes. Typically, each process gets its own memory space, but processes belonging to a single user can share memory (in which case we'll call them threads).

2.2.4 Device tree and ATAGs

The Linux kernel needs information about the system on which it runs. Although a kernel binary must be compiled for a target architecture (e.g., Arm), a kernel binary should be able to run on a wide variety of platforms for this architecture. This means that the kernel has to be provided with information about the hardware at boot time, e.g., number of CPUs, amount of memory, location of memory, devices and their location in the memory map, etc. The traditional way to do this on Arm systems was using a format called ATAGs, which provided a data structure in the kernel that would be populated with information that the bootloader provided. A more modern and flexible approach is called Device Tree[3]. It defines a format and syntax to describe system hardware in a Device Tree Source file. A device tree is a tree data structure with nodes that describe the physical devices in a system. The Device Tree source files can be compiled using a special compiler into a machine-architecture-independent binary format called Device Tree Blob.

2.2.5 Files and persistent storage

The Linux Information Project defines a *file* as:

A file is a named collection of related data that appears to the user as a single, contiguous block of information and that is retained in storage.[2]

In this definition, *storage* refers to computer devices or media which can retain data for relatively long periods (e.g., years or decades), such as solid state drives and other types of non-volatile memory, magnetic hard disk drives (HDDs), CDROMs and magnetic tape, in other words, persistent storage. This is in contrast with RAM memory, the content of which is retained only temporarily (i.e., only while in use or while the power supply remains on).

A persistent storage medium (which I will call 'disk') such as an SD card, USB memory stick or hard disk, stores data in a linear fashion with sequential access. However, in practice, the disk does not contain a single array of bytes. Instead, it is organized using *partitions* and *file systems*. We discuss these in more detail in Chapter 9, but below is a summary of these concepts.

Partition

A disk can be divided into partitions, which means that instead of presenting as a single blob of data, it presents as several different blobs. Partitions are logical rather than physical, and the information about how the disk is partitioned (i.e., the location, size, type, name, and attributes of each partition) is stored in a partition table. There are several standards for the structure of partitions and partition tables, e.g., GUID Partition Table and MBR.

---

[1] Assuming the system does not run a hypervisor. Otherwise, it is the memory available to the Virtual Machine running the kernel.
[2] http://www.linfo.org/file.html   [3] https://www.devicetree.org/specifications

File system

Each partition of a disk contains a further system for logical organization. The purpose of most file systems is to provide the *file* and *directory (folder)* abstractions. There are a great many different file systems (e.g., fat32, ext4, hfs+, ...) and we will cover the most important ones in Chapter 9. For the purpose of this chapter, what you need to know is that a file system not only allows to store information in the form of files organized in directories but also information about the permissions of usages for files and directories, as well as timestamp information (file creation, modification, etc.).

The information in a file system is typically organized as a hierarchical tree of directories, and the directory at the root of the tree is called the root directory. To use a file system, the kernel performs an operation called *mounting*. As long as a file system has not been mounted, the system can't access the data on it.

Mounting a file system attaches that file system to a directory (mount point) and makes it available to the system. The root (/) file system is always mounted. Any other file system can be connected or disconnected from the root file system at any point in the directory tree.

2.2.6 'Everything is a file'

One of the key characteristics of Linux and other UNIX-like operating systems is the often-quoted concept of 'everything is a file.' This does not mean that all objects in Linux are files as defined above, but rather that Linux prefers to treat all objects from which the OS can read data or to which it can write data using a consistent interface. So it might be more accurate to say 'everything is a stream of bytes.' Linux uses the concept of a file descriptor, an abstract handle used to access an input/output resource (of which a file is just one type). So one can also say that in Linux, 'everything is a file descriptor.'

What this means in practice is that the interface to, e.g., a network card, keyboard or display is represented as a file in the file system (in the /dev directory); system information about both hardware and software is available under /proc. For example, Figure 2.2 shows the listing of `/dev` and `/proc` on the Raspberry Pi. We can see device files representing memory (ram*), terminals (tty*), modem (ppp),

```
wim@rpi:~ $ ls /dev
autofs           gpiochip1  loop7                pts    ram8     tty11 tty25 tty39 tty52 tty9       vcs5
block            gpiochip2  loop-control         ram0   ram9     tty12 tty26 tty4  tty53 ttyAMA0    vcs6
btrfs-control    gpiomem    mapper               ram1   random   tty13 tty27 tty40 tty54 ttyprintk  vcsa
bus              hwrng      mem                  ram10  raw      tty14 tty28 tty41 tty55 uhid       vcsa1
cachefiles       initctl    memory_bandwidth     ram11  rfkill   tty15 tty29 tty42 tty56 uinput     vcsa2
char             input      mmcblk0              ram12  serial1  tty16 tty3  tty43 tty57 urandom    vcsa3
console          kmsg       mmcblk0p1            ram13  shm      tty17 tty30 tty44 tty58 vc-cma     vcsa4
cpu_dma_latency  log        mmcblk0p2            ram14  snd      tty18 tty31 tty45 tty59 vchiq      vcsa5
cuse             loop0      mqueue               ram15  stderr   tty19 tty32 tty46 tty6  vcio       vcsa6
disk             loop1      net                  ram2   stdin    tty2  tty33 tty47 tty60 vc-mem     vcsm
fb0              loop2      network_latency      ram3   stdout   tty20 tty34 tty48 tty61 vcs        vhci
fd               loop3      network_throughput   ram4   tty      tty21 tty35 tty49 tty62 vcs1       watchdog
full             loop4      null                 ram5   tty0     tty22 tty36 tty5  tty63 vcs2       watchdog0
fuse             loop5      ppp                  ram6   tty1     tty23 tty37 tty50 tty7  vcs3       zero
gpiochip0        loop6      ptmx                 ram7   tty10    tty24 tty38 tty51 tty8  vcs4
wim@rpi:~ $ ls /proc
1   245  327 4347 482  514  57  69  722 82  93           execdomains    locks          sysvipc
10  251  328 4351 4876 5149 58  690 723 83  94           fb             meminfo        thread-self
11  252  33  4354 488  515  59  691 724 84  95           filesystems    misc           timer_list
12  2564 332 4363 5    5158 592 699 725 844 96           fs             modules        timer_stats
120 2566 34  4366 5008 52   60  7   73  845 asound       interrupts     mounts         tty
13  26   35  4394 5012 520  600 70  74  846 buddyinfo    iomem          net            uptime
14  2621 355 4456 506  521  61  704 75  847 bus          ioports        pagetypeinfo   vc-cma
156 2624 359 450  507  524  615 71  76  848 cgroups      irq            partitions     version
16  27   36  457  508  5248 619 714 77  85  cmdline      kallsyms       sched_debug    vmallocinfo
17  28   365 458  509  525  62  715 78  862 consoles     keys           schedstat      vmstat
18  29   371 459  5095 526  63  716 799 88  cpu          key-users      self           zoneinfo
19  299  38  4612 510  53   64  717 8   9   cpuinfo      kmsg           slabinfo
2   3    39  463  5107 54   65  718 80  90  crypto       kpagecgroup    softirqs
21  30   40  470  511  547  66  719 800 91  devices      kpagecount     stat
22  31   402 471  5111 548  67  72  808 922 device-tree  kpageflags     swaps
23  32   41  4753 512  55   675 720 81  923 diskstats    latency_stats  sys
24  3240 42  476  513  56   68  721 815 924 driver       loadavg        sysrq-trigger
wim@rpi:~ $
```

Figure 2.2: Listing of /dev and /proc on the Raspberry Pi running Raspbian.

and many others. In particular, there is `/dev/null` which is a special device which discards the information written to it, and `/dev/zero` which returns an endless stream of zero bytes (i.e., 0x00, so when you try cat `/dev/zero` you will see nothing. Try `cat/dev/zero  |  hd` instead.)

2.2.7 Users
A Linux system is typically a multi-user system. What this means is that it supports another level of separation, permissions, and protection above the level of processes. A user can run and control multiple processes, each in their own memory space, but with shared access to system resources. In particular, the concept of users and permission is tightly connected with the file system. The file system permissions for a given user control the access of that user in terms of reading, writing, and executing files in different parts of the file system hierarchy.

Just as the kernel runs in privileged mode to control the user space processes, there is also a need for a privileged user to control the other users (similar to the 'Administrator' on Windows systems). In Linux, this user is called *root*[3] and when the system boots, the first process (*init*, which has PID=1) is run as the root user. The init process can create new processes. In fact, in Linux, any process can create new processes (as explained in more detail in Chapter 4). However, a process owned by the root user can assign ownership of a created process to another user, whereas processes created by a non-root user process can only be owned by itself.

2.2.8 Credentials
In Linux, *credentials* is the term for the set of privileges and permissions associated with any object. Credentials express, e.g., ownership, capabilities, and security management properties. For example, for files and processes, the key credentials are the user id and group id. To decide what a certain object (e.g., a task) can do to another object (e.g., a file), the Linux kernel performs a security calculation using the credentials and a set of rules. In practice, processes executed as root can access all files and other resources in the system; for a non-root user, file and directory access is determined by a system of permissions on the files and by the membership of groups: a user can belong to one or more groups of users.

File access permissions can be specified for individual users, groups, and everyone. For example, in Figure 2.3, we see that the directory /home/wim can be written to by user wim in group wim. If we try to create an (empty) file using the touch command, this succeeds. However, if we try to do the same in the directory /home/pleroma, owned by user pleroma in group pleroma, we get 'permission denied' because only user pleroma has write access to that directory.

```
[wim@rpi:~ $ ls -ld /home/wim/
drwxr-xr-x 6 wim wim 4096 Dec 22 15:42 /home/wim/
[wim@rpi:~ $ touch /home/wim/test
[wim@rpi:~ $ ls -l /home/wim/test
-rw-r--r-- 1 wim wim 0 Dec 22 15:45 /home/wim/test
[wim@rpi:~ $ ls -ld /home/pleroma/
drwxr-xr-x 6 pleroma pleroma 4096 Dec 18 12:03 /home/pleroma/
[wim@rpi:~ $ touch /home/pleroma/test
touch: cannot touch '/home/pleroma/test': Permission denied
wim@rpi:~ $
```

Figure 2.3: Example of restrictions on file creation on the Raspberry Pi running Raspbian.

[3] For more info about the origin of the name, root see www.linfo.org/root.html

Note that because of the 'everything is a file' approach, this system of permissions extends in general to devices, system information, etc. However, the actual kernel security policies can restrict access further. For example, in Figure 2.2, the numbers in the /proc listing represent currently running processes by their PID.

To illustrate the connection between users, permissions, and processes, Figure 2.4 shows how user wim can list processes in /proc belonging to two different non-root users, wim, and pleroma. The command cat /proc/548/maps prints out the entire memory map for the process with PID 548. The map is quite large, so for this example, only the heap memory allocation is shown (using grep heap).

```
[wim@rpi:~ $ ls -l /proc/ | grep wim
dr-xr-xr-x  8 wim          wim          0 Dec 22 11:47 4351
dr-xr-xr-x  8 wim          wim          0 Dec 22 15:02 4354
dr-xr-xr-x  8 wim          wim          0 Dec 22 15:02 4363
dr-xr-xr-x  8 wim          wim          0 Dec 22 15:02 4366
dr-xr-xr-x  8 wim          wim          0 Dec 22 15:01 548
dr-xr-xr-x  8 wim          wim          0 Dec 22 15:02 592
dr-xr-xr-x  8 wim          wim          0 Dec 22 15:23 9491
dr-xr-xr-x  8 wim          wim          0 Dec 22 15:23 9492
[wim@rpi:~ $ ls -l /proc/ | grep wim
dr-xr-xr-x  8 wim          wim          0 Dec 22 11:47 4351
dr-xr-xr-x  8 wim          wim          0 Dec 22 15:02 4354
dr-xr-xr-x  8 wim          wim          0 Dec 22 15:02 4363
dr-xr-xr-x  8 wim          wim          0 Dec 22 15:02 4366
dr-xr-xr-x  8 wim          wim          0 Dec 22 15:01 548
dr-xr-xr-x  8 wim          wim          0 Dec 22 15:02 592
dr-xr-xr-x  8 wim          wim          0 Dec 22 15:23 9494
dr-xr-xr-x  8 wim          wim          0 Dec 22 15:23 9495
[wim@rpi:~ $ ls -l /proc/548/maps
-r--r--r-- 1 wim wim 0 Dec 22 15:09 /proc/548/maps
[wim@rpi:~ $ cat /proc/548/maps | grep heap
020ac000-020cd000 rw-p 00000000 00:00 0              [heap]
[wim@rpi:~ $ ls -l /proc/600/maps
-r--r--r-- 1 pleroma pleroma 0 Dec 22 15:05 /proc/600/maps
[wim@rpi:~ $ cat /proc/600/maps
cat: /proc/600/maps: Permission denied
wim@rpi:~ $ 
```

Figure 2.4: Example of restrictions on process memory access via /proc on the Raspberry Pi running Raspbian.

However, when we try to do the same with /proc/600/maps, we get 'Permission denied' because the cat process owned by user wim does not have the right to inspect the memory map of a process owned by another user. This is despite the file permissions allowing read access.

2.2.9 Privileges and user administration

The system administrator creates user accounts and decides on access to resources using groups (using tools such as useradd(8), groupadd(8), chgrp(1), etc.). The kernel manages credentials per process using struct cred which is a field of the task_struct.

The admin also decides how many resources each user and process gets, e.g., using ulimit.

Resource limits are set in /etc/security/limits.conf and can be changed at runtime via the shell command ulimit. Internally, the ulimit implementation uses the getrlimit and setrlimit system calls which modify the kernel struct rlimit in include/uapi/linux/resource.h.

2.3 Booting Linux on Arm-based systems (Raspberry Pi 3)

In this section, we discuss the boot process for Linux on the Raspberry Pi 3. The boot sequence of Linux on Arm-based systems varies significantly from platform to platform. The differences sometimes arise due to the needs of the target market but can also be due to choices made by SoC and platform vendors. The boot sequence discussed here is a specific example to demonstrate what happens on a particular platform.

This Raspberry Pi 3 (Figure 2.5) runs Raspbian Linux on an Arm Cortex-A53 processor which is part of the Broadcom BCM2837 System-on-Chip (SoC). This SoC also contains a GPU (Broadcom VideoCore IV) which shares the RAM with the CPU. The GPU controls the initial stages of the boot process. The SoC also has a small amount of One Time Programmable (OTP) memory which contains information about the boot mode and a boot ROM with the initial boot code.

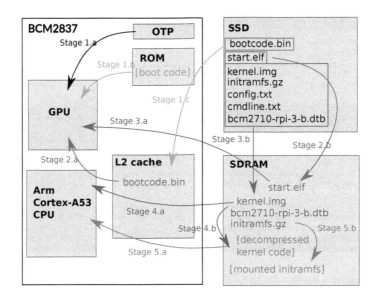

Figure 2.5: Boot Process for Raspbian Linux on the Raspberry Pi 3.

2.3.1 Boot process stage 1: Find the bootloader

Stage 1 of the boot process begins with reading the OTP to check which boot modes are enabled. By default, this is SD card boot, followed by a USB device boot. The code for this stage is stored in the on-chip ROM. The boot code checks each of the boot sources for a file called `bootcode.bin` in the root directory of the first partition on the storage medium (FAT32 formatted); if it is successful, it will load the code into the local 128K (L2) cache and jump to its first instruction to start Stage 2.

Note: The boot ROM supports GUID partitioning and MBR-style partitioning.

2.3.2 Boot process stage 2: Enable the SDRAM

Stage 2 is controlled by `bootcode.bin`, which is closed-source firmware. It enables the SDRAM and loads Stage 3 (`start.elf`) from the storage medium into the SDRAM.

2.3.3 Boot process stage 3: Load the Linux kernel into memory

Stage 3 is controlled by `start.elf`, which is a closed-source ELF-format binary running on the GPU.

`start.elf` loads the compressed Linux kernel binary `kernel.img` and copies it to memory. It reads `config.txt, cmdline.txt` and `bcm2710-rpi-3-b.dtb` (Device Tree Binary).

The file `config.txt` is a text file containing system configuration parameters which would on a conventional PC be edited and stored using a BIOS.

The file `cmdline.txt` contains the command line arguments to be passed on to the Linux kernel (e.g., the file system type and location of the root file system) using ATAGs, and the `.dtb` file contains the Device Tree Blob.

2.3.4 Boot process stage 4: Start the Linux kernel

Stage 4 starts `kernel.img` on the CPU: releasing reset on the CPU causes it to run from the address where the kernel.img data was written. The kernel runs some Arm-specific code to populate CPU registers and turn on the cache, then decompresses itself, and runs the decompressed kernel code. The kernel initializes the MMU using Arm-specific code and then run the rest of the kernel code which is processor-independent.

2.3.5 Boot process stage 5: Run the processor-independent kernel code

Stage 5 is the processor-independent kernel code. This code consists mainly of initialization functions to set up interrupts, perform further memory configuration, and load the initial RAM disk `initramfs`.

This is a complete set of directories that you would find on a normal root file system and was loaded into memory by the Stage 3 boot loader. It is copied into kernel space memory and mounted. This initramfs serves as a temporary root file system in RAM and allows the kernel to fully boot and perform user-space operations without having to mount any physical disks.

A single Linux kernel image can run on multiple platforms with support for a large number of devices/ peripherals. To reduce the overhead of loading and running a kernel binary bloated with features that aren't widely used, Linux supports runtime loading of components (modules) that are not needed during early boot. Since the necessary modules needed to interface with peripherals can be part of the initramfs, the kernel can be very small, but still, support a large number of possible hardware configurations. After the kernel is booted, the initramfs root file system is unmounted, and the real root file system is mounted. Finally, the `init` function is started, which is the first user-space process. After this, the idle task is started, and the scheduler starts operation.

2.3.6 Initialization

After the kernel has booted it launches the first process, called *init*. This process is the parent of all other processes. In the Raspbian Linux distribution that runs on the Raspberry Pi 3, this `init` is actually an alias for `/lib/systemd/systemd` because Raspbian, as a Debian-derived distribution, uses systemd as its init system. Other Linux distributions can have different implementations of init, e.g., SysV init or upstart.

The *systemd* process executes several processes to initialize the system: keyboard, hardware drivers, file systems, network, services. It has a sophisticated system for configuring all the processes under its control as well as for starting and stopping processes, checking their status, logging, changing privileges, etc.

The systemd process performs many tasks, but the principle is always the same: it starts a process under the required user name and monitors its state. If the process exits, systemd takes appropriate action, e.g., restarting the process or reporting the error that caused it to exit.

2.3.7 Login
One of the systemd responsibilities is running the processes that let users log into the system (systemd-logind). To login via a terminal (or virtual console), Linux uses two programs: *getty* and *login* (originally, the tty in getty meant 'teletype,' a precursor to modern terminals). Both run as root.

A basic *getty* program opens the terminal device, initializes it, prints the login prompt, and waits for a user name to be entered. When this happens, *getty* executes the *login* program, passing it the user name to log in as. The *login* program then prompts the user for a password. If the password is wrong, *login* simply exits. The systemd process will notice this and spawn another *getty* process. If the password is correct, *login* executes the user's shell program as that user. From then on, the user can start processes via the shell.

The reason why there are two separate programs is that both *getty* and *login* can be used on their own, for example, a remote login over SSH does not use a terminal but still uses *login*: each new connection is handled by a program called *sshd* that starts a login process.

A graphical login is conceptually not that different from the above description. The difference is that instead of the getty/login programs, a graphical login program called the *display manager* is run, and after authentication, this program launches the graphical shell.

In Raspbian the display manager is LightDM, and the graphical shell is LXDE (Lightweight X11 Desktop Environment). Like most Linux distributions, the graphical desktop environment is based on the X Window System (X11), a project originally started at MIT and now managed by the X.Org Foundation.

2.4 Kernel administration and programming
The administrator of a Linux system does not need to know the inner workings of the Linux kernel but needs to be familiar with tools to configure the operating system, including adding functionality to the kernel through kernel modules, and compilation of a custom kernel.

2.4.1 Loadable kernel modules and device drivers
As explained above, the Linux kernel is modular, and functionality can be loaded at run time using Loadable Kernel Modules (LKM). This feature is used in particular to configure drivers for the system hardware. Therefore the administrator needs to be familiar with the main concepts of the module system and a basic understanding of the role of a device driver.

■ To insert a module into the Linux kernel, the command *insmod (8)* can be used. *insmod* makes an *init_module()* system call to load the LKM into kernel memory.

■ The *init_module()* system call invokes the LKM's initialization routine immediately after it loads the LKM. *insmod* passes to *init_module()* the address of the initialization subroutine in the LKM using the *macro module_init()*.

■ The LKM author sets up the module's init_module to call a kernel function that registers the subroutines that the LKM contains. For example, a character device driver's init_module subroutine might call the *register_chrdev* kernel subroutine, passing the major and minor number of the device it intends to drive and the address of its own *open()* routine as arguments. *register_chrdev* records that when the kernel wants to open that particular device, it should call the *open()* routine in our LKM.

■ When an LKM is unloaded (e.g., via the rmmod(8) command), the LKM's cleanup subroutine is called via the macro *module_exit()*.

■ In practice, the administrator will want to use the more intelligent modprobe(8) command to handle module dependencies automatically. Finally, to list all loaded kernel modules, the command lsmod(8) can be used.

For the curious, the details of implementation are init_module, load_module, and do_init_module in kernel/module.c.

2.4.2 Anatomy of a Linux kernel module

As an administrator, sometimes you may have to add a new device to your system for which the standard kernel of your system's Linux distro does not provide a driver. That means you will have to add this driver to the kernel.

A trivial kernel module is very simple. The following module will print some information to the kernel log when it is loaded and unloaded.

Listing 2.4.1: A trivial kernel module   C

```c
1   #include <linux/init.h>          // For macros __init __exit
2   #include <linux/module.h>        // Kernel LKM functionality
3   #include <linux/kernel.h>        // Kernel types and function definitions
4
5   static int __init hello_LKM_init(void){
6       printk(KERN_INFO "Hello from our LKM!\n");
7       return 0;
8   }
9
10  static void __exit hello_LKM_exit(void){
11      printk(KERN_INFO "Goodbye from our LKM!\n");
12  }
13
14  module_init(hello_LKM_init);
15  module_exit(hello_LKM_exit);
```

However, note that a kernel module is not an application; it is a piece of code to be used by the kernel. As you can see, there is no *main()* function. Furthermore, kernel modules:

- do not execute sequentially: a kernel module registers itself to handle requests using its initialization function, which runs and then terminates. The types of request that it can handle are defined within the module code. This is quite similar to the event-driven programming model that is commonly utilized in graphical-user-interface (GUI) applications.

- do not have automatic resource management (memory, file handles, etc.): any resources that are allocated in the module code must be explicitly deallocated when the module is unloaded.

- do not have access to the common user-space system calls, e.g., *printf()*. However, there is a *printk()* function that can output information to the kernel log, and which can be viewed from user space.

- can be interrupted: kernel modules can be used by several different programs/processes at the same time, as they are part of the kernel. When writing a kernel module you must, therefore, be very careful to ensure that the module behavior is consistent and correct when the module code is interrupted.

- have to be very resource-aware: as a module is kernel code, its execution contributes to the kernel runtime overhead, both in terms of CPU cycles and memory utilization. So you have to be very aware that your module should not harm the overall performance of your system.

The macros *module_init* and *module_exit* are used to identify which subroutines should be run when the module is loaded and unloaded. The rest of the module functionality depends on the purpose of the module, but the general mechanism used in the kernel to connect a specific module to a generic API (e.g., the file system API) is via a struct with function pointers, which functions in the same way as an object interface declaration in Java or C++. For example, the file system API provides a struct file_operations (defined in include/linux/fs.h) which looks as follows:

Listing 2.4.2: file_operations struct from <include/linux/fs.h>

```c
struct file_operations {
    struct module *owner;
    loff_t (*llseek) (struct file *, loff_t, int);
    ssize_t (*read) (struct file *, char __user *, size_t, loff_t *);
    ssize_t (*write) (struct file *, const char __user *, size_t, loff_t *);
    ssize_t (*read_iter) (struct kiocb *, struct iov_iter *);
    ssize_t (*write_iter) (struct kiocb *, struct iov_iter *);
    int (*iterate) (struct file *, struct dir_context *);
    int (*iterate_shared) (struct file *, struct dir_context *);
    __poll_t (*poll) (struct file *, struct poll_table_struct *);
    long (*unlocked_ioctl) (struct file *, unsigned int, unsigned long);
    long (*compat_ioctl) (struct file *, unsigned int, unsigned long);
    int (*mmap) (struct file *, struct vm_area_struct *);
    unsigned long mmap_supported_flags;
    int (*open) (struct inode *, struct file *);
    int (*flush) (struct file *, fl_owner_t id);
    int (*release) (struct inode *, struct file *);
    int (*fsync) (struct file *, loff_t, loff_t, int datasync);
```

```
19     int (*fasync) (int, struct file *, int);
20     int (*lock) (struct file *, int, struct file_lock *);
21     ssize_t (*sendpage) (struct file *, struct page *, int, size_t, loff_t *, int);
22     unsigned long (*get_unmapped_area)(struct file *,
23         unsigned long, unsigned long, unsigned long, unsigned long);
24     int (*check_flags)(int);
25     int (*flock) (struct file *, int, struct file_lock *);
26     ssize_t (*splice_write)(struct pipe_inode_info *, struct file *, loff_t *,
27         size_t, unsigned int);
28     ssize_t (*splice_read)(struct file *, loff_t *, struct pipe_inode_info *,
29         size_t, unsigned int);
30     int (*setlease)(struct file *, long, struct file_lock **, void **);
31     long (*fallocate)(struct file *file, int mode, loff_t offset,
32         loff_t len);
33     void (*show_fdinfo)(struct seq_file *m, struct file *f);
34 #ifndef CONFIG_MMU
35     unsigned (*mmap_capabilities)(struct file *);
36 #endif
37     ssize_t (*copy_file_range)(struct file *, loff_t, struct file *,
38         loff_t, size_t, unsigned int);
39     int (*clone_file_range)(struct file *, loff_t, struct file *, loff_t,
40     u64);
41     ssize_t (*dedupe_file_range)(struct file *, u64, u64, struct file *,
42         u64);
43 } __randomize_layout;
```

So if you want to implement a module for a custom file system driver, you will have to provide implementations of the calls you want to support with the signatures as provided in this struct. Then in your module code, you can create an instance of this struct and populate it with pointers to the functions you've implemented, for example, assuming you have implemented *my_file_open, my_file_read, my_file_write, and my_file_close*, you would create the following struct:

Listing 2.4.3: Example file_operations struct   C

```
1     static struct file_operations my_file_ops =
2     {
3         .open = my_file_open,
4         .read = my_file_read,
5         .write = dmy_file_write,
6         .release = dmy_file_close,
7     };
```

Now all that remains is to make the kernel use this struct, and this is achieved using yet another API call which you call in the initialization subroutine. In the case of a driver for a character file (e.g., a serial port or audio device), this call would be `register_chrdev(0, DEVICE_- NAME, &my_file_ops)`. This API call is also defined in include/linux/fs.h. Other types of devices have similar calls to register new functionality with the kernel.

2.4.3 Building a custom kernel module

If you want to create your own kernel module, you don't need the entire kernel source code, but you do need the kernel header files. On a Raspberry Pi 3 running Raspbian, you can use the following commands to install the kernel headers:

```
Listing 2.4.4: Installing kernel headers on Raspbian                              Bash

1    $ sudo apt-get update
2    $ sudo apt-get install raspberrypi-kernel-headers
```

The Linux kernel has a dedicated Makefile-based system to build modules (and to build the actual kernel) called kbuild. The kernel documentation provides a good explanation of how to build a kernel module in Documentation/kbuild/modules.txt.

The disadvantage to building a kernel module from source is that you have to rebuild it every time you upgrade the kernel. The Dynamic Kernel Module Support (dkms) framework offers a way to ensure that custom modules are automatically rebuilt whenever the kernel version changes.

2.4.4 Building a custom kernel

In some cases, it might be necessary or desirable for the system administrator to build a custom kernel. Building a custom kernel gives fine-grained control over many of the kernel configurations and can be used to achieve better performance or a smaller footprint.

The process to build a custom kernel is explained on the Raspberry Pi web site. For this, you will need the complete kernel sources. Again the kernel documentation is a great source for additional information, have a look at Documentation/kbuild/kconfig.txt, Documentation/kbuild/kbuild.txt, and Documentation/kbuild/makefiles.txt.

If you compile the Linux kernel on a Raspberry Pi device, it will take several hours—even with parallel compilation threads enabled. On the other hand, cross-compiling the kernel on a modern x86-64 PC only takes a few minutes at most.

2.5 Administrator and programmer view of the key chapters

From a systems programmer or administrator perspective, Linux is a POSIX-compliant system. POSIX (the Portable Operating System Interface) is a family of IEEE standards aimed at maintaining compatibility between operating systems. POSIX defines the application programming interface (API) used by programs to interact with the operating system. In practice, the standards are maintained by The Open Group, the certifying body for the UNIX trademark, which publishes the Single UNIX Specification, an extension of the IEEE POSIX standards (currently at version 4). The key chapters in this book discuss both the general (non-Linux specific) concepts and theory as well as the POSIX-compliant Linux implementations.

2.5.1 Process management

Linux administrators and programmers need to be familiar with processes, what they are, and how they are managed by the kernel. Chapter 4 'Process management' introduces the process abstraction. We outline the state that needs to be encapsulated. We walk through the typical lifecycle of a process from forking to termination. We review the typical operations that will be performed on a process.

2.5.2 Process scheduling

Scheduling of processes and threads has a huge impact on system performance, and therefore Linux administrators and programmers need a good understanding of scheduling in general and the scheduling capabilities of the Linux kernel in particular. It is important to understand how to manage process priorities, per-process and per-user resources, and how to make efficient use of the scheduler. Chapter 5 'Process scheduling,' discusses how the OS schedules processes on a processor. This includes the rationale for scheduling, the concept of context switching, and an overview of scheduling policies (FCFS, priority, ...) and scheduler architectures (FIFO, multilevel feedback queues, priorities, ...). The Linux scheduler is studied in detail, with particular attention to the Completely Fair Scheduler but also discussing soft and hard real-time scheduling in the Linux kernel.

2.5.3 Memory management

While memory itself is remarkably straightforward, OS architects have built lots of abstraction layers on top. Principally, these abstractions serve to improve performance and/or programmability. For both the administrator and the programmer, it is important to have a good understanding of how the memory system works and what its performance trade-offs are. This is tightly connected with concepts such as virtual memory, paging, swap space, etc. The programmer also needs to understand how memory is allocated and what the memory protection mechanisms are. All this is covered in Chapter 6, 'Memory Management.' We briefly review caches (in hardware and software) to improve access speed. We go into detail about virtual memory to improve the management of physical memory resource. We will provide highly graphical descriptions of address translation, paging, page tables, page faults, swapping, etc. We explore standard schemes for page replacement, copy-on-write, etc. We will examine concrete examples in Arm architecture and Linux OS.

2.5.4 Concurrency and parallelism

Concurrency and parallelism are more important for the programmer than the administrator, as concurrency is needed for responsive, interactive applications and parallelism for performance. From an administrator perspective, it is important to understand the impact of the use of multiple hardware threads by a single application. In Chapter 7, 'Concurrency and parallelism,' we discuss how the OS supports concurrency and how the OS can assist in exploiting hardware parallelism. We define concurrency and parallelism and discuss how they relate to threads and processes. We discuss the key issue of resource sharing, covering locking, semaphores, deadlock, and livelock. We look at OS support for concurrent and parallel programming via POSIX threads and present an overview of practical parallel programming techniques such as OpenMP, MPI, and OpenCL.

2.5.5 Input/output

Chapter 8 'Input/output,' presents the OS abstraction of an I/O device. We review device interfacing, covering topics like polling, interrupts, and DMA, and we discuss memory-mapped I/O. We investigate a range of device types, to highlight their diverse features and behavior. We cover hardware registers, memory mapping, and coprocessors. Furthermore, we examine the ways in which devices are exposed to programmers, and we review the structure of a typical device driver.

2.5.6 Persistent storage

Because Linux, as a Unix-like operating system, is designed around the file system abstraction, a good understanding files and file systems is important for the administrator, in particular of concepts such as mounting, formatting, checking, permissions and links. Chapter 9 'Persistent storage' focuses on file systems. We discuss the use cases and explain how the raw hardware (block- and sector-based storage, etc.) is abstracted at the OS level. We talk about mapping high-level concepts like files, directories, permissions, etc. down to physical entities. We review allocation, space management, and recovery from failure. We present a case study of a Linux file system. We also discuss Windows-style FAT, since this is how USB bulk storage operates.

2.5.7 Networking
Networking is important at many levels: when booting, the firmware deals with the MAC layer, the kernel starts the networking subsystem (arp, dhcp and init starts daemons; then user processes start clients and/or daemons. The administrator may need to tune the TCP/IP stack and configure the kernel firewall. Most applications today require network access. As the Linux networking stack is handled by the kernel, the programmer needs to understand how Linux manages networking as well as the basic APIs.

Chapter 10 'Networking' introduces networking from a Linux kernel perspective: why is networking treated differently from other types of IO, what are the OS requirements to support the network stack, etc.. We introduce socket programming with a focus of the role the OS plays (e.g.~buffering, file abstraction, supporting multiple clients, ...).

2.6 Summary
In this chapter, we have introduced several basic operating system concepts and illustrated how they relate to Linux. We have discussed what happens when a Linux system (in particular on the Raspberry Pi) boots and initializes. We have introduced kernel modules and kernel compilation. Finally, we have presented a roadmap of the key chapters in the book, highlighting their relevance to Linux system administrators and programmers.

2.7 Exercises and questions
2.7.1 Installing Raspbian on the Raspberry Pi 3
1. Following the instructions on raspberrypi.org, download the latest Raspbian disk image and install it either as a Virtual Machine using qemu or on an actual Raspberry Pi 3 device.
2. Boot the device or VM and ping it (as explained on the Raspberry Pi web site).

2.7.2 Setting up SSH under Raspbian
1. Configure your Raspberry Pi to start an ssh server when it boots (this is not discussed in the text).
2. Log in via ssh and create a dedicated user account.
3. Forbid access via ssh to any account except this dedicated one.

2.7.3 Writing a kernel module
1. Write a simple kernel module that prints some information to the kernel log file when loaded, as explained in the text.
2. Write a more involved kernel module that creates a character device in /dev.

2.7.4 Booting Linux on the Raspberry Pi
1. Describe the stages of the Linux boot process for the Raspberry Pi.
2. Explain the purpose of the `initramfs` RAM disk.

2.7.5 Initialization
1. After the kernel has booted it launches the first process, called *init*. What does this process do?
2. Are there specific requirements on the *init* process?

2.7.6 Login
1. Which are the programs involved in logging in to the system via a terminal?
2. Explain the login process and how the kernel is involved.

2.7.7 Administration
1. Explain the role of the /dev and /proc file systems in system administration.
2. Explain the Linux approach to permissions: who are the participants, what are the restrictions, what is the role of the kernel?
3. As a system administrator, which tools do you have at your disposal to control and limit the behavior of your user processes in terms of CPU and memory utilization.

Chapter 3

Hardware architecture

A brief history of Arm, based on an interview from 2012 with Sophie Wilson FRS FREng, a British computer scientist and software engineer who designed the Acorn Micro-Computer and later the instruction set of the Arm processor, which became the de facto model used in 21st-century smartphones.

Image ©2013 Chris Monk, CC BY 2.0, commons.wikimedia.org

In 1983 Acorn Computers had produced the BBC Microcomputer. It was designed as a two-processor system from the outset in order to be able to build both a small cheap machine and a big expensive workstation-style machine. This was possible by using two processors: an IO processor and a second processor that would do the actual heavy lifting. Acorn made many variants of the second processor based on existing microprocessors.

In Sophie's words, "We could see what all these processors did and what they didn't do. So, the first thing they didn't do was they didn't make good use of the memory system. The second thing they didn't do was that they weren't fast, they weren't easy to use." Regarding the rationale behind the design of the original Arm processor, Sophie said, "We rather hoped that we could get to a power level such that if you wrote in a higher-level language, you could , e.g., write 3D graphics games. For the processors that were on sale at the time that wasn't true. They were too slow. So we felt we needed a better processor. We particularly felt we needed a better processor in order to compete with what was just beginning to be a flood of IBM PC compatibles. So, we gave ourselves a project slogan which was *MIPS for the masses*". "This was very different to what other people were doing at the time. RISC processor research had just been sort of released by IBM, by Berkeley, by Stanford, and they were all after making workstation-class machines that were quite high end. We ended up wanting to do the same thing but at the low end, a machine for the masses that would be quite powerful but not super powerful."

"ARM was that machine: a machine that was MIPS for the masses. We started selling Arm powered machines in 1986, 1987. The things that we'd endowed it with, what we'd set Arm up to be, with its cheap and powerful mindset, were the things that became valuable. When people wanted to put good amounts of processing into something, that was the really important attribute."

"We designed a deeply embedded processor, or an embedded processor, without consciously realizing it in our striving for what we thought would be ideal for our marketplace; that's been what's really mattered. As a sort of side effect of making it cheap and simple to use, we also ended up making it power efficient; that wasn't intentional. In hindsight, it was an obvious accident. We only had 25,000 transistors in the first one. We were worried about power dissipation. We needed to be extremely careful for something that would be mass manufactured and put into cheap machines without heat sinks and that sort of thing. So there were already some aspects of power conservation in the design, but we performed way better than that and as the world has gone increasingly mobile that aspect of Arm has mattered as well. But to start off, we designed a really good, deeply embedded processor."

3.1 Overview

In this chapter, we discuss the hardware on which the operating system runs, with a focus on the Linux view on the hardware system and the OS support of the Arm Cortex series processors. The purpose of this chapter is to provide you with a useable mental model for the hardware system and to explain the need for an operating system and how the hardware supports the OS.

What you will learn
After you have studied the material in this chapter, you will be able to:

1. Discuss the support that modern hardware offers for operating systems (dedicated registers, timers, interrupt architecture, DMA).

2. Compare and contrast instruction sets for the Arm Cortex M0+ and Arm Cortex A53 in terms of purpose, capability and OS support.

3. Explain the role and structure of the address map.

4. Explain the hardware structure of the memory subsystem (caches, TLB, MMU).

3.2 Arm hardware architecture

Figure 3.1 [1] shows the entire Arm processor family, with the most recent members on the right, and the highest performance and capability processors at the top. We will illustrate the Arm hardware architecture using two quite different processors as examples: the Arm Cortex M0+ is a single-core, very low gate count, highly energy-efficient processor that is intended for microcontroller and deeply embedded applications that require an area optimized processor and low power consumption, such as IoT devices. It does not have a cache and uses the 16-bit Armv6-M Thumb instruction set. In general, such processors will not run Linux, however many of the main OS support features are still available.

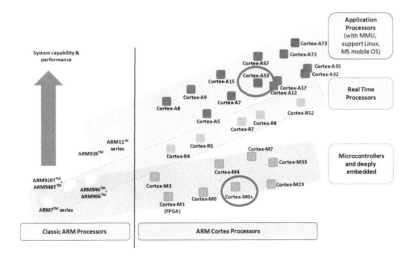

Figure 3.1: Arm processor family.

By contrast, the Arm Cortex A53, used in the Raspberry Pi 3, is a mid-range, low-power processor that implements the Armv8-A architecture. The Cortex-A53 processor has one to four cores, each with an L1 memory system and a single shared L2 cache. It is a 64-bit processor which supports the AArch64 and AArch32 (including Thumb) execution modes. It is intended as an Application Processor for application domains such as mobile computing, smartphones, and energy-efficient servers.

All Arm processor systems use the Advanced Microcontroller Bus Architecture (AMBA), an open-standard specification for the connection and management of functional blocks in system-on-chip (SoC) designs.

All Arm processors have a RISC (Reduced Instruction Set Computing) architecture[1]. RISC architecture based processors typically require fewer transistors than those with a complex instruction set computing (CISC) architectures (e.g., x86), which can result in lower cost and lower power consumption. Furthermore, as the instructions are simpler, most instructions can be executed in a single cycle, which makes instruction pipelining simpler and more efficient. The complex functionality supported in a CISC instruction set is achieved through a combination of multiple RISC instructions.

Typically, RISC machines have a large number of general-purpose registers (while CISC machines have more special-purpose registers). In a RISC architecture, any register can contain either data or an address. Furthermore, a RISC processor typically operates on data held in registers. Separate load and store instructions transfer data between the register bank and external memory (this is called a load-store architecture).

3.3 Arm Cortex M0+

The Arm Cortex-M0+ processor is a low-spec embedded processor, typically used for applications that need lower power and don't need full OS support. Figure 3.2 shows the Arm MPS2+ Prototyping Board for Cortex-M based designs, an FPGA development platform supporting the entire Cortex-M processor range except for the M23 and M33. The functional block diagram of the Cortex-M0+ processor [2] is shown in Figure 3.3. The Cortex-M0+ uses the AHB-Lite (Advanced High-performance Bus Lite) Lite bus standard [3]. AHB-Lite is a bus interface that supports a single bus master and provides high-bandwidth operation.

Figure 3.2: Arm MPS2+ FPGA Prototyping Board for Cortex-M based designs. Photo by author.

[1] The name ARM was originally an acronym for Acorn RISC Machine and was altered to Advanced RISC Machines.

It is typically used to communicate with internal memory devices, external memory interfaces, and high bandwidth peripherals. Low-bandwidth peripherals can be included as AHB-Lite slaves but typically reside on the AMBA Advanced Peripheral Bus (APB). Bridging between AHB and APB is done using a AHB-Lite slave, known as an APB bridge.

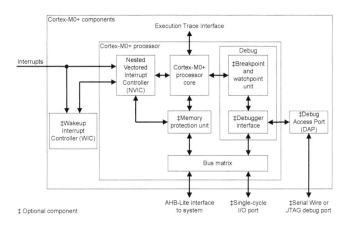

Figure 3.3: Cortex-M0 processor functional block diagram.

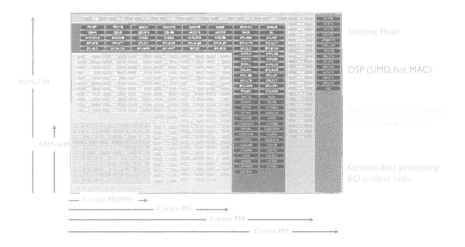

Figure 3.4: Thumb instruction set support in the Cortex-M processors.

3.3.1 Interrupt control
The Cortex-M0+ handles interrupts via a programmable controller called the Nested Vectored Interrupt Controller (NVIC). This controller supports up to 240 dynamically re-prioritizable interrupts each with up to 256 levels of priority. It keeps track of stacked/nested interrupts to enable back-to-back processing ("tail-chaining") of interrupts.

3.3.2 Instruction set
As mentioned, the Cortex-M0+ implements the Armv6-M Thumb instruction set; this is a subset of the Armv7-M Thumb instruction set and includes a number of 32-bit instructions that use Thumb-2 technology. The Thumb instruction set is a 16-bit instruction set formed of a subset of the

most commonly used 32-bit Arm instructions. Thumb instructions have corresponding 32-bit Arm instructions that have the same effect on the processor model. Thumb instructions operate with the standard Arm register configuration. On execution, 16-bit Thumb instructions are transparently decompressed to full 32-bit Arm instructions in real-time, without performance loss. For more details, we refer to [2]. Figure 3.4 illustrates the various Arm Thumb instruction sets and the purposes of the instructions. The key points to notice is that the Armv6-M Thumb instruction set is very small and that it is a very reduced subset of the complete Thumb instruction set.

3.3.3 System timer

An interesting feature of the Cortex-M0+ is the optional 24-bit System Timer (SysTick). This timer can be used by an operating system. It can be polled by software or can be configured to generate an interrupt. The SysTick interrupt has its own entry in the vector table and therefore can have its own handler. The SysTick timer is controlled via a set of special system control registers.

3.3.4 Processor mode and privileges

The Cortex-M0+ processor supports the Armv6-M Thread and Handler mode through a control register (CONTROL) and two different stack pointers, Main Stack Pointer (MSP) and Process Stack Pointer (PSP) as explained in Chapter 1. Thread mode is used to execute application software. The processor enters Thread mode when it comes out of reset. Handler mode is used to handle exceptions. The processor returns to Thread mode when it has finished all exception processing.

It also (optionally) supports different privilege levels for software execution as follows:

- Unprivileged: The software has limited access to the MSR and MRS instructions, and cannot use the CPS instruction or access the system timer, NVIC, or system control block. It might have restricted access to memory or peripherals.

- Privileged: The software can use all the instructions and has access to all resources.

In Thread mode, the CONTROL register controls whether software execution is privileged or unprivileged. In Handler mode, software execution is always privileged. Only privileged software can write to the CONTROL register to change the privilege level for software execution in Thread mode. Unprivileged software can use the SVC instruction to make a supervisor call to transfer control to privileged software.

3.3.5 Memory protection

The Cortex-M0+ (optionally) supports memory protection through an optional Memory Protection Unit (MPU). When implemented, the processor supports the Armv6 Protected Memory System Architecture model [2]. The MPU provides support for protection regions with priorities and access permissions. The MPU can be used to enforce privilege rules, separate processes, and manage memory attributes.

Considering the above features, in principle, the M0+ is capable of running an OS like Linux. In practice, embedded systems with a Cortex-M0+ will not have sufficient storage and memory to run Linux, but they can support other OSs such as freeRTOS.[2]

[2] https://www.freertos.org/

3.4 Arm Cortex A53

This processor is used in the Raspberry Pi 3, shown in Figure 3.5. The functional block diagram of the Cortex-A53 processor [4] is shown in Figure 3.6. It is immediately clear that this is a much more complex processor, with up to 4 cores and a 2-level cache hierarchy. Each core (bottom row) has a dedicated Floating-point Unit (FPU) and the Neon SIMD (single instruction multiple data) architecture extension. From the Governor blocks at the top, the main features of interest from an OS perspective are "Arch timer" and "GIC CPU interface." The other blocks (CTI, Retention control, and Debug over power down) provide advanced debug and power-saving support.

Figure 3.5: Raspberry Pi 3 Model B with Arm Cortex-A53. Photo by author.

Cortex-A53 processor											
APB decoder			APB ROM			APB multiplexer			CTM		
Governor											
Core 0 governor			Core 1 governor			Core 2 governor			Core 3 governor		
CTI	Retention control	Debug over power down	CTI	Retention control	Debug over power down	CTI	Retention control	Debug over power down	CTI	Retention control	Debug over power down
Clock and reset	Arch timer	GIC CPU interface	Clock and reset	Arch timer	GIC CPU interface	Clock and reset	Arch timer	GIC CPU interface	Clock and reset	Arch timer	GIC CPU interface
Core 0			Core 1			Core 2			Core 3		
FPU and NEON extension		Crypto extension	FPU and NEON extension		Crypto extension	FPU and NEON extension		Crypto extension	FPU and NEON extension		Crypto extension
L1 ICache	L1 DCache	Debug and trace	L1 ICache	L1 DCache	Debug and trace	L1 ICache	L1 DCache	Debug and trace	L1 ICache	L1 DCache	Debug and trace
Level 2 memory system											
L2 cache		SCU		ACE/AMBA 5 CHI master bus interface			ACP slave				

Figure 3.6: Cortex-A53 processor functional block diagram.

3.4.1 Interrupt control
The "GIC CPU interface" block represents the Generic Interrupt Controller CPU Interface, an implementation of the Generic Interrupt Controller (GIC) architecture defined as part of the Armv8-A architecture. The GIC defines the architectural requirements for handling all interrupt sources for any processing element connected to a GIC and a common interrupt controller programming

interface applicable to uniprocessor or multiprocessor systems. The GIC is a much more advanced and flexible interrupt handling system than the NVIC of the Cortex-M0+ because it needs to support heterogeneous multicore systems and virtualization. Rather than the simple set of registers used by the NVIC, the GIC uses a memory-mapped interface of 255KB as well as a set of GIC control registers (GICC*) and registers to support virtualization of interrupts (GICH*, GICV*) in the CPU.

3.4.2 Instruction set

The Cortex-A53 supports both the AArch32 and AArch64 instruction set architectures. The AArch32 includes the Thumb instruction set used in the Cortex-M series. Consequently, code compiled for the Cortex-M0+, for example, can run on the Cortex-A53. More to the point, the Raspbian Linux distribution for the Raspberry Pi 3 is a 32-bit distribution, so the processor is running the OS and all applications in the AArch32 state.

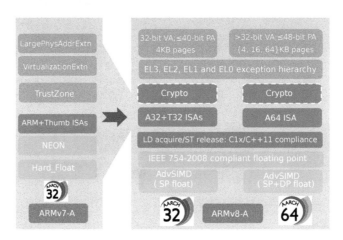

Figure 3.7: Arm architecture evolution.

Figure 3.7, adapted from [5], shows how the Armv7-A architecture has been incorporated into the Armv8-A architecture. In addition, Armv8 supports two execution states: AArch32, in which the A32 and T32 instruction sets (Arm and Thumb in Armv7-A) are supported and AArch64, in the 64-bit instruction set. Armv8-A is backwards compatible with Armv7-A, but the exception, privilege, and security model has been significantly extended as discussed below. In AArch32, the Armv7-A Large Physical Address Extensions are supported, providing 32-bit virtual addressing and 40-bit physical addressing. In AArch64, this is extended in a backward compatible way to provide 64-bit virtual addresses and a 48-bit physical address space. Another addition is the cryptographic at the instruction level, i.e., dedicated instructions to speed up cryptographic computations.

The latest ISO/IEC standards for C (C11, ISO/IEC 9899:2011) and C++ (ISO/IEC 14882:2011) introduce standard capabilities for multi-threaded programming. This includes the requirement for standard implementations of mutexes and other forms of "uninterruptible object access." The Load-Acquire and Store-Release instructions introduced in AArch64 have been added to comply with these standards.

Floating-point and SIMD support

The Armv8 architecture provides support for IEEE 754-2008 floating-point operations and SIMD (Single Instruction Multiple Data) or vector operations through dedicated registers and instructions.

The Armv8 architecture provides two register files, a general-purpose register file, and a SIMD and floating-point register (SIMD&FP) register file. In each of these, the possible register widths depend on the Execution state.

- In AArch64 state, there is:

    - A general-purpose register file containing 31 64-bit registers. Many instructions can access these registers as 64-bit registers or as 32-bit registers, using only the bottom 32 bits.

    - A SIMD&FP register file containing 32 128-bit registers. The quadword integer and floating-point data types only apply to the SIMD&FP register file. The AArch64 vector registers support 128-bit vectors (the effective vector length can be 64-bits or 128-bits depending on the instruction encoding used).

- In AArch32 state, there is:

    - A general-purpose register file containing 32-bit registers. Two 32-bit registers can support a doubleword; vector formatting is supported.

    - A SIMD&FP register file containing 64-bit registers. AArch32 state does not support quadword integer or floating-point data types.

Both AArch32 and AArch64 states support SIMD and floating-point instructions:

- AArch32 state provides:

    - SIMD instructions in the base instruction sets that operate on the 32-bit general-purpose registers.

    - Advanced SIMD instructions that operate on registers in the SIMD&FP register file.

    - Floating-point instructions that operate on registers in the SIMD&FP register file.

- AArch64 state provides:

    - Advanced SIMD instructions that operate on registers in the SIMD&FP register file.

    - Floating-point instructions that operate on registers in the SIMD&FP register file.

3.4.3 System timer

The Arm Cortex-A53 implements the Arm Generic Timer architecture [6]. The Generic Timer can schedule events and trigger interrupts based on an incrementing counter value. It provides:

■ Generation of timer events as interrupt outputs.

■ Generation of event streams.

The Generic Timer can schedule events and trigger interrupts based on an incrementing counter value. It provides a system counter that measures the passing of time in real-time but also supports virtual counters that measure the passing of virtual-time, i.e., the "equivalent real-time" on a Virtual Machine.

The Cortex-A53 processor provides a set of timer registers within each core of the cluster. The timers are:

■ An EL1 Non-secure physical timer.

■ An EL1 Secure physical timer.

■ An EL2 physical timer.

■ A virtual timer.

The Cortex-A53 processor does not include the system counter. This resides in the SoC. The system counter value is distributed to the Cortex-A53 processor with a synchronous binary encoded 64-bit bus. For more details, we refer to the Technical Reference Manual [4].

3.4.4 Processor mode and privileges

In terms of privileges, the Cortex-A53 defines the Armv8 exception model, with four Exception levels, EL0-EL3, that provide an execution privilege hierarchy:

■ *EL0* has the lowest software execution privilege, and execution at EL0 is called unprivileged execution.

■ Increased values of n, from 1 to 3, indicate increased software execution privilege. The OS would run in *EL1*.

■ *EL2* provides support for processor virtualization.

■ *EL3* provides support for two security states, as part of the TrustZone architecture:

  ☐ In *Secure* state, the processor can access both the Secure and the Non-secure memory address space. When executing at EL3, it can access all the system control resources.

  ☐ In *Non-secure* state, the processor can access only the Non-secure memory address space and cannot access the Secure system control resources.

The addition of EL3 allows, e.g. to run a trusted OS in parallel with a hypervisor supporting non-trusted OSs on a single system.

It is possible to switch at run time between the AArch32 and AArch64 instruction set architectures, but there are certain restrictions relating to the exception levels, explained in Figure 3.8. Essentially, code running at a higher exception level can only be AArch64 if the lower exception levels are also AArch64.

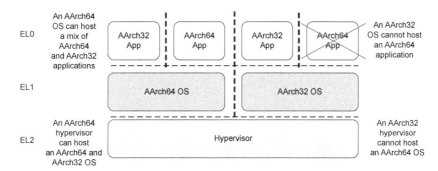

Figure 3.8: Moving between AArch32 and AArch64.

For each implemented Exception level, in AArch64 state, a dedicated stack pointer register is implemented. In AArch32 state, the stack pointer depends on the "PE mode" (these do not exist in AArch64). PE modes support normal software execution and handle exceptions. The current mode determines the set of general-purpose and special-purpose registers that are available. The AArch32 modes are:

- Monitor mode. This mode always executes at Secure EL3.

- Hyp (hypervisor) mode. This mode always executes at Non-secure EL2.

- System, Supervisor, Abort, Undefined, IRQ, and FIQ modes. The Exception level these modes execute at depends on the Security state:

  - In Secure state: Execute at EL3 when EL3 is using AArch32.

  - In Non-secure state: always execute at EL1.

- User mode. This mode always executes at EL0.

3.4.5 Memory management unit
As explained in Chapter 1, modern processors provide hardware support for address translation and memory protection. We also explained briefly the concept of memory pages and the page table. A more detailed discussion is provided in Chapter 6, "Memory management." For the purpose of the discussion of the Cortex-A53 MMU, we can consider the terms "virtual memory" and "logical memory" to be the same. An additional complexity is caused by the support for Virtual Machines (hypervisor) in

the Armv8 architecture: as each VM must provide the illusion of running on real hardware, there is an extra level of addressing called Intermediate Physical Address (IPA) required.

The MMU controls table walk hardware that accesses translation tables in main memory. It translates virtual addresses to physical addresses and provides fine-grained memory system control through a set of virtual-to-physical address mappings and memory attributes held in page tables.

These are loaded into the Translation look-aside buffer (TLB) when a location is accessed. In practice, the TLB is split into a very small, very fast micro TLB and a larger main TLB.

The MMU in each core comprises the following components:

Translation look-aside buffer
The TLB consists of two levels:

1. A 10-entry fully-associative instruction micro TLB and 10-entry fully-associative data micro TLB. We explained the concept of a fully-associative cache in Chapter 1. There are two separate micro TLBs for instructions and data to allow parallel access for performance reasons.

2. A 4-way set-associative 512-entry unified main TLB (Figure 3.9). "Unified" means that this TLB is used for both instructions and data. The main TLB is not fully associative but 4-way set-associative. Remember that "fully associative" means that every address can be stored at any possible entry of the TLB. If the cache or TLB is not fully associative, it means that there are restrictions on where a given address can be stored. A very common approach is an n-way set-associative cache, which means that the cache is divided into blocks of n entries, and each block is mapped to a fixed region of memory. An address from a given region of memory can only be stored in a given block, but it can be stored in any of the n entries in that block. For example, on the Raspberry Pi 3, the RAM is 1GB. Given a page size of 4kB, this means 256K pages. This is mapped to 128 blocks (4 entries per block in the TLB), so every physical memory block has 2k frames, each of which can be stored in one of 4 entries in the TLB.

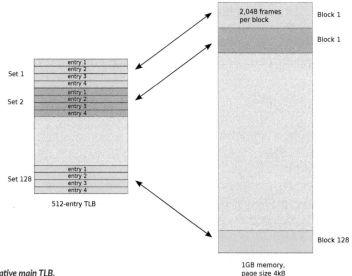

Figure 3.9: 4-way set-associative main TLB.

Additional caches

As we will see in Chapter 6, in practice page tables are hierarchical and address translation in a hypervisor-based environment has two stages (Figure 3.10). The Cortex-53 MMU, therefore, provides additional caches:

- 4-way set-associative 64-entry walk cache.
  The walk cache RAM holds the partial result of a stage 1 translation. For more details, see Chapter 6.

- 4-way set-associative 64-entry IPA cache.
  The Intermediate Physical Address (IPA) cache RAM holds mappings between intermediate physical addresses and physical addresses. Only Non-secure EL1 and EL0 stage 2 translations use this cache.

Note that it is possible to disable stage 1 or stage 2 of the address translation.

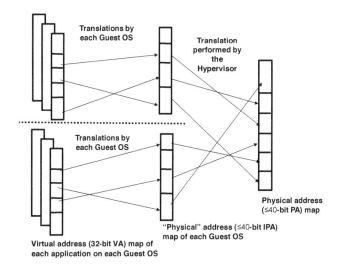

Figure 3.10: Two-stage address translation.

3.4.6 Memory system

In Chapter 1, we introduced the concept of caching and a simple model for a cache, a small, fast memory for often-used data. The actual memory system in the Cortex-A53 is more complicated, but the same concepts apply (Figure 3.6).

L1 Cache

The L1 memory system consists of separate per-core instruction and data caches. The implementer configures the instruction and data caches independently during implementation, to sizes of 8KB, 16KB, 32KB, or 64KB. The Raspberry Pi 3 configuration has 16KB for both Instruction and Data. Note that the instruction cache is read-only because instruction memory is read-only.

The L1 instruction cache has the following key features:

- Cache line size of 64 bytes.

- 2-way set associative.

- 16-byte read interface to the L2 memory system. This means it takes 4 cycles to read a cache line from the L2 cache.

The L1 data memory system has the following features:

- Cache line size of 64 bytes.

- 4-way set associative.

- 32-byte write and 16-byte read interface to the L2 memory system.

- 64-bit read and 128-bit write path from the data L1 memory system to the datapath. In other words, the CPU can read one 64-bit word and write 2 64-bit words directly from the L1 data cache.

- Support for three outstanding data cache misses. This means that instead of immediately fetching a cache line on a cache miss, the requests are deferred. So the cache will not block to fetch the cache line on the first miss but allow the CPU to continue executing instructions (and hence potentially create more misses).

The L1 data cache supports only a Write-Back policy (remember from Chapter 1, this means that initial writes are to the cache, and write back to memory only occurs on eviction of the cache line). It normally[3] allocates a cache line on either a read miss or a write miss (i.e., both write-allocate and read-allocate). A special feature of the L1 data cache is that it includes logic to switch into pure read allocate mode for certain scenarios. When in read allocate mode, loads behave as normal, and writes still lookup in the cache but, if they miss, they write out to L2 only.

The L1 data cache uses physical memory addresses. The micro TLB produces the physical address from the virtual address before performing the cache access.

L2 Cache
The L2 cache is a unified cache shared by all cores, with a configurable cache size of 128KB, 256KB, 512KB, 1MB, and 2MB. The Raspberry Pi 3 configuration is 512KB.

Data is allocated to the L2 cache only when evicted from the L1 memory system, not when first fetched from the system. Instructions are allocated to the L2 cache when fetched from the system and can be invalidated during maintenance operations.

The L2 cache has the following key features:

- Cache line size of 64 bytes;

- 16-way set-associative cache structure;

- Uses physical addresses.

---

[3] This behavior can be altered by changing the inner cache allocation hints in the page tables.

Data cache coherency

Cache coherency refers to the need to ensure that local caches on different cores in a multicore system with a shared memory have present a coherent view on the memory. This essentially means that the system should behave as if there are no caches. We note for completeness that the Cortex-A53 processor uses the MOESI protocol to maintain data coherency between multiple cores. In this protocol, each cache line is in one of five states: Modified, Owned, Exclusive, Shared, or Invalid. The L2 memory system includes a Snoop Control Unit (SCU) which implements this protocol. For more information, we refer to the "Arm Cortex-A Series Programmer's Guide for ARMv8-A", [7].

3.5 Address map

The description of the purpose, size, and position of the address regions for memory and peripherals in a system is called the *address map or memory map*. Because Arm system can be 32 or 64-bit, the address space ranges from 4GB (32-bit) to 1TB (40-bit). The white paper Principles of Arm Memory Maps describes Arm address maps for 32, 36 and 40-bit systems, and proposes extensions for 44 and 48-bit systems.

Arm has harmonized the memory maps across its various systems to provide internal consistency and software portability, and to address the constraints that come with mixing 32-bit components within larger address spaces. The introduction of Large Physical Address Extension (LPAE) to ARMv7 class CPUs has grown the physical address spaces to 36-bit and 40-bits, providing 64GB or 1024GB (1TB) memory space. The 64-bit ARMv8 architecture can address 48-bits, providing 256TB.

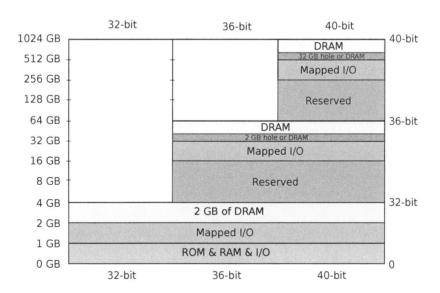

Figure 3.11: Arm 40-bit address map.

Figure 3.11 shows how the address maps for different bit widths are related. The address maps are defined as nested sets. As each memory map increases by 4-bits of address space, it contains all of the smaller address maps, at the lower addresses. Each increment of 4 address bits results in a 16-fold increase in addressable space. The address space is partitioned in a repeatable way:

8/16 DRAM;

4/16 Mapped I/O;

3/16 Reserved space;

1/16 Previous memory map (i.e., without the additional 4 address bits).

For example, the 36-bit address map contains the entire 32-bit address map in the lowest 4GB of address space.

The address maps are partitioned into four types or regions:

1. Static I/O and Static Memories, for register, mapped on-chip peripherals, boot ROMs, and scratch RAMs.

2. Mapped I/O, for dynamically configured, memory-mapped buses, such as PCIe.

3. DRAM, for main system dynamic memory.

4. Reserved space, for future use.

The "DRAM holes" mentioned in the Figure are an optional mechanism to simplify the decoding scheme when partitioning a large capacity DRAM device across the lower physically addressed regions, at the cost of leaving a small percentage of the address space unused.

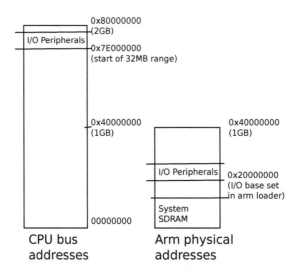

Figure 3.12: Broadcom BCM2835 Arm-based SoC (Raspberry Pi) address maps.

If we consider the 32-bit address space in the case of the Broadcom BCM2835 System-on-Chip used in the Raspberry Pi 3, the picture (Figure 3.12) is a bit more complicated because the actual 32-bit address space is used for the addresses on the system bus, but an MMU translates these addresses to a different set of "physical" addresses for the Arm CPU. The lowest 1GB of the Arm physical address map is effectively the Linux kernel memory. For addressing of user memory, an additional MMU is used.

3.6 Direct memory access

Direct memory access (DMA) is a mechanism that allows blocks of data to be transferred to or from devices with no CPU overhead. The CPU manages DMA operations by submitting DMA requests to a DMA controller. While the DMA transfer is in progress, the CPU can continue executing code. When the DMA transfer is completed, the DMA controller signals the CPU via an interrupt.

DMA is advantageous if large blocks of memory have to be copied or if the transfer is repetitive because both cases would otherwise consume a considerable amount of CPU time. Like most modern operating systems, Linux supports DMA transfers through a kernel API, if the hardware has DMA support. It should be noted that this does not require special instructions:the DMA controller is memory-mapped, and the CPU simply writes the request to that region of memory.

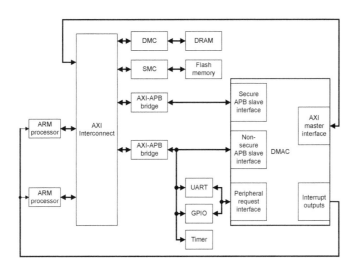

Figure 3.13: Example system with Cortex-A and CoreLink DMA controller.

Arm processors do not include a DMA engine as part of the CPU core. Arm provides dedicated DMA controllers such as the lightweight PrimeCell μDMAController [8], a very low gate count DMA controller compatible with the AMBA AHB-Lite protocol as used in the Cortex-M series, and the more advanced CoreLink DMA-330 DMA Controller [9] which has a full AMBA-compliant interface or the SoC manufacturers can provide their own DMA engines. Figure 3.13 shows an example system with the CoreLink DMAC. In the Arm Cortex M series, the DMA controller will be a peripheral on the AHB bus.

However, in the higher-end Arm Cortex-A series, a special interface called Accelerator Coherency Port (ACP) is provided as part of the AMBA AXI standard. The reason is that on multicore processors with cache coherency, the cache system complicates the DMA transfer because it is possible that some data has not been written to the main memory at the time of the transfer. With the ACP, the Cortex-A series implement a hardware mechanism to ensure that accesses to shared DMA memory regions are cache-coherent. Without such a mechanism, the operating system (or end-user software on a bare-metal system) must ensure the coherency. More details on integrating a DMA engine in an Arm-based multiprocessor SoC are provided in the Application Note Implementing DMA on ARM SMP Systems [10].

On the Arm Cortex A53, the ACP port is optional, and it is not provided on the SoC in the Raspberry Pi 3. The DMA controller on the Raspberry Pi SoC is not a ARM IP core. It is part of the I/O Peripheral address space. An additional complication, in this case, is that the DMA controller uses CPU bus addresses so for a DMA transfer the software needs to translate between the Arm physical addresses and the CPU bus addresses.

In general, DMA controllers are complex devices that usually have their own instruction set as well as a register file. This means that the Linux kernel needs a dedicated driver for the DMA controller.

3.7 Summary

In this chapter, we had a look a two different types of Arm processors: the Arm Cortex M0+, a single-core, very low gate count, highly energy-efficient processor intended for microcontroller and deeply embedded applications that implements the ARMv6-M architecture, and the Arm Cortex A53 used in the Raspberry Pi 3, a mid-range, low-power processor that implements the Armv8-A architecture and has all features required to run an OS like Linux. We have discussed these processors in terms of their instruction set, interrupt model, security model, and memory system. We have also introduced the Arm address maps and Direct memory access (DMA) support.

3.8 Exercises and questions

3.8.1 Bare-bones programming

The aim of this exercise is to implement some of the basic operating system functionality. To do this from scratch is quite a lot of work but we suggest you start from existing code provided in the tutorial series Bare-Metal Programming on Raspberry Pi 3 on GitHub.

1. Create a cyclic executive with three tasks where each task creates a continuous waveform: task 1 creates a sine; task 2, a block wave; and task 3, a triangle; each with a different period. Print either the values of the waveforms or a text-based graph on the terminal.

2. Make your cyclic executive preemptive.

3. Share a resource between the three tasks. This can be a simple shared variable with read and write access.

Other, harder suggestions:
1. Make memory allocation dynamic, i.e., write your own *malloc()* and *free()*.
2. Create a minimal memory file system.

3.8.2 Arm hardware architecture

1. What was the meaning of "MIPS for the masses"?
2. What are the advantages of a RISC architecture over a CISC architecture?

3.8.3 Arm Cortex M0+

1. For what kind of projects would you use an Arm Cortex M0+?
2. Why is the Arm Cortex M0+ not suitable for running Linux?

3.8.4 Arm Cortex A53

1. Discuss floating-point and SIMD support in the Arm Cortex A53
2. Discuss the processor modes and privileges in the Arm Cortex A53
3. Discuss the cache and TLB architecture of the Arm Cortex A53

3.8.5 Address map

1. Explain why Arm systems share a common address map for 32, 36 and 40-bit systems.
2. What is the purpose of "DRAM holes"?

3.8.6 Direct memory access

1. What is the role of the Accelerator Coherency Port (ACP) in the DMA architecture?

References

[1] J. Yiu, *Arm Cortex-M for Beginners – An overview of the Arm Cortex-M processor family and comparison*, Arm Ltd, 3 2017, v2. [Online].
Available: https://developer.arm.com/-/media/Files/pdf/Porting%20to%20ARM%2064-bit%20v4.pdf

[2] *Cortex™-M0+ Technical Reference Manual Revision: r0p1*, Arm Ltd, 12 2012, revC. [Online].
Available: http://infocenter.arm.com/help/topic/com.arm.doc.ddi0484c/DDI0484C_cortex_m0p_r0p1_trm.pdf

[3] *AMBA 3 AHB-Lite Protocol – Specification*, Arm Ltd, 3 2017, v1.0. [Online].
Available: https://silver.arm.com/download/download.tm?pv=1085658

[4] *Arm® Cortex®-A53 MPCore Processor – Technical Reference Manual Rev: r0p4*, Arm Ltd, 2 2016, revision: r0p4. [Online].
Available: http://infocenter.arm.com/help/topic/com.arm.doc.ddi0500g/DDI0500G_cortex_a53_trm.pdf

[5] C. Shore, *Porting to 64-bit Arm*, Arm Ltd, 7 2014, revC. [Online].
Available: https://developer.arm.com/-/media/Files/pdf/Porting%20to%20ARM%2064-bit%20v4.pdf

[6] *ARM® Architecture Reference Manual – ARMv8, for ARMv8-A architecture profile*, Arm Ltd, 12 2017, issue: C.a. [Online].
Available: https://silver.arm.com/download/download.tm?pv=4239650&p=1343131

[7] *Arm Cortex-A Series - Programmer's Guide for ARMv8-A - Version: 1.0*, Arm Ltd, 3 2015, issue A. [Online].
Available: http://infocenter.arm.com/help/topic/com.arm.doc.den0024a/DEN0024A_v8_architecture_PG.pdf

[8] *PrimeCell uDMA Controller (PL230) Technical Reference Manual Revision: r0p0*, Arm Ltd, 1 2007, issue: A. [Online].
Available: http://infocenter.arm.com/help/index.jsp?topic=/com.arm.doc.ddi0417a/index.html

[9] *CoreLink DMA-330 DMA Controller Technical Reference Manual Revision: r1p2*, Arm Ltd, 1 2012, issue: D. [Online].
Available: http://infocenter.arm.com/help/index.jsp?topic=/com.arm.doc.ddi0424d/index.html

[10] *Implementing DMA on ARM SMP Systems*, Arm Ltd, 8 2009, issue: A. [Online].
Available: http://infocenter.arm.com/help/index.jsp?topic=/com.arm.doc.dai0228a/index.html

Chapter 4

Process management

4.1 Overview

Processes are **programs in execution**. Have you ever seen a whale skeleton displayed in a museum? This is like a **program**—it's a *static* object, see Figure 4.1. Although it has shape and structure, it's never going to 'do' anything of interest. Now think about a live whale swimming through the ocean, see Figure 4.2. This is like a **process**—it's a *dynamic* object. It incorporates the skeleton structure, but it has more attributes and is capable of activity.

In this chapter, we explore what Linux processes look like, how they operate, and how they enable multi-program execution. We outline the context that needs to be encapsulated in a process. We walk through the process lifecycle, considering typical operations that will be performed on a process.

Figure 4.1: Blue whale skeleton at the Natural History Museum in London. Photo by author.

Figure 4.2: Blue whale swimming in the ocean. Public domain photo by NOAA.

What you will learn
After you have studied the material in this chapter, you will be able to:

1. Describe why processes are used in operating systems.

2. Justify the need for relevant metadata to be maintained for each process.

3. Sketch an outline data structure for the process abstraction.

4. Recognize the state of processes on a running Linux instance.

5. Develop simple programs that interact with processes in Linux.

4.2 The process abstraction

A process is a program in execution. A **program** consists only of executable code and static data. These are stored in a binary artifact, such as an ELF object or a Java class file. On the other hand, a **process** also encapsulates the runtime execution context. This includes the program counter, stack pointer and other hardware register values for each thread of execution, so we know whereabouts we are in the program execution. The process also records memory management information. Further, the process needs to keep track of owned resources such as open file handles and network connections.

A process maps onto a user application (e.g., spreadsheet), a background utility (e.g., file indexer) or a system service (e.g., remote login daemon). It is possible that multiple processes might be executing the same program at once. These would be different runtime instances of the same program. Some complex applications only permit a single instance of the process to be executed at once. For instance, the Firefox web browser has a lock file, that prevents multiple instances of the application from executing with the same user profile, see Figure 4.3.

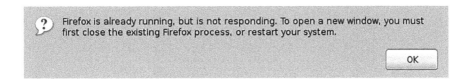

Figure 4.3: Firefox displays an error message and refuses to run multiple application instances for a single user profile.

4.2.1 Discovering processes

How many processes are executing on your system right now? In an interactive shell session, type:

```
1   ps aux | wc -l
```

The `ps` command displays information about processes currently registered with the OS. The options we use are as follows:

a	Include all users' processes
u	Display user-friendly output
x	Include processes not started from a user terminal

My Linux server shows 257 processes. How many processes are on your machine? Every time you invoke a new program, a new process starts. This might occur if you click a program icon in an app launcher bar, or if you type an executable file name at a shell prompt.

4.2.2 Launching a new process

Let's find out how to start a new process programmatically, using the `fork` system call. This is the standard Unix approach to create a new process. The fork-ing process (known as the *parent*) generates an exact copy (known as the *child*), that is executing the same code. The only difference between the parent and the child (i.e., the only way to distinguish between the two processes) is the *return value* of the `fork` call. In the child process, this return value is 0. In the parent process, the return value is a positive integer which denotes the allocated process identifier (or *pid*) of the child. Figure 4.4 shows this sequence schematically. Note that if we can't fork a new process, `fork` returns 1.

Below we show a simple Python script. This runs a program that creates a second copy of itself.

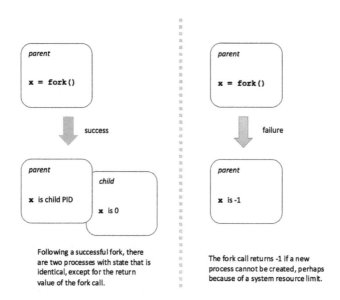

Figure 4.4: Schematic diagram of the behavior of the fork system call.

Listing 4.2.2: Example of fork() in Python — Python

```python
import os

def child():
    print ("Child process has PID {:d}".format(os.getpid()))

def parent():
    # only parent executes this code
    print ("Parent process has PID {:d}".format(os.getpid()))
    child_pid = os.fork()
    # both parent and child will execute subsequent if statement
    if child_pid==0:
        # child executes this
        child()
    else:
        # parent executes this
        print ("Parent {:d} has just forked child {:d}".format(
            os.getpid(), child_pid))

parent()
```

The child process is a *copy* of the parent process, with the only difference being the return value of fork. However, the child process occupies an entirely separate virtual address space—so any subsequent changes made to either the parent or the child memory will not be visible in the other process. This duplication of memory is done in a lazy way, using the *copy on write* technique to avoid massive memory copy overheads. Data is shared until one process (either parent or child) tries to modify it; then the two processes are each allocated a private copy of that data. Copy on write is explained in more detail in Section 6.5.7.

4.2.3 Doing something different

The `fork` call allows us to start a new process, but the child is almost exactly a replica of the parent. How do we execute a *different* program in a child process? Linux supports this with the `execve` system call, which replaces the currently running process with data from a specified program binary. The first parameter is the name of the executable file, the second parameter is the argument vector (effectively `argv` in C programs), and the third parameter is a set of environment variables, as key/value pairs.

Listing 4.2.3: Example of execve() in Python   *Python*

```
1   import os
2
3   os.execve("/bin/ls", ["ls", "-l", "*"], {})
```

This is precisely how an interactive shell, like bash, launches a new program; first, the shell calls `fork` to start a new process, then the shell calls `execve` to load the new program binary that the user wants to run.

The `execve` call does not return unless there is an error that prevents the new program from being executed. See `man execve` for details of such errors, in which case `execve` returns -1. There are several other variants of `execve`, which you can find via `man execl`.

In Linux, the `fork` operation is implemented by the underlying `clone` system call. The `clone` function allows the programmer to specify explicitly which parts of the old process are *duplicated* for the new process, and which parts are *shared* between the two processes. A `clone` call enables the child process to share parts of its context, such as the virtual address space, with the parent process. This allows us to support threads as well as processes with a single API, which is the implementation basis of the Native Posix Threads Library (NPTL) in Linux. For instance, the `pthread_create` function invokes the `clone` system call. Torvalds [1] gives a description of the design rationale for `clone`.

4.2.4 Ending a process

A parent process can block, waiting for a child process to complete. The parent calls the `wait` function for this purpose. Conversely, a child process can complete by calling the `exit` function with a status code argument (a non-zero value conventionally indicates an error). Alternatively, the child process may terminate by returning from its `main` routine.

The example C code below illustrates the duality between `wait` in the parent and `exit` in the child processes.

Listing 4.2.4: Example use of wait() in C code   *C*

```
1   #include <stdio.h>
2   #include <stdlib.h>
3   #include <sys/types.h>
4   #include <sys/wait.h>
5   #include <unistd.h>
6
7   int main() {
```

```
 8
 9      pid_t child_pid, pid;
10      int status;
11
12      child_pid = fork();
13
14      if (child_pid == 0) {
15          //child process
16          pid = getpid();
17          printf("I'm child process %d\n", pid);
18          printf("... sleep for 10 seconds, then exit with status 42\n");
19          sleep(10);
20          exit(42);
21      }
22      else if (child_pid > 0) {
23          //parent
24          //waiting for child to terminate
25          pid = wait(&status);
26          if (WIFEXITED(status)) {
27              printf("Parent discovers child exit with status: %d\n", WEXITSTATUS(status));
28          }
29      }
30      else {
31
32          perror("fork failed");
33          exit(1);
34      }
35      return 0;
36 }
```

Figure 4.5 illustrates the sequence of Linux system calls that are executed by a parent and a child process during the lifetime of the child.

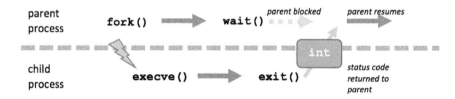

Figure 4.5: Schematic diagram showing how to start and terminate a child process.

If the parent process completes before the child process, then the child becomes an *orphan* process. It is 'adopted' by one of the parent's ancestors, known as a *subreaper*. See man prctl for details. If there are no nominated subreapers in the process ancestors, then the child is adopted by the init process. In either case, the parent field of the child process' task_struct is updated when its original parent exits. This process is known as *re-parenting*.

4.3 Process metadata

A great deal of information is associated with each process. The OS requires this metadata to identify, execute, and manage each process. Generally, the relevant information is encapsulated in a data structure known as a *process control block*.

The most basic metadata is the unique, positive integer identifier associated with a process, conventionally known as the process *pid*. Some metadata is related to context switch saved data, such as register values, open file handles, or memory configuration. This information enables the process to resume execution after it has been suspended by the OS. Further metadata relates to the interactions between a process and the OS—e.g., profiling statistics and scheduling details. Figure 4.6 shows a high-level schematic diagram of the metadata stored in a process control block.

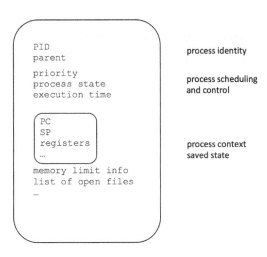

Figure 4.6: Generic OS management metadata required for each process, stored in a per-process data structure known as the process control block.

4.3.1 The /proc file system

The Linux kernel exposes some process metadata as part of a virtual file system. Let's look in the /proc directory on your Linux system:

Listing 4.3.1: The /proc file system   *Bash*

```
1    cd /proc
2    ls
```

You should see a list of directories, many of which will have names that are integers. Each integer corresponds to a pid, and the files inside these pid directories capture information about the relevant process.

cmdline	The textual command that was invoked to start this process
cwd	A symbolic link to the current working directory for this process
exe	A symbolic link to the executable file for this process
fd/	A folder containing file descriptors for each file opened by the process
maps	A table showing how data is arranged in memory
stat	A list of counters for various OS events, specific to this process

Table 4.1: Virtual files associated with a process in /proc/[pid]/.

Table 4.1 lists a few of these files and the information they contain. For the full list, execute man 5 proc at a Linux terminal prompt. The /proc/[pid] files are not 'real'—look at the file sizes with ls -l. These pseudo-files are not stored on the persistent file system: instead, they are file-like representations of in-memory kernel metadata for each process.

Let's list the commands that all the processes in our system are executing:

```
Listing 4.3.2: Finding all processes in the system via /proc                              Bash

1    cd /proc
2    for CMD in `find . -maxdepth 2 -name "cmdline"`; do cat $CMD; echo "";done | sort
```

We observe that some commands are blank—these processes do not have a corresponding command-line invocation.

4.3.2 Linux kernel data structures
The Linux kernel spreads process metadata across several linked blocks of memory. In this section, we will examine three key data structures:

■ thread_info

■ task_struct

■ thread_struct

The C struct called thread_info is architecture-specific; for the Arm platform the struct is defined in arch/arm/include/asm/thread_info.h. Each thread of execution has its own unique thread_info instance, embedded at the base of the thread's runtime kernel stack. (Each thread has a dedicated 8KB stack in kernel memory for use when executing kernel code; this is distinct from the regular user-mode stack.) We can extract the thread_info pointer by a low-overhead bitmask operation on the stack pointer register, see code below.

```
Listing 4.3.3: Snippet from function current_thread_info(void)                              C

1    return (struct thread_info *)
2        (current_stack_pointer & ~(THREAD_SIZE - 1));
```

The majority of information in thread_info relates to the low-level processor context, such as register values and status flags. The data structure includes a pointer to the corresponding task_-struct instance for the process.

The C struct called task_struct is the Linux-specific instantiation of the process control block. It is necessarily a large data structure, storing all the context for the process. The data structure is defined in the architecture-independent kernel header file linux/sched.h. In the kernel, the C macro current returns a pointer to the task_struct for the current process. On 32-bit Arm Linux kernel 4.4 the code sizeof(*current) measures the data structure size as 3472 bytes.

The `thread_struct` data structure is defined in the header file `arch/arm/include/asm/processor.h`. This is a small block of memory, referenced by `task_struct`, which stores more processor-specific context relating to fault events and debugging information.

Each thread has its own unique instances of these three key data structures, although references to other metadata elements might be shared (e.g., for memory maps or open files, recall the earlier discussion of the `clone` system call). Figure 4.7 shows a schematic diagram of these per-thread data structures and their relationships.

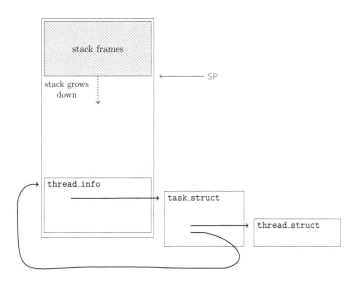

Figure 4.7: Runtime layout of Linux data structures that encapsulate process metadata, residing in kernel memory space.

When a process starts, it runs with a single thread. Its process identifier (PID) has the same integer value as its thread group identifier (TGID). If the process creates a new thread, then the new thread shares the original process address space. The new thread acquires its own PID but retains the original TGID.

As we will see in the next chapter, the Linux scheduler handles all threads in a process as separate items: in other words, a thread is a kernel-visible schedulable execution entity, but a process is a user-visible execution context. Process tools like `top` generally merge multiple threads that share a TGID into a single process.

4.3.3 Process hierarchies

Every process p has a *parent*, which is the process that created *p*. The initial system process is the ancestor of all other processes. In Linux, this is the `init` process, which has pid 1. The global variable `init_task` contains a pointer to the `init` process' `task_struct`.

There are two ways to iterate over processes:

1. Chase the linked list of pointers from one process to the next. This circular doubly-linked list runs through the processes. Each `task_struct` instance has a `next` and `prev` pointer. The macro `for_each_process` iterates overall tasks.

2. Chase the linked list of pointers from child process to parent. Each `task_struct` instance has a `parent` pointer. This linear linked list terminates at the `init_task`.

The C code below will iterate over the linked list from the current task's process control block to the init task. It prints out the 'family tree' of the processes.

When you invoke this program, how deep is the tree? On my machine, it traverses 5 levels of process until it reaches the init process.

Note that this code needs to run in the kernel. It is privileged code since it accesses critical OS data structures. The easiest way to implement this is to wrap up the code as a kernel module, which is explained in Section 2.4.3. The `printk` function is like `printf` only it outputs to the kernel log, which you can read with the `dmesg` utility.

Listing 4.3.4: C code to trace a task's ancestry

```
1   #include <linux/module.h>        /* Needed by all modules */
2   #include <linux/kernel.h>        /* Needed for KERN_INFO */
3   #include <linux/sched.h>         /* for task_struct */
4
5   int init_module(void)
6   {
7       struct task_struct *task;
8
9       for (task = current; task != &init_task; task = task->parent) {
10          printk(KERN_INFO " %d (%s)  -> ", task->pid, task->comm);
11      }
12      printk(KERN_INFO " %d (%s) \n", task->pid, task->comm);
13
14      return 0;
15  }
```

In general, it is more efficient to avoid kernel code. Where possible, utilities remain in 'userland,' as the non-kernel code is often called.

For this reason, most Linux process information utilities like `ps` and `top` gather process metadata from the `/proc` file system, which can be accessed without expensive kernel-level system calls or special privileges. The `pstree` tool is another example utility—it displays similar information to our process family tree code outlined above, but `pstree` uses the /proc pseudo-files rather than expensive system calls. The `pstree` utility is part of the `psmisc` Debian package, which you may need to install explicitly. Figure 4.8 shows typical output from `pstree`, for a Pi with a single user logged in via ssh.

```
pi@raspberrypi:~ $ pstree
systemd──┬─2*[agetty]
         ├─avahi-daemon───avahi-daemon
         ├─cron
         ├─dbus-daemon
         ├─dhcpcd
         ├─ntpd
         ├─rsyslogd──┬─{in:imklog}
         │           ├─{in:imuxsock}
         │           └─{rs:main Q:Reg}
         ├─sshd───sshd───sshd───bash──┬─emacs───{gmain}
         │                            └─pstree
         ├─systemd───(sd-pam)
         ├─systemd-journal
         ├─systemd-logind
         ├─systemd-udevd
         └─thd
```

Figure 4.8: Process hierarchy output from pstree.

4.4 Process state transitions

When a process begins execution, it can move between various scheduling states. Figure 4.9 shows a simple state transition diagram, which indicates the state a process might be in, and the action that will transfer the process to a different state. A more complex version is presented in the next chapter.

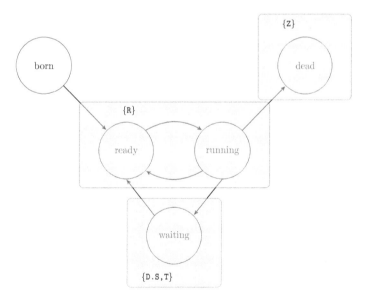

Figure 4.9: The state transition diagram for a Linux process, states named in circles, with possible ps state codes indicated.

Table 4.2 lists the different process states, and their standard Linux abbreviations, which you might see in the output of the `ps` or `top` command. Each state corresponds to a bitflag value, stored in the corresponding `task->state` field. The values are defined in `include/linux/sched.h`, which we explore in more detail in the next chapter.

Let's play with some processes in Linux. Start a process in your terminal, perhaps a text editor like vim. While it is running, make it stop by pressing CTRL + z. This sends the STOP signal to the process. Effectively we have paused its execution. This is how program debugging works.

Now let's run another process that incurs heavy disk overhead, perhaps

R	Running, or runnable
S	Sleeping, can be interrupted
D	Waiting on IO, not interruptible
T	Stopped, generally by a signal
Z	Zombie, a dead process

Table 4.2: Linux process states, see man ps for full details.

Listing 4.4.1: find   *Bash*

```
1    find / -name "foo" &
```

or

Listing 4.4.2: dd   *Bash*

```
1    dd if=/dev/zero of=/tmp/foo bs=1K count=200K &
```

Now you can observe your processes with the ps command. Use the watch tool to see how the states change over time.

Listing 4.4.3: watch   *Bash*

```
1    watch ps u
```

You should see that some processes are running (R) and others are sleeping (S), waiting for I/O (D), or stopped (T). Press CTRL + c to exit the watch program.

A *zombie* process is a completed child process that is waiting to be 'tidied up' by its parent process. A process remains in the zombie state until its parent calls the wait function, or the parent terminates itself. The example Python code below will demonstrate a zombie child, as the parent is sleeping for one minute after the fork, but the child process exits immediately.

Listing 4.4.4: Python zombie example   *Python*

```
1    import os
2    import time
```

```
3
4   def main():
5       child_pid = os.fork()
6       # both parent and child will execute subsequent if statement
7       if child_pid==0:
8           # child executes this
9           pid = os.getpid()
10          print ("To see the zombie, run ps u -p {:d}".format(os.getpid()))
11          exit()
12      else:
13          # parent executes this
14          time.sleep(60)
15          print ("Zombie process disappears now")
16
17  main()
```

4.5 Context switch

The earliest electronic computers were **single-tasking**. These systems executed one program exclusively until another program was loaded into memory. For instance, the early EDSAC machine at Cambridge would ring a warning bell when a program completed execution, so the technician could read off the results and load in a new program. Up until the 1980s, micro-computers ran single-program operating systems like DOS and CP/M. For such computers, process management was unnecessary.

Processes are the basis of **multi-programming**, where the operating system executes multiple programs concurrently. Effectively, the operating system multiplexes many processes onto a smaller number of physical processor cores.

The **context switch** operation enables this multiplexing. All the runtime data required for a process (as we outlined in Section 4.3) is saved into a process control block (effectively the `task_struct` in Linux). The OS serializes the process metadata. Then the process is paused, and another process resumes execution.

If processes are switched in and out of execution at sufficiently high frequency, then it appears that all the processes are executing simultaneously. This is analogous to a person who is juggling, see Figure 4.10. In the same way, as the OS handles more processes than there are processors, the persons deals with more juggling balls than s/he has hands.

Figure 4.10: Juggling with more balls than hands is like multi-tasking execution. Image owned by the author.

For short-term process scheduling, the process context data is stored in RAM (i.e., kernel memory). For processes that are not likely to be executed again in the short-term, the process memory is paged out to disk. Given that the context captures all we need to know to resume the process, this paging is relatively straightforward (see Chapter 6). Another possibility is that the process might be migrated across a network link to another machine, perhaps within a cloud datacenter (see Chapter 11).

There are three practical questions to ask, in terms of context switching on a Linux system.

Q1: How long does a process actually execute before it is switched out?
We will cover process scheduling in more detail in the next chapter. However, Linux specifies a *scheduling quantum* which is a notional amount of time each process will be executed in a round-robin style before a context switch. This quantum time value is specified on my Raspberry Pi as 10ms. You can check the default value on your Linux system with:

Listing 4.5.1: Default Linux timeslice *Bash*

```
1    cat /proc/sys/kernel/sched_rr_timeslice_ms
```

Q2: How much data do we need to save for a process context?
For each thread, there is a `thread_info` struct, to capture saved register values and other processor context. This data structure can be up to around 500 bytes on a 32-bit Arm processor with hardware floating-point support. There is also process control information; however, much of this data will already be resident in memory, so probably only minor updates required at a context switch event.

Q3: How long does a context switch take, on a standard Linux machine?
The *context switch overhead* measures the time taken to suspend one process and resume another. This overhead must be made as low as possible on interactive systems, to enable rapid and smooth context switching between user processes.

The open-source lmbench utility [2] contains code to measure a range of low-level system performance characteristics, including the context switch overhead. Download the code tarball, then execute the following commands:

Listing 4.5.2: Using lmbench *Bash*

```
1    tar xvzf lmbench3.tar.gz
2    cd lmbench3/src
3    make results
4    # ignore errors
5    cd ../bin/armv7l-linux-gnu/
6    ./lat_ctx -s 0 10
```

This reports the context switch overhead for your machine. On my Raspberry Pi 2 Model B v1.1 running Linux kernel 4.4, lmbench reports a context switch overhead of around 12 μs. What do you measure on your machine?

4.6 Signal communications

Inter-process communication will be covered in a future chapter. For now, we focus only on sending signals to processes. A signal is like an interrupt — it's an event generated by the kernel to invoke a signal handler in another process. Signals are a mechanism for one-way asynchronous notifications, with a minimal data payload. The recipient process only knows the signal number and the identity of the sender. Check out the `siginfo_t` struct definition in the `<sys/siginfo.h>` header for more details.

4.6.1 Sending signals

The simplest way to send a signal to a process is to use the `kill` command, at a shell prompt, also specifying the target pid. Below is an example to kill an annoying repeat print loop.

Name	Number	Description	Interactive
SIGINT	2	Terminal interrupt	CTRL + c
SIGQUIT	3	Terminal quit	
SIGILL	4	Illegal instruction	
SIGKILL	9	Kill process (cannot be caught/ignored)	
SIGSEGV	11	Segmentation fault (bad memory access)	
SIGPIPE	13	Write on a pipe with no reader, broken pipe	
SGALRM	14	Alarm clock	Use alarm function to set an alarm
SIGCHLD	17	Child process has stopped or exited	
SIGCONT	18	Continue executing, if stopped	bg or fg
SIGSTOP	19	Stop executing (cannot be caught/ignored)	CTRL + z

Table 4.3: A selection of Linux signal codes, consult signal.h for the full set.

Listing 4.6.1: Example kill process *Bash*

```bash
while ((1)) ; do echo "hello $BASHPID"; sleep 5; done &
# suppose this prints out hello 15082
# ... then you should type
kill 15082
```

Effectively, this kill command is like interactively pressing CTRL + c on the console. Study the table of selected signals below to see some other events that a process may handle and their equivalent interactive key combinations.

Note that some signals are standardized across all Unix variants, whereas other signals may be system-specific. Execute the command `man kill` or `kill -l` for details.

4.6.2 Handling signals

We have looked at sending signals to processes. Now let's consider how to handle such signals when a process receives them. A *signal handler* is a callback routine which is installed by the process to deal with a particular signal. Below is a simple example of a program that responds to the SIGINT signal.

```c
1   #include <stdio.h>
2   #include <signal.h>
3   #include <string.h>
4   #include <unistd.h>
5
6   struct sigaction act;
7
8   void sighandler(int signum, siginfo_t *info, void *p) {
9       printf("Received signal %d from process %lu\n",
10          signum, (unsigned long)info->si_pid);
11      printf("goodbye\n");
12  }
13
14  int main() {
15      // instructions for interactive user
16      printf("Try kill -2 %lu, or just press CTRL+C\n", (unsigned long)getpid());
17      // zero-initialize the sigaction instance
18      memset(&act, 0, sizeof(act));
19      // set up the callback pointer
20      act.sa_sigaction = sighandler;
21      // set up the flags, so the signal handler receives relevant info
22      act.sa_flags = SA_SIGINFO;
23      // install the handler
24      sigaction(SIGKILL, &act, NULL);
25      // wait for something to happen
26      sleep(60);
27      return 0;
28  }
```

Listing 4.6.2: Simple signal handler in C

Some signals cannot be handled by the user process, in particular, SIGKILL and SIGSTOP. Even if you attempt to install a handler for these signals, it will never be executed.

If we don't install a handler for a signal, then the default OS handler is used instead. This will generally report the signal then cause the process to terminate. For example, consider what happens when your C programs dereference a null pointer; normally the default SIGSEGV handler supplied by the OS is invoked, see Figure 4.11.

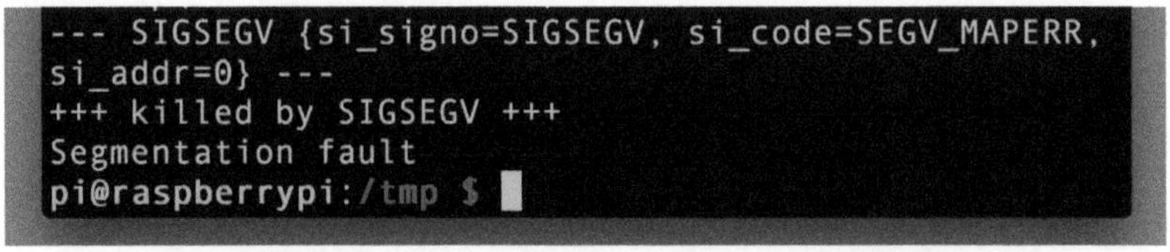

```
--- SIGSEGV {si_signo=SIGSEGV, si_code=SEGV_MAPERR,
si_addr=0} ---
+++ killed by SIGSEGV +++
Segmentation fault
pi@raspberrypi:/tmp $ 
```

Figure 4.11 When a program deferences a null pointer, a segmentation fault occurs and the appropriate OS signal handler reports the error.

4.7 Summary

In this chapter, we have explored the concept of a process as a program in execution. We have seen how to instantiate processes using Linux system calls. We have reviewed the typical lifecycle of a process and considered the various states in which a process can be found. We have explored the runtime data structures that encapsulate process metadata. Finally, we have seen how to attract the attention of a process using the signaling mechanism. Future chapters will explore how processes are scheduled by the OS and how one process can communicate with other concurrently executing processes.

4.8 Further reading

O'Reilly's book on *Linux System Programming* [3] covers processes from a detailed user code perspective. The companion volume on *Understanding the Linux Kernel* [4] goes into much greater depth about process management in Linux; although this textbook covers earlier kernel versions, most of the material is still directly relevant.

4.9 Exercises and questions

4.9.1 Multiple choice quiz

1. **Which of these is not a mechanism for allowing two processes to communicate with each another?**
a) message passing
b) context switch
c) shared memory

2. **What happens when a process receives a signal?**
a) The processor switches to privileged mode.
b) Control jumps to a registered signal handler.
c) The process immediately quits.

3. **Which of the following items is shared by two threads that are cloned by the same process?**
a) thread_info runtime metadata
b) program memory
c) call stack

4. **Immediately after a successful fork system call, the only observable difference between parent and child processes is:**
a) the return value of the fork call
b) the stack pointer
c) the program counter value

4.9.2 Metadata mix

1. Process metadata may be divided into three different kinds: (1) identity, (2) context switch saved state, and (3) scheduling control information. Look at the following fields from the Linux `task_struct` data structure in the `linux/sched.h` header file. For each field, identify which sort of metadata it is. You may want to look at the comments in the header file for more information.

a) `unsigned int rt_priority`
b) `pid_t pid`
c) `volatile long state;`
d) `struct files_struct *files;`
e) `void *stack;`
f) `unsigned long maj_flt;`

4.9.3 Russian doll project

A *matryoshka* doll is a set of wooden dolls of decreasing size placed one inside another. This challenge involves creating a matryoshka process. Define a constant called `MATRYOSHKA`, and set it to a small integer value. Now write a C program with a `main` function that sets a local variable x to the `MATRYOSHKA` value. Then construct a loop that checks the value of x. If x is less than or equal to 0, then return, otherwise decrement the value of x and fork a new process. Recall from Section 4.2 that the `fork` call should be wrapped in an `if` statement to ensure different behavior for the parent and child processes. To make your code more interesting, each individual process could print out its unique id and its value of x. The output should look like this:

```
Listing 4.9.1: Matryoshka program output                                           C

1    " I'm 1173: x is 4 "
2    " I'm 1174: x is 3 "
3    " I'm 1175: x is 2 "
4    " I'm 1176: x is 1 "
5    " I'm 1177: x is 0 "
```

4.9.4 Process overload

When one user starts too many processes rapidly, the entire system can become unusable. Discuss why this might happen. Effectively, rapid process creation is an OS denial-of-service attack. Search online for 'fork-bomb' attacks to find out more details [5]. How does the `ulimit` command mitigate such denial-of-service attacks?

4.9.5 Signal frequency

Consider the signals listed in Table 4.3. Which of these signals are likely to be received frequently? Which signals are rarer? In what circumstances might you use a custom signal handler for your application?

4.9.6 Illegal instructions

You can attempt to execute an illegal instruction on your Raspberry Pi with the assembler code block shown below:

Listing 4.9.2: Execute an illegal instruction

```c
1   int main() {
2       asm volatile (".word 0xe7f0000f\n");
3       return 0;
4   }
```

Compile this code and execute it. You should see an `Illegal Instruction` error message. Now define a signal handler for `SIGILL`. At first, the signal handler should just report the illegal instruction and exit the program. As an advanced step, try to get the signal handler to advance the user program counter by one instruction (4 bytes) and return. You will need to access and modify the `context->uc_mcontext.arm_pc` data field.

References

[1] L. Torvalds, *The Linux Edge*. O'Reilly, 1999, http://www.oreilly.com/openbook/opensources/book/linus.html

[2] L. W. McVoy, C. Staelin *et al.*, "lmbench: Portable tools for performance analysis." in *USENIX annual technical conference*, 1996, pp. 279–294, download code from http://www.bitmover.com/lmbench/

[3] R. Love, *Linux System Programming: Talking Directly to the Kernel and C Library*, 2nd ed. O'Reilly, 2013.

[4] D. P. Bovet and M. Cesati, *Understanding the Linux Kernel*, 3rd ed. O'Reilly, 2005.

[5] E. S. Raymond, "The new hacker's dictionary: Fork bomb," 1996, see also http://www.catb.org/~esr/jargon/html/F/fork-bomb.html

Chapter 5

Process scheduling

5.1 Overview

This chapter discusses how the OS schedules processes on a processor. This includes the rationale for scheduling, the concept of context switching, and an overview of scheduling policies (FCFS, priority, ...) and scheduler architectures (FIFO, multilevel feedback queues, priorities, ...). The Linux scheduler is studied in detail.

What you will learn
After you have studied the material in this chapter, you will be able to:

1. Explain the rationale for scheduling and relationship to the process lifecycle.

2. Discuss the pros and cons of different policies for scheduling in terms of the principles and criteria.

3. Calculate scheduling criteria and reason about scheduling policy performance with respect to the criteria.

4. Analyze the implementation of scheduling in the Linux kernel.

5. Control scheduling of threads and processes as a programmer or system administrator.

5.2 Scheduling overview: what, why, how?

In Chapter 1, we introduced the concept of tasks and explained what a processor needs to do to allow multiple tasks to execute concurrently. Each task constitutes an amount of work for the CPU, and scheduling is the method by which this work is assigned to the CPU. The operating system scheduler is the component responsible for the scheduling activity.

5.2.1 Definition
According to the Oxford dictionary [1], *a schedule*[1] is "a plan for carrying out a process or procedure, giving lists of intended events and times: we have drawn up an engineering schedule"; *to schedule* means to "arrange or plan (an event) to take place at a particular time" or to "make arrangements for (someone or something) to do something". In the context of operating systems, both meanings hold: the scheduler arranges events (i.e., execution of task code on the CPU) to take place at a particular time and makes arrangements for the task to run.

5.2.2 Scheduling for responsiveness
Scheduling is primarily motivated by the need to execute multiple tasks concurrently. In a modern computing system, many tasks are active at the same time. For example, on a desktop system, every tab in a web browser is a task; the graphical user interface requires a number of tasks, there are tasks taking care of networking, etc. At the time of writing this text, my laptop was running 317 processes. From these, 106 were superuser tasks, 24 were services, and the remaining 190 were owned by my user account. Most of these tasks are long-running, i.e., they only exit when the system shuts down. In fact, out of the 190 processes under my user name, only 33 belonged to applications that I had actually launched.

---

[1] The origin is late Middle English (in the sense 'scroll, explanatory note, appendix'): from Old French cedule, from late Latin schedula 'slip of paper,' diminutive of scheda, from Greek σχεδη 'papyrus leaf.'

Now assume for a moment that the system would execute these tasks one by one, waiting until a task completes, then execute the next task. The very first task would occupy the processor forever, so none of the other tasks would be able to run. Therefore the operating system gives each process, in turn, a slice of CPU time.

5.2.3 Scheduling for performance

However, there is another important benefit of scheduling. The processor is very fast (remember, even the humble Raspberry Pi executes 10 million instructions in a single Linux time slice). But when accessing peripherals for I/O, the processor has to wait for the peripheral, and this can take a long time because peripherals such as disks are comparatively slow. For example, simply accessing DRAM without a cache takes between 10 and 100 clock cycles; accessing a hard disk takes several milliseconds, i.e., millions of clock cycles. Without concurrent execution, the CPU would idle until the I/O request had completed. Instead, the operating system will schedule the next task on the CPU.

5.2.4 Scheduling policies

A scheduling policy is used to decide what share of CPU time a process will get and when it will be scheduled. In practice, processes have different needs. For example, when playing a video, it is important that the image does not freeze or stutter, so it is better to give such a process frequent short slices than infrequent long slices. On the other hand, many of the system processes that run invisibly in the background are not timing critical, so the operating system might decide to schedule them when with low priority.

In the rest of the chapter, we will look in detail at the scheduling component of the kernel and its relationship to the process management infrastructure discussed in the previous chapter.

5.3 Recap: the process lifecycle

Recall from the previous chapter that the operating system manages each process through a data structure called the Process Control Block, which in Linux is implemented using the `task_- struct` datastructure. With respect to the process lifecycle, the main attribute of interest is the `state` which can be one of the following (from linux/sched.h)

```
#define TASK_RUNNING    0x0000
#define TASK_INTERRUPTIBLE   0x0001
#define TASK_UNINTERRUPTIBLE   0x0002
#define __TASK_STOPPED   0x0004
#define __TASK_TRACED   0x0008
#define TASK_PARKED   0x0040
#define TASK_DEAD   0x0080
#define TASK_WAKEKILL   0x0100
#define TASK_WAKING   0x0200
#define TASK_NOLOAD   0x0400
#define TASK_NEW   0x0800
#define TASK_STATE_MAX   0x1000
#define TASK_NORMAL (TASK_INTERRUPTIBLE | TASK_UNINTERRUPTIBLE)
#define TASK_IDLE (TASK_UNINTERRUPTIBLE | TASK_NOLOAD)
```

as well as the exit_state which can be one of the following:

```
#define EXIT_DEAD  0x0010
#define EXIT_ZOMBIE  0x0020
```

Observe that each of these states represents a unique bit in the state value. Figure 5.1 shows the actual states a process can be in, annotated with the state values. Scheduling is concerned with moving tasks between these states, in particular from the run queue to the CPU and from the CPU to the run queue or the waiting state.

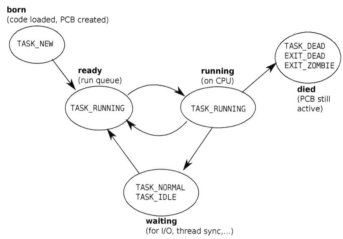

Figure 5.1: Linux process lifecycle.

The key point to note is that when the task is running on the CPU, the OS is not running until an interrupt occurs. Typically the interrupt is caused by the timer that controls the time slice allocated to the running process, or raised by peripherals. Another point to note is that most processes actually spend most of their time in the *waiting* state. This is because most processes frequently perform I/O operations (e.g., disk access, network access, keyboard/mouse/touch screen input, …) and these I/O operations usually take a relatively long time to complete. You can check this using the time command, for example, we can *time* a command that waits for user input, e.g.

Listing 5.3.1: Timing a command that waits for user input *Bash*

```
1   wim@rpi:~ $ time man man
2
3   real 0m5.275s
4   user 0m0.620s
5   sys 0m0.060s
```

The *man* command displays the man page for a command (in this case its own man page) and waits until the user hits 'q' to exit. I hit 'q' after about five seconds.

To interpret the output of the time, we need the definitions of *real*, *user*, and *sys*. According to the man page:

The *time* command runs the specified program command with the given arguments. When the command finishes, *time* writes a message to standard error giving timing statistics about this program run. These statistics consist of

the elapsed *real* time between invocation and termination,

the *user* CPU time (the sum of the `tms_utime` and `tms_cutime` values in a struct `tms` as returned by times(2)), and

the *system* CPU time (the sum of the `tms_stime` and `tms_cstime` values in a struct `tms` as returned by times(2)).

The man page of times gives us some more details:

The struct tms is as defined in `<sys/times.h>`:

Listing 5.3.2: struct tms from <sys/times.h>

```c
struct tms {
    clock_t tms_utime;  /* user time */
    clock_t tms_stime;  /* system time */
    clock_t tms_cutime; /* user time of children */
    clock_t tms_cstime; /* system time of children */
};
```

The `tms_utime` field contains the CPU time spent executing instructions of the calling process. The `tms_stime` field contains the CPU time spent in the system while executing tasks on behalf of the calling process. The `tms_cutime` field contains the sum of the `tms_utime` and `tms_cutime` values for all waited-for terminated children. The `tms_cstime` field contains the sum of the `tms_stime` and `tms_cstime` values for all waited-for terminated children.

So what the example tells us is that the process spent only 620 ms out of 5.275 s running user instructions and the OS spent 60 ms performing work on behalf of the user process. So for about 4.6 seconds the process was waiting for I/O, i.e., the interrupt from the keyboard caused by hitting the 'q' key. Most processes will alternate many times between *running* and *waiting*. The time a process spends in the running state is called the *burst time*.

5.4 System calls

When a user process wants to perform I/O or any other system-related operation, it needs to instruct the operating system to perform the required action. This operation is called a *system call*. Because the operating system is interrupt-driven, the user process needs to raise a software interrupt to give control to the operating system. Furthermore, Linux system calls are identified by a unique number and take a variable number of arguments. Linux allows us to implement system calls via the `syscall()` library function (although this is not the used for the common system calls in the C library). The *syscall(2) man page* provides a very good discussion of the details. The following section gives a summary of the man page, omitting specific details for non-Arm architectures.

5.4.1 The Linux syscall (2) function

Listing 5.4.1: Linux syscall

```c
1    #define _GNU_SOURCE /* See feature_test_macros(7) */
2    #include <unistd.h>
3    #include <sys/syscall.h> /* For SYS_xxx definitions */
4    long syscall(long number, ...);
```

`syscall()` is a small library function that invokes the system call whose assembly language interface has the specified *number* with the specified *arguments*. Employing `syscall()` is useful, for example, when invoking a system call that has no wrapper function in the C library. `syscall()` saves CPU registers before making the system call, restores the registers upon return from the system call, and stores any error code returned by the system call in *errno(3)* if an error occurs. Symbolic constants for system call numbers can be found in the header file <sys/syscall.h>.

The return value is defined by the system call being invoked. In general, a 0 return value indicates success. A −1 return value indicates an error, and an error code is stored in *errno*.

Architecture calling conventions
Each architecture ABI (Application Binary Interface) has its own requirements on how system call arguments are passed to the kernel. For system calls that have a *glibc* wrapper (e.g., most system calls), *glibc* handles the details of copying arguments to the right registers in a manner suitable for the architecture.

Every architecture has its own way of invoking and passing arguments to the kernel. The details for the (32-bit) EABI and arm64 (i.e., AArch64) architectures are listed in the two tables below.

Table 5.1 lists the instruction used to transition to kernel mode (which might not be the fastest or best way to transition to the kernel, so you might have to refer to vdso(7)), the register used to indicate the system call number, the register used to return the system call result, and the register used to signal an error.

ABI	Instruction	Syscall#	Retval	Error
arm/EABI	swi #0	r7	r0	-
arm64	svc #0	x8	x0	-

Table 5.1: Instruction used to transition to kernel mode.

Table 5.2 shows the registers used to pass the system call arguments.

ABI	arg1	arg2	arg3	arg4	arg5	arg6	arg7
arm/EABI	r0	r1	r2	r3	r4	r5	r6
arm64	x0	x1	x2	x3	x4	x5	x-

Table 5.2: Registers used to pass the system call arguments.

The Cortex-A53 is an AArch64 core which supports both ABIs. However, the Raspbian Linux shipped with the Raspberry Pi 3 is a 32-bit Linux, so it uses the EABI. This means that it uses `swi` (Software Interrupt) rather than `svc` (Supervisor Call) to perform a system call. However, in practice, they are synonyms, and their purpose is to provide a mechanism for unprivileged software to make a system call to the operating system. The X^* registers in AArch64 indicated that the general-purpose R^* registers are accessed as 64-bit registers. [2]

For example (taken from the *syscall* man page), using *syscall()*, the *readahead()* system call would be invoked as follows on the Arm architecture with the EABI in little-endian mode:

Listing 5.4.2: Example syscall: readahead()   C

```c
1    syscall(SYS_readahead, fd, 0,
2    (unsigned int) (offset & 0xFFFFFFFF),
3    (unsigned int) (offset >> 32),
4    count);
```

5.4.2 The implications of the system call mechanism

Whenever a user process wants to perform I/O or any other system-related operation, the operating system takes over. This means that every system call involves a context switch, with overheads, as discussed in the previous chapter. Note that in the time taken to perform a context switch time (around $10\mu s$) the CPU could have executed 10,000 operations, so the overhead of context switching is considerable.

> **Virtual dynamic shared object (vDSO)**
>
> To reduce the overhead of system calls, over time two mechanisms have been introduced into the Linux kernel: vsyscall (virtual system call) and vDSO Dynamic Shared Object). The original vsyscall mechanism is now obsolete so we only discuss the vDSO. The purpose of both mechanism is the same: to allow system calls without the need for a context switch. The rationale behind this mechanism is that some system calls that are frequently used do not actually require kernel privileges, and therefore handing control over these operations to the kernel is an unnecessary overhead. As the name indicates, these calls are implemented in a special dynamically shared library (linux-vdso.so) which is automatically provided by the kernel to any process created. In practice, for the Arm architecture only two system calls are implemented this way: *clock_gettime() and gettimeofday()*.

5.5 Scheduling principles

After this detour into the process lifecycle and the role of system calls, let's have a look at the principles of OS scheduling and what criteria an OS can use to make scheduling decisions.

Let's assume a number of tasks are active in the system, and that each of these tasks spends a certain portion of its lifetime *running* on the CPU and another portion *waiting*. It is also possible that the task is *ready* to run, but the CPU is occupied by another task.

5.5.1 Preemptive versus non-preemptive scheduling

A first design decision to make is if the scheduler will be able to interrupt *running* tasks, for example, to run a task that it considers more important (i.e., it has a higher priority). If this is the case, the scheduler is called pre-emptive. In Linux, all scheduling is preemptive. The opposite, non-preemptive scheduling, can be used if the tasks voluntarily yield the CPU to other tasks. This is called cooperative multitasking and is not commonly used in modern operating systems.

Note that we do not use the term preemption when a task is moved to the *waiting* state because this is not a scheduling activity. From a scheduling perspective, the remainder of the task can be considered as a new task (belonging to the same process or thread).

5.5.2 Scheduling policies

The *scheduling policy* is the approach to scheduling taken by the scheduler. To understand the concept better, consider that the scheduler must keep a list of tasks that are ready to run. This list is ordered in some way, and the task at the head of the list is the one that will run next. Therefore the main decision of the scheduler is in which position in the list to put a new ready task. Furthermore, the scheduler must also decide for how long a task can run if it is not pre-empted by another task or interrupted by a system call. Essentially, these two decisions form the scheduling policy. Linux has several different scheduling policies, each task (i.e., each process or thread) can be set to one of these policies. The practical implementation of a policy is an algorithm, so sometimes we will use the term *scheduling algorithm* instead.

5.5.3 Task attributes

We mentioned above (Section 5.5.1) that the scheduler can consider one task more important than another, and therefore give a higher priority of execution to the more important task. This means that the more important task can either be run sooner, or for longer, or both. The importance of a task depends on its attributes. A task attribute could, for example, be the time when the task was put in the task list, or its position in the task list; or the time it takes for the task to run; or the amount of CPU time that has already been spent by the task. Or the task can have an explicit *priority* attribute, which in practice is a small integer value used by the kernel to assess how important a process is.

The Linux kernel uses several of the above-mentioned attributes, depending on the scheduling policy used, and all threads have a priority attribute.

5.6 Scheduling criteria

When selecting a scheduling policy, we can use different criteria, e.g., depending on the typical process mix on the system, or depending on the requirements on the threads in an application. The most commonly used criteria are:

CPU utilization: Ideally, the CPU would be busy 100% of the time, so that we don't waste any CPU cycles.

Throughput: The number of processes completed per unit time.

Turnaround time: The elapsed (wall clock) time required for a particular task to complete, from birth time to death.

Waiting time: The time spent by a task in the ready queue waiting to be run on the CPU.

Response time: The time taken between submitting a request and obtaining a response.

Load average: The average number of processes in the ready queue. On Linux, it is reported by "uptime" and "who."

In general, we want to optimize the average value of criteria, i.e., maximize CPU utilization and throughput, and minimize all the others. It is also desirable to minimize the variance of a criteria because users prefer a consistently predictable system over an inconsistent one, even if the latter performs better on average.

5.7 Scheduling policies

In this section, we discuss some common scheduling policies that make it easier to understand the actual design choices and implementation details are for the Linux kernel scheduler. To analyze the behavior and performance of the various scheduling algorithms we use a Gantt chart, i.e., a simple plot of the task id on a discrete timeline. Table 5.3 shows the example task configuration that will be used to create the Gantt charts for the different scheduling policies.

Pid	Burst time	Arrival time	Priority
1	12	0	0
2	6	2	1
3	2	4	1
4	4	8	2
5	8	16	0
6	8	20	1
7	2	20	0
8	10	24	0

Table 5.3: Example task configuration.

5.7.1 First-come, first-served (FCFS)

This is a very simple scheduling policy where the attribute deciding its priority is simply its relative arrival time in the list of runnable tasks. In this context, this lists is a FIFO queue called the run queue. The scheduler simply takes the task at the head of the queue and runs it on the CPU until it either finishes or gets interrupted by a system call and hence moves to the *waiting* state. When the tasks have finished waiting, it will be re-added at the tail of the run queue. FCFS scheduling can either be preemptive or non-preemptive, as illustrated in Figures 5.2 and 5.3.

FCFS, non-preemptive

time	0	2	4	6	8	10	12	14	16	18	20	22	24	26	28	30	32	34	36	38	40
arrival	1	2	3		4					5	6,7		8								
run	1	1	1	1	1	1	2	2	2	3	4	4	5	5	5	5	6	6	6	6	7

Figure 5.2: Schedule for the example task configuration with non-preemptive FCFS.

FCFS, preemptive

time	0	2	4	6	8	10	12	14	16	18	20	22	24	26	28	30	32	34	36	38	40
arrival	1	2	3		4				5		6,7		8								
run	1	1	2	3	4	4	1	1	5	5	6	6	8	8	8	8	8	1	1	2	2

Figure 5.3: Schedule for the example task configuration with preemptive FCFS.

5.7.2 Round-robin (RR)

Round robin is another very simple scheduling policy that is nevertheless very widely used. We introduced it already in Chapter 1. This policy consists of running every task for a fixed amount of time.This amount of time is known as the *time slice* or *scheduling quantum*. The choice of the quantum is crucial: if it is too long, the system will become unresponsive; if it is too short, the context switching overhead will be considerable. As mentioned in the previous chapter, you can check this value on your Linux system using:

Listing 5.7.1: Linux round-robin quantum from /proc   *Bash*

```bash
1    cat /proc/sys/kernel/sched_rr_timeslice_ms
```

On the Raspberry Pi 3, it is 10 ms.

The schedule for the example task configuration using RR is shown in Figure 5.4.

RR, q=4

time	0	2	4	6	8	10	12	14	16	18	20	22	24	26	28	30	32	34	36	38	40
arrival	1	2	3		4				5		6,7		8								
run	1	1	2	2	3	4	4	1	5	5	6	6	7	8	8	1	1	2	5	5	6

Figure 5.4: Schedule for the example task configuration with Round-Robin scheduling.

5.7.3 Priority-driven scheduling

In priority-driven scheduling, the order in the run queue is determined by the priority of the process or thread; in other words, the run queue is a priority queue. In general, we can observe the following:

- A priority-driven scheduler is an on-line scheduler.

- It does NOT precompute a schedule of tasks/jobs.

- It assigns priorities to jobs when they are released and places them on a ready job queue in priority order.

- When preemption is allowed, a scheduling decision is made whenever a job is released or completed.

- At each scheduling decision time, the scheduler updates the ready job queue and then schedules and executes the job at the head of the queue.

We can distinguish between fixed-priority and dynamic-priority algorithms:

- A fixed-priority algorithm assigns the same priority to all the jobs in a task.

- A dynamic-priority algorithm assigns different priorities to the individual jobs in a task.

The priority of a job is usually assigned upon its release and does not change. The next two example scheduling policies use time-related information as the priority.

5.7.4 Shortest job first (SJF) and shortest remaining time first (SRTF)

If we knew how long it would take for a task to run, we could reorder the run queue so that the shortest task would be at the head of the queue. This policy is called shortest job first (SJF) or sometimes shortest job next, and an illustrative schedule is shown in Figure 5.5. I mention it because it is a very common one in other textbooks, e.g. [3], but it is not very practical as in general the scheduler can't know how long a task will take to complete. It is, however, the simplest example of the use of a task attribute as a priority (the priority is inverse to the predicted remaining CPU time). Furthermore, SJF is provably optimal, in that for a given set of tasks and their execution times, it gives the least average waiting time for each process.

SJF

time	0	2	4	6	8	10	12	14	16	18	20	22	24	26	28	30	32	34	36	38	40
arrival	1	2	3		4					5		6,7		8							
run	1	1	1	1	1	1	3	4	4	2	2	2	7	5	5	5	5	6	6	6	6

Figure 5.5: Schedule for the example task configuration with Shortest Job First scheduling.

The preemptive version of SJF is called shortest remaining time first (SRTF). The criterion for preemption, in this case, is that a newly arrived task has a shorter remaining run time than the currently running task (Figure 5.6). This policy has been proven to be the optimal preemptive policy [4]. Both SJF and SRTF have an additional drawback: it is possible that some tasks will never run until because their remaining time is always considered to be longer than that of any other task in the system. This is known as starvation.

SRTF

time	0	2	4	6	8	10	12	14	16	18	20	22	24	26	28	30	32	34	36	38	40
arrival	1	2	3		4					5		6,7		8							
run	1	2	3	2	2	4	4	1	5	5	5	5	7	6	6	6	6	1	1	1	1

Figure 5.6: Schedule for the example task configuration with Shortest Remaining Time First scheduling.

SETF

time	0	2	4	6	8	10	12	14	16	18	20	22	24	26	28	30	32	34	36	38	40
arrival	1	2	3		4					5		6,7		8							
run	1	2	3	1	4	4	2	1	5	5	6	6	8	8	8	8	8	7	2	5	5

Figure 5.7: Schedule for the example task configuration with Shortest Elapsed Time First scheduling.

5.7.5 Shortest elapsed time first (SETF)

SJF and SRTF are so-called *clairvoyant* algorithms, as they require the scheduler to know information that is not available, in this case, the *remaining* run time of the process. A more practical approach is to use the *elapsed* run time of a process instead, which is of course easily measurable by the OS. The paper "Speed Is as Powerful as Clairvoyance" [5] proved that SETF not only obtains good average-case response time but also does not starve any job.

5.7.6 Priority scheduling

The term "priority scheduling" is used for priority-driven scheduling where the priority of the task is an entirely separate attribute, not related to other task attributes. Priority driven scheduling can either be preemptive or non-preemptive, as illustrated in Figures 5.8 and 5.9.

Priority, non-preemptive

time	0	2	4	6	8	10	12	14	16	18	20	22	24	26	28	30	32	34	36	38	40
arrival	1	2	3		4				5		6,7		8								
run	1	1	1	1	1	1	2	2	2	5	5	5	5	7	8	8	8	8	8	3	6

Figure 5.8: Schedule for the example task configuration with non-preemptive Priority scheduling.

Priority, preemptive

time	0	2	4	6	8	10	12	14	16	18	20	22	24	26	28	30	32	34	36	38	40
arrival	1	2	3		4				5		6,7		8								
run	1	1	1	1	1	1	2	2	5	5	5	5	7	8	8	8	8	8	3	6	6

Figure 5.9: Schedule for the example task configuration with preemptive Priority scheduling.

The advantage of using a separate priority rather than, e.g. a time-based attribute of the task is that the priority can be changed if required. This is essential to prevent starvation, as mentioned for SJF. Any priority-based scheduling policy carries the risk that low-priority processes may never execute because there is always a higher-priority process taking precedence. To remedy this, the priority should not be static but increased with the age of the process. This is called *aging*.

5.7.7 Real-time scheduling

Real-time applications are applications that process data in real-time, i.e., without delays. From a scheduling perspective, this means that the tasks have well defined time constraints. Processing must be done within the defined constraints to be considered correct, in particular, not finishing a process within a given deadline can cause incorrect functionality.

We can distinguish two types of real-time systems:

- Soft real-time systems give no guarantee as to when a critical real-time process will be scheduled, but only guarantee that the critical process will have a higher priority. A typical example is video and audio stream processing: missing deadlines will affect the quality of the playback bit is not fatal.

- In hard real-time systems, a task must be serviced by its deadline, so the scheduler must be able to guarantee this. This is, for example, the case for the controls of an airplane or other safety-critical systems.

5.7.8 Earliest deadline first (EDF)

The Linux kernel supports both types of real-time scheduling. For soft real-time scheduling, it uses Round-Robin or FIFO. For hard real-time scheduling, it uses an algorithm known as Earliest Deadline First (EDF). This is a dynamic priority-driven scheduling algorithm for periodic tasks, i.e., tasks that periodically need some work to be done. This periodic activity is usually called a *job*. The period and the deadline for the jobs of each task must be known.

The job queue is ordered by the earliest deadline of the jobs. To compute this deadline, the scheduler must be aware of the period of each task, the phase differences between those periods and the execution times and deadlines for each job. Usually, the deadline is the same as the period, i.e., a job for a given task must finish within one period. In that case, each task can be described by a tuple (phase, period, execution time).

Algorithm 5.1 EDF Schedule for example tasks `T1 = (0,2,1)`, `T2 = (0,5,2.5)`

```
Time     Ready to Run             Scheduled
0        J1,1[2]; J2,1[5]         J1,1
1        J2,1[5]                  J2,1
2        J1,2[4]; J2,1[5]         J1,2
3        J2,1[5]                  J2,1
4        J2,1[5]; J1,3[6]         J2,1
4.5      J1,3[6]                  J1,3
5        J1,3[6]; J2,2[10]        J1,3
5.5      J2,2[10]                 J2,2
6        J1,4[8]; J2,2[10]        J1,4
7        J2,2[10]                 J2,2
8        J1,5[10]; J2,2[10]       J1,5
9        J2,2[10]                 J2,2
```

For example, consider a system with two tasks which both started at time t=0, so the phase is 0 for both. T1 has a period of 2 and an execution time of 1; T2 has a period of 5 and an execution time of 2.5:

```
T1 = (0 , 2, 1)
T2 = (0 , 5, 2.5)
```

In other words, both tasks are active half of the time, so in principle together, they will use the CPU 100%. Because the tasks are periodic, it is sufficient to calculate a schedule for the least common multiple of the periods of T1 and T2, in this task 2*5=10. The schedule is shown below. This is an important property of EDF: it guarantees that all deadlines are met provided that the total CPU utilization is not more than 100%. In other words, it is always possible to create a valid schedule.

5.8 Scheduling in the Linux kernel

The Linux kernel supports two categories of scheduling, normal and *real-time*. A good explanation is provided in the *sched(7) man page*. With regards to scheduling, the *thread* is the main abstraction, i.e., the scheduler schedules threads rather than processes.

Each thread has an associated *scheduling policy* and a *static scheduling priority*. The scheduler makes its decisions based on knowledge of the static scheduling policy and priority of all threads in the system.

There are currently (kernel 4.14) three normal scheduling policies: SCHED_OTHER, SCHED_IDLE and SCHED_BATCH, and three real-time policies, SCHED_FIFO, SCHED_RR and SCHED_DEADLINE. Of these, SCHED_OTHER, SCHED_FIFO and SCHED_RR are required by the POSIX 1003.1b real-time standard [6].

For threads scheduled using one of the normal policies, the static priority is not used in scheduling decisions (it is set to 0). Processes scheduled under one of the real-time policies have a static priority value in the range 1 (low) to 99 (high). Thus real-time threads always have higher static priority than normal threads.

The scheduler maintains a list of runnable threads per static priority value. To determine which thread to run next, it looks for the non-empty list with the highest static priority and selects the thread at the head of this list.

The scheduling policy determines where a thread is to be inserted into the list of threads with equal priority and how it will progress to the head of the list.

In Linux, all scheduling is preemptive: if a thread with a higher static priority becomes ready to run, the currently running thread will be pre-empted and returned to the run list for its priority level. The scheduling policy of the thread determines the ordering within the run list. This means that, e.g. for the run list with static priority 0, i.e., the normal scheduling category (SCHED_- NORMAL), there can be up to three different policies that decide the relative ordering of the threads. For each of the higher static priority run lists (real-time), there can be one or two.

5.8.1 User priorities: niceness

Niceness or nice value is the relative, dynamic priority of a process. Niceness values range from -20 (most favorable to the process) to 19 (least favorable to the process) and the value affects how the process is scheduled, but not in a direct way. The nice value of a running process can be changed by the user via the *nice(1)* command or the *nice(2)* system call. We will see further how the different schedulers use these values. Note that nice values are only for non-real-time processes.

5.8.2 Scheduling information in the task control block

As mentioned before, the task control block is implemented in the Linux kernel in the `task_struct` data structure, defined in *include/linux/sched.h*. Let's have a look at the scheduling-specific information stored in the task_struct (all other fields have been removed for conciseness).

```c
Listing 5.8.1: task_struct from <include/linux/sched.h>

1    struct task_struct {
2
3      int       on_rq;
4    /** - int prio, static_prio;
5        priority of a process used when scheduled. Variable prio, which is the
6        user-nice values can be converted to static priority to better scale
7        various scheduler parameters.
8    */
9      int       prio, static_prio, normal_prio;
10     unsigned int      rt_priority; // for soft real-time
11
12     const struct sched_class *sched_class; // see below
```

```
13    struct sched_entity  se; // see below
14    struct sched_rt_entity  rt; // for soft real-time
15    struct sched_dl_entity  dl; // for hard real-time
16
17    /**      the scheduling policy used for this process, as listed above*/
18    unsigned int       policy;
19    };
```

This structure includes a number of other scheduling-related data structures. We will discuss `sched_entity` and the real-time variants `sched_rt_entity` and `sched_dl_entity`. in the sections on the CFS and real-time schedulers. The `sched_class` struct is effectively an interface for the actual scheduling class in use: all functionality is implemented in each of the separate scheduling classes *fair, idle,rt,deadline*.

Listing 5.8.2: sched_class from <include/linux/sched.h>

```
1    struct sched_class {
2        const struct sched_class *next;
3
4        void (*enqueue_task) (struct rq *rq, struct task_struct *p, int flags);
5        void (*dequeue_task) (struct rq *rq, struct task_struct *p, int flags);
6        void (*yield_task) (struct rq *rq);
7        bool (*yield_to_task)
8            (struct rq *rq, struct task_struct *p, bool preempt);
9
10       void (*check_preempt_curr)
11           (structt rq *rq, struct task_struct *p, int flags);
12
13       struct task_struct * (*pick_next_task)
14           (struct rq *rq,struct task_struct *prev,struct rq_flags *rf);
15       void (*put_prev_task) (struct rq *rq, struct task_struct *p);
16
17       void (*set_curr_task) (struct rq *rq);
18       void (*task_tick) (struct rq *rq, struct task_struct *p, int queued);
19       void (*task_fork) (struct task_struct *p);
20       void (*task_dead) (struct task_struct *p);
21
22       void (*switched_from) (struct rq *this_rq, struct task_struct *task);
23       void (*switched_to) (struct rq *this_rq, struct task_struct *task);
24       void (*prio_changed)
25           (struct rq *this_rq, struct task_struct *task,int oldprio);
26
27       unsigned int (*get_rr_interval) (struct rq *rq,
28           struct task_struct *task);
29
30       void (*update_curr) (struct rq *rq);
31
32   };
```

So in order to perform a scheduling operation for a process p, all the scheduler has to do is call

```
p->sched_class-><name of the operation>
```

and the corresponding operation for the particular scheduling class for that process will be carried out. The Linux kernel keeps a per-CPU runqueue (`struct rq`) which contains different runqueues per scheduling class as follows (from sched.h):

Listing 5.8.3: runqueue struct from <include/linux/sched.h>

```c
1   /*
2    * This is the main, per-CPU runqueue data structure.
3    *
4    */
5   struct rq {
6   /* runqueue lock: */
7     raw_spinlock_t lock;
8     unsigned int nr_running;
9   #define CPU_LOAD_IDX_MAX 5
10    unsigned long cpu_load[CPU_LOAD_IDX_MAX];
11    struct load_weight load;
12    unsigned long nr_load_updates;
13    u64 nr_switches;
14    struct cfs_rq cfs;
15    struct rt_rq rt;
16    struct dl_rq dl;
17    struct task_struct *curr, *idle, *stop;
18  };
```

5.8.3 Process priorities in the Linux kernel

The kernel uses the priorities as set or reported by nice() and as static priorities and represents them on a scale from 0 to 139. Priorities from 0 to 99 are reserved for real-time processes and 100 to 139 (which are the nice values from -20 through to +19 shifted by 120) are for normal processes. The kernel code implementing this can be found in include/linux/sched/prio.h, together with some macros to convert between nice values and priorities.

Listing 5.8.4: Linux kernel priority calculation

```c
1   #define MAX_NICE 19
2   #define MIN_NICE -20
3   #define NICE_WIDTH (MAX_NICE - MIN_NICE + 1)
4
5   /*
6    * Priority of a process goes from 0..MAX_PRIO-1, valid RT
7    * priority is 0..MAX_RT_PRIO-1, and SCHED_NORMAL/SCHED_BATCH
8    * tasks are in the range MAX_RT_PRIO..MAX_PRIO-1. Priority
9    * values are inverted: lower p->prio value means higher priority.
10   *
11   * The MAX_USER_RT_PRIO value allows the actual maximum
12   * RT priority to be separate from the value exported to
13   * user-space. This allows kernel threads to set their
14   * priority to a value higher than any user task. Note:
15   * MAX_RT_PRIO must not be smaller than MAX_USER_RT_PRIO.
16   */
17
18  #define MAX_USER_RT_PRIO 100
19  #define MAX_RT_PRIO    MAX_USER_RT_PRIO
20
21  #define MAX_PRIO (MAX_RT_PRIO + NICE_WIDTH)
22  #define DEFAULT_PRIO   (MAX_RT_PRIO + NICE_WIDTH / 2)
23
24  /*
25   * Convert user-nice values [ -20 ... 0 ... 19 ]
26   * to static priority [ MAX_RT_PRIO..MAX_PRIO-1 ],
```

```
27    * and back.
28    */
29  #define NICE_TO_PRIO(nice)   ((nice) + DEFAULT_PRIO)
30  #define PRIO_TO_NICE(prio)   ((prio) - DEFAULT_PRIO)
31
32  / *
33    * 'User priority' is the nice value converted to something we
34    * can work with better when scaling various scheduler parameters,
35    * it's a [ 0 ... 39 ] range.
36    */
37  #define USER_PRIO(p)         ((p)-MAX_RT_PRIO)
38  #define TASK_USER_PRIO(p)  USER_PRIO((p)->static_prio)
39  #define MAX_USER_PRIO      (USER_PRIO(MAX_PRIO))
```

Priority info in task_struct

The task_struct contains several priority-related fields:

```
int prio, static_prio, normal_prio;
unsigned int rt_priority; // for soft real-time
```

static_prio is the priority set by the user or by the system itself:

```
p->static_prio = NICE_TO_PRIO(nice_value);
```

normal_priority is based on static_prio and on the scheduling policy of a process, i.e., real-time or "normal" process. Tasks with the same static priority that use different policies will get different normal priorities. Child processes inherit the normal priorities.

p->prio is the so-called "dynamic priority." It is called dynamic because it can be changed by the system, for example when the system temporarily raises a task's priority to a higher level, so that it can preempt another high-priority task. Initially, prio is set to the same value as static_prio. The actual dynamic priority is computed as:

```
p->prio = effective_prio(p);
```

This function, defined in kernel/sched/core.c, returns the normal_prio unless the task is a real-time task, in which case it uses normal_prio() to recompute the normal priority

---

Listing 5.8.5: Implementation of effective_prio()   C

```
1    static int effective_prio(struct task_struct *p)
2    {
3      p->normal_prio = normal_prio(p);
4    / *
5    * If we are RT tasks or we were boosted to RT priority,
6    * keep the priority unchanged. Otherwise, update priority
7    * to the normal priority:
8    */
9      if (!rt_prio(p->prio))
```

```
10        return p->normal_prio;
11     return p->prio;
12   }
```

For a real-time task, it calculates normal_prio as

Listing 5.8.6: Implementation of normal_prio()   C

```
1    static inline int normal_prio(struct task_struct *p)
2    {
3      int prio;
4      if (task_has_dl_policy(p))
5          prio = MAX_DL_PRIO-1;
6      else if (task_has_rt_policy(p))
7          prio = MAX_RT_PRIO-1 - p->rt_priority;
8      else
9          prio = p->static_prio;
10     return prio;
11   }
```

In other words, if the task is not real-time, then prio, static_prio, and normal_prio have the same value.

Priority and load weight

The way the priorities are used is not simply to order tasks but to compute a "load weight," which is then used to calculate the CPU time allowed for a task.

The structure task_struct->se.load contains the weight of a process in a struct load_weight:

Listing 5.8.7: load_weight struct   C

```
1    struct load_weight {
2      unsigned long weight;
3      u32 inv_weight;
4    };
```

The weight is roughly equivalent to 1024/(1.25)^(nice), the actual values are hardcoded in the array sched_prio_to_weight (in kernel/sched/core.c):

Listing 5.8.8: Scheduling priority-to-weight conversion   C

```
1    const int sched_prio_to_weight[40] = {
2    /* -20 */ 88761, 71755, 56483, 46273, 36291,
3    /* -15 */ 29154, 23254, 18705, 14949, 11916,
4    /* -10 */ 9548, 7620, 6100, 4904, 3906,
5    /* -5 */ 3121, 2501, 1991, 1586, 1277,
6    /* 0 */ 1024, 820, 655, 526, 423,
7    /* 5 */ 335, 272, 215, 172, 137,
8    /* 10 */ 110, 87, 70, 56, 45,
9    /* 15 */ 36, 29, 23, 18, 15,
10   };
```

This conversion is used in set_load_weight

```c
Listing 5.8.9: Implementation of set_load_weight()                              C
1    static void set_load_weight(struct task_struct *p)
2    {
3      int prio = p->static_prio - MAX_RT_PRIO;
4      struct load_weight *load = &p->se.load;
5      /*
6       * SCHED_IDLE tasks get minimal weight:
7       */
8      if (idle_policy(p->policy)) {
9        load->weight = scale_load(WEIGHT_IDLEPRIO);
10       load->inv_weight = WMULT_IDLEPRIO;
11       return;
12     }
13     load->weight = scale_load(sched_prio_to_weight[prio]);
14     load->inv_weight = sched_prio_to_wmult[prio];
15   }
```

Here scale_load is a macro which increases resolution on 64-bit architectures; SCHED_IDLE is a scheduler policy for very low priority system background tasks. The inv_weight field is used to speed up reverse computations. So in essence, the operation is

```
load->weight = sched_prio_to_weight[prio];
```

The way the weight is used depends on the scheduling policy.

5.8.4 Normal scheduling policies: the completely fair scheduler

All normal scheduling policies in the Linux kernel (SCHED_OTHER, SCHED_IDLE, and SCHED_BATCH) are implemented as part of what is known as the "Completely Fair Scheduler" (CFS). The philosophy behind this scheduler, which was introduced in kernel version 2.6.23 in 2009, is stated in the kernel documentation (https://elixir.bootlin.com/linux/latest/source/kernel/sched/sched.h) as follows:

80% of CFS's design can be summed up in a single sentence: CFS basically models an "ideal, precise multi-tasking CPU" on real hardware.

"Ideal multi-tasking CPU" is a (non-existent :-)) CPU that has 100% physical power and which can run each task at precise equal speed, in parallel, each at 1nr_running speed. For example: if there are 2 tasks running, then it runs each at 50% physical power --- i.e., actually in parallel.

On real hardware, we can run only a single task at once, so we have to introduce the concept of "virtual runtime." The virtual runtime of a task specifies when its next timeslice would start execution on the ideal multi-tasking CPU described above. In practice, the virtual runtime of a task is its actual runtime normalized to the total number of running tasks.

In other words, the CFS attempts to balance the virtual runtime overall tasks. The CFS scheduler run queue (`struct cfs_rq cfs` in `struct rq` in sched.h) is a priority queue with the task with the smallest virtual runtime at the head of the queue.

Listing 5.8.10: Implementation of CFS runqueue

```c
/* CFS-related fields in a runqueue */
struct cfs_rq {
  struct load_weight load;
  unsigned long runnable_weight;
  unsigned int nr_running, h_nr_running;
  u64 exec_clock;
        u64 min_vruntime;
  struct rb_root_cached tasks_timeline;
  / *
   * 'curr' points to currently running entity on this cfs_rq.
   * It is set to NULL otherwise (i.e., when none are currently running).
   */
  struct sched_entity *curr, *next, *last, *skip;
};
```

The CFS algorithm computes the duration of the next time slice for this task based on the priorities of all tasks in the queue and runs it.

The calculation of the virtual runtime is done in the functions `sched_slice()`, `sched_- vslice()` and `calc_delta_fair()` in fair.c, using information from the sched_entity struct se:

Listing 5.8.11: sched_entity struct for calculation of virtual runtime

```c
struct sched_entity {
  /* For load-balancing: */
  struct load_weigh    load;
  struct rb_node     run_node;
  struct list_head    group_node;
  unsigned int      on_rq;

  u64        exec_start;
  u64        sum_exec_runtime;
  u64        vruntime;
  u64        prev_sum_exec_runtime;

  u64        nr_migrations;

  struct sched_statistics    statistics;

};
```

As the actual C code in the kernel is quite convoluted, below we present equivalent Python code:

Listing 5.8.12: Calculation of virtual runtime slice

```python
# Targeted preemption latency for CPU-bound tasks.
# NOTE: this latency value is not the same as the concept of 'timeslice length'
# - timeslices in CFS are of variable length and have no persistent notion
# like in traditional, time-slice based scheduling concepts.
   sysctl_sched_latency = 6 ms * (1 + ilog(ncpus))
# Minimal preemption granularity for CPU-bound tasks:
   sysctl_sched_min_granularity = 0.75 ms * (1 + ilog(ncpus))
   sched_nr_latency = sysctl_sched_latency/sysctl_sched_min_granularity #6/0.75=8
```

```
9
10   def sched_slice(cfs_rq, tasks):
11       se =head(tasks)
12       # The idea is to set a period (slice) in which each task runs once.
13       # When there are too many tasks (sched_nr_latency)
14       # we have to stretch this period because otherwise, the slices get too small.
15       nrr = cfs_rq.nr_running + (not se.on_rq)
16       slice = sysctl_sched_latency
17       if nrr > sched_nr_latency:
18           slice = nrr * sysctl_sched_min_granularity
19       # slice is scaled using the weight of every other task in the run queue
20       for se in tasks:
21           cfs_rq = cfs_rq_of(se)
22           if not se.on_rq:
23               cfs_rq.load.weight += se.load.weight
24           slice = slice*se.load.weight/cfs_rq.load.weight
25       return slice
26
27
28   # The vruntime slice of a to-be-inserted task is: vslice = slice / weight
29
30   def calc_delta_fair(slice,task):
31       return slice*1024/task.load.weight
32
33   def sched_vslice(cfs_rq, tasks):
34       slice = sched_slice(cfs_rq, tasks)
35       se = head(tasks)
36       vslice = calc_delta_fair(slice,se)
37        return vslice
```

The actual position of a task in the queue depends on vruntime, which is calculated as follows:

Listing 5.8.13: Calculation of vruntime *Python*

```
1    # Update the current task's runtime statistics.
2    def update_min_vruntime(cfs_rq):
3      curr = cfs_rq.curr
4      leftmost = rb_first_cached(cfs_rq.tasks_timeline)
5      vruntime = cfs_rq.min_vruntime
6      if curr:
7        if curr.on_rq:
8          vruntime = curr.vruntime
9        else:
10         curr = None
11
12     if leftmost: /* non-empty tree */
13       se = rb_entry(leftmost)
14       if not curr:
15         vruntime = se.vruntime
16          else:
17         vruntime = min_vruntime(vruntime, se.vruntime)
18
19       # ensure we never gain time by being placed backwards.
20     cfs_rq.min_vruntime = max_vruntime(cfs_rq.min_vruntime, vruntime)
21
22   def update_curr(cfs_rq):
23     curr = cfs_rq.curr
24     now = rq_clock_task(rq_of(cfs_rq))
25     delta_exec = now - curr.exec_start
26     curr.exec_start = now
27     curr.sum_exec_runtime += delta_exec
```

```
28      curr.vruntime += calc_delta_fair(delta_exec,curr)
29        cfs_rq = update_min_vruntime(cfs_rq)
30
31  def update_curr_fair(rq):
32      update_curr(cfs_rq_of(rq.curr.se))
```

In other words, the kernel calculates the difference between the time the process started (exec_- start) and the current time (now) and then updates exec_start to now. Then it uses this delta_exec and the load weight to calculate vruntime. Finally, the min_vruntime is calculated as the minimum of the vruntime of the task at the head of the queue (i.e., the leftmost node in the red-black tree) and the vruntime of the current task. The code checks if there is a current task, and if the queue is not empty and provides fallbacks. This calculated value is then compared with the currently stored value (cfs_rq.min_vruntime) and the largest of the two becomes the new cfs_rq.min_vruntime.

5.8.5 Soft real-time scheduling policies

The Linux kernel supports both soft real-time scheduling policies SCHED_RR and SCHED_FIFO required by the POSIX real-time specification [7]. Real-time processes are managed by a separate scheduler, defined in <kernel/sched/rt.c>.

From the kernel's perspective, real-time processes have one key difference compared to other processes: if there is a runnable real-time task, it will be run—unless there is another real-time task with a higher priority.

There are currently two scheduling policies for soft real-time tasks:

▪ SCHED_FIFO: This is a First-Come. First-Served scheduling algorithm as discussed in Section 5.7.1. Tasks following this policy do not have timeslices; they run until they block, yield the CPU voluntarily or get pre-empted by a higher priority real-time task. A SCHED_FIFO task must have a static priority > 0 so that it always preempts any SCHED_NORMAL, SCHED_BATCH or SCHED_IDLE process. Note that this means that a SCHED_FIFO task will use the CPU until it finished, and no non-real-time tasks will be scheduled on that CPU. Several SCHED_FIFO tasks of the same priority run round-robin. A task can be pre-empted by a higher-priority task, in which case it will stay at the head of the list for its priority and will resume execution as soon as all tasks of higher priority are blocked again. When a blocked SCHED_FIFO thread becomes runnable, it will be inserted at the end of the list for its priority.

▪ SCHED_RR: This is a Round-Robin (as explained in Section 5.7.2) enhancement of SCHED_FIFO scheduler, so it runs every task for a maximum fixed time slice. Tasks of the same priority run round-robin until pre-empted by a more important task. If after running for a time quantum, a task is not finished, it will be put at the end of the list for its priority. A task that has been pre-empted by a higher priority task and subsequently resumes execution will complete the remaining portion of its round-robin time quantum. As mentioned before, the length of the time quantum can be retrieved via /proc/sys/kernel/sched_rr_timeslice_ms or by using sched_rr_get_interval(2).

The kernel gives real-time tasks a static priority, which does not get dynamically recalculated; the only way to change this priority is by using the chrt(1) command. This ensures that a real-time task always preempts a normal one and that strict order is kept between real-time tasks of different priorities.

Soft real-time processes use a separate scheduling entity struct sched_rt_entity (rt in the task_struct):

Listing 5.8.14: Soft real-time scheduling entity struct

```c
struct sched_rt_entity {
  struct list_head    run_list;
  unsigned long    timeout;
  unsigned long    watchdog_stamp;
  unsigned int    time_slice;
  unsigned short    on_rq;
  unsigned short    on_list;

  struct sched_rt_entity    *back;
#ifdef CONFIG_RT_GROUP_SCHED
  struct sched_rt_entity    *parent;
  /* rq on which this entity is (to be) queued: */
  struct rt_rq    *rt_rq;
  /* rq "owned" by this entity/group: */
  struct rt_rq    *my_q;
#endif
};
```

As explained in Section 5.8.2, the main runqueue contains dedicated runqueues for the normal (CFS), soft real-time (rt) and hard real-time (dl) scheduling classes. The soft real-time queue uses a priority queue implemented using a static array of linked lists and a bitmap. All real-time tasks of a given priority prio are kept in a linked list in active.queue[prio] and a bitmap (active.bitmap), keeps track of whether a particular queue is empty or not.

Listing 5.8.15: Soft real-time runqueue

```c
/* Real-Time classes' related field in a runqueue: */
struct rt_rq {
  struct rt_prio_array active;
  unsigned int rt_nr_running;
  unsigned int rr_nr_running;
#if defined CONFIG_SMP || defined CONFIG_RT_GROUP_SCHED
  struct {
    int curr; /* highest queued rt task prio */
  } highest_prio;
#endif
  int rt_queued;

  int rt_throttled;
  u64 rt_time;
  u64 rt_runtime;
  /* Nests inside the rq lock: */
  raw_spinlock_t rt_runtime_lock;

#ifdef CONFIG_RT_GROUP_SCHED
  unsigned long rt_nr_boosted;

  struct rq *rq;
```

```
23     struct task_group *tg;
24  #endif
25  };
26
27  /*
28   * This is the priority-queue data structure of the RT scheduling class:
29   */
30  struct rt_prio_array {
31    DECLARE_BITMAP(bitmap, MAX_RT_PRIO+1);  /* include 1 bit for delimiter */
32    struct list_head queue[MAX_RT_PRIO];
33  };
34
35  struct rt_bandwidth {
36    /* nests inside the rq lock: */
37    raw_spinlock_t      rt_runtime_lock;
38    ktime_t         rt_period;
39    u64     rt_runtime;
40    struct hrtimer      rt_period_timer;
41    unsigned int    rt_period_active;
42  };
```

Similar to `update_curr()` in the CFS, there is an `update_curr_rt()` function, defined in kernel/sched/rt.c in real-time scheduler. This function keeps track of the CPU time spent by soft real-time tasks, collects some statistics, updates timeslices where needed, and calls the scheduler when appropriate. All calculations are done using actual time; no virtual clock is used.

5.8.6 Hard real-time scheduling policy

Since kernel version 3.14 of the Linux kernel (2014), Linux supports hard real-time scheduling via the SCHED_DEADLINE scheduling class. This is an implementation of the Earliest Deadline First (EDF) algorithm discussed in Section 5.7.8, combined with the Constant Bandwidth Server (CBS) algorithm [8].

According to the sched(7) Linux manual page:

The SCHED_DEADLINE (sporadic task model deadline scheduling) policy is currently implemented using GEDF (Global Earliest Deadline First) in conjunction with CBS (Constant Bandwidth Server). A sporadic task is one that has a sequence of jobs, where each job is activated at most once per period. Each job also has a relative deadline, before which it should finish execution, and a computation time, which is the CPU time necessary for executing the job. The moment when a task wakes up because a new job has to be executed is called the arrival time. The start time is the time at which a task starts its execution. The absolute deadline is thus obtained by adding the relative deadline to the arrival time.

A SCHED_DEADLINE task is guaranteed to receive a given runtime every period, and this runtime is available within deadline from the beginning of the period.

The runtime, period, and deadline are stored in the struct sched_dl_entity struct (dl in the `task_struct`) and can be set using the sched_setattr() system call:

Listing 5.8.16: Hard real-time scheduling entity struct

```c
1   struct sched_dl_entity {
2       /* the node in the red-black tree.
3    The red-black tree is used as priority queue
4    */
5    struct rb_node          rb_node;
6
7    /*
8     * Original scheduling parameters.
9     */
10   u64        dl_runtime;   /* Maximum runtime for each instance */
11   u64        dl_deadline;   /* Relative deadline of each instance */
12   u64        dl_period;   /* Separation of two instances (period) */
13   u64        dl_bw;   /* dl_runtime / dl_period */
14   u64        dl_density;   /* dl_runtime / dl_deadline   */
15
16   /*
17    * Actual scheduling parameters. Initialized with the values above,
18    * they are continuously updated during task execution.
19    */
20   s64        runtime;   /* Remaining runtime for this instance */
21   u64        deadline;   /* Absolute deadline for this instance */
22   unsigned int    flags;   /* Specifying the scheduler behavior */
23
24   /*
25    * Some bool flags
26    */
27   unsigned int        dl_throttled        : 1;
28   unsigned int        dl_boosted        : 1;
29   unsigned int        dl_yielded        : 1;
30   unsigned int        dl_non_contending : 1;
31
32   /*
33    * Per-task bandwidth enforcement timer.
34    */
35   struct hrtimer          dl_timer;
36
37   /*
38    * Inactive timer
39    */
40   struct hrtimer inactive_timer;
41   };
```

Time budget allocation

When a task wakes up because a new job has to be executed (i.e., at arrival time), `deadline` and `runtime` are recalculated as follows (this is the Constant Bandwidth Server or CBS algorithm [8]):

if $deadline < currentTime$ or $\dfrac{runtime}{deadline - currentTime} > \dfrac{dl\_runtime}{dl\_period}$ then

```
deadline = currentTime+dl+deadline
runtime = dl_runtime
```

else deadline and runtime are left unchanged.

This calculation is done in setup_new_dl_entity in kernel/sched/deadline.c:

```c
Listing 5.8.17: Deadline and runtime recalculation                              C

1   static inline void setup_new_dl_entity(struct sched_dl_entity *dl_se)
2   {
3     struct dl_rq *dl_rq = dl_rq_of_se(dl_se);
4     struct rq *rq = rq_of_dl_rq(dl_rq);
5
6     if (dl_se->dl_throttled)
7       return;
8
9     dl_se->deadline = rq_clock(rq) + dl_se->dl_deadline;
10    dl_se->runtime = dl_se->dl_runtime;
11  }
```

This function is called via

```
enqueue_task_dl() → enqueue_dl_entity() → eupdate_dl_entity()
```

- As explained in Section 5.7.8, the EDF algorithm selects the task with the smallest deadline like the one to be executed first. In other words, we have a priority queue where the deadline is the priority. Just like for the CFS, in the kernel, this priority queue is implemented using a red-black tree. The leftmost node in the tree has the smallest deadline and is cached so that selecting this node is O(1).

- When a task executes for an amount of time Δt, its runtime is decreased as

runtime = runtime − Δt

This is done in `update_curr_dl` in kernel/sched/deadline.c:

```c
Listing 5.8.18: Runtime update for EDF scheduling                               C

1   static void update_curr_dl(struct rq *rq)
2   {
3     struct task_struct *curr = rq->curr;
4     struct sched_dl_entity *dl_se = &curr->dl;
5     u64 delta_exec;
6
7     if (!dl_task(curr) || !on_dl_rq(dl_se))
8       return;
9
10    delta_exec = rq_clock_task(rq) - curr->se.exec_start;
11    if (unlikely((s64)delta_exec <= 0)) {
12      return;
13    }
14
15    dl_se->runtime -= delta_exec;
16
17  throttle:
18    if (dl_runtime_exceeded(dl_se) ) {
19      dl_se->dl_throttled = 1;
20      __dequeue_task_dl(rq, curr, 0);
21      if (unlikely(dl_se->dl_boosted || !start_dl_timer(curr)))
22        enqueue_task_dl(rq, curr, ENQUEUE_REPLENISH);
```

```
23
24        if (!is_leftmost(curr, &rq->dl))
25            resched_curr(rq);
26    }
27
28    if (rt_bandwidth_enabled()) {
29        struct rt_rq *rt_rq = &rq->rt;
30
31        raw_spin_lock(&rt_rq->rt_runtime_lock);
32        if (sched_rt_bandwidth_account(rt_rq))
33            rt_rq->rt_time += delta_exec;
34        raw_spin_unlock(&rt_rq->rt_runtime_lock);
35    }
36 }
```

This function is called via

```
scheduler_tick() → task_tick_dl() → update_curr_dl()
```

When the runtime becomes less than or equal to 0, the task cannot be scheduled until its deadline. The CBS feature in the kernel throttles tasks that attempt to over-run their specified runtime. This is done by setting a timer for the replenishment of the time budget to the deadline (`start_dl_timer(curr)`).

When this replenishment time is reached, the budgets are updated:

```
deadline = currentTime+dl+deadline
runtime = dl_runtime
```

5.8.7 Kernel preemption models
User space programs are always preemptible. However, in certain real-time scenarios, it may be desirable to preempt kernel code as well.

The Linux kernel provides several preemption models, which have to be selected when compiling the kernel. For hard real-time performance, the "Fully Preemptible Kernel" preemption model must be selected. The last two entries below are available only with the PREEMPT_RT patch set. This is an official kernel patch set which gives the Linux kernel hard real-time capabilities. We refer to HOWTO setup Linux with PREEMPT_RT properly for more details. The possible preemption models are detailed in the kernel configuration file kernel/Kconfig.preempt:

- No Forced Preemption (Server): The traditional Linux preemption model, geared towards throughput. System call returns and interrupts are the only preemption points.

- Voluntary Kernel Preemption (Desktop): This option reduces the latency of the kernel by adding more "explicit preemption points" to the kernel code at the cost of slightly lower throughput. In addition to explicit preemption points, system call returns and interrupt returns are implicit preemption points.

▨ Preemptible Kernel (Low-Latency Desktop): This option reduces the latency of the kernel by making all kernel code (that is not executing in a critical section) preemptible. An implicit preemption point is located after each preemption disables section.

▨ Preemptible Kernel (Basic RT): This preemption model resembles the "Preemptible Kernel (Low-Latency Desktop)" model. Besides the properties mentioned above, threaded interrupt handlers are forced (as when using the kernel command line parameter threadirqs). This model is mainly used for testing and debugging of substitution mechanisms implemented by the PREEMPT_RT patch.

▨ Fully Preemptible Kernel (RT): All kernel code is preemptible except for a few selected critical sections. Threaded interrupt handlers are forced. Furthermore, several substitution mechanisms, like sleeping spinlocks and rt_mutex are implemented to reduce preemption disabled sections. Additionally, large preemption disabled sections are substituted by separate locking constructs. This preemption model has to be selected in order to obtain real-time behavior.

5.8.8 The red-black tree in the Linux kernel

The Linux kernel uses a red-black tree as the implementation of its priority queues. The red-black tree is a self-balancing binary search tree with O(log(n)) guarantees on accessing (search), insertion and deletion of node. More specifically, the height H of a red-black tree with n nodes (the length of the path from the root to the deepest node in the tree) is bounded by:

$$log\ (n + 1) \leq H \leq 2log\ (n + 1)$$

The implementation of the red-black tree in the linux kernel is lib/rbtree.c, the API is include/linux/rbtree.h and the data structure is documented in rbtree.txt. The API is quite simple, as illustrated by example in the documentation:

Creating a new rbtree

Data nodes in a rbtree tree are structures containing a struct rb_node member:

```
Listing 5.8.19: Node in a rbtree                                             C

1    struct mytype {
2      struct rb_node node;
3      char *keystring;
4    };
```

When dealing with a pointer to the embedded struct rb_node, the containing data structure may be accessed with the standard container_of() macro. In addition, individual members may be accessed directly via rb_entry(node, type, member).

At the root of each rbtree is a rb_root structure, which is initialized to be empty via:

```
Listing 5.8.20: Root for rbtree                                             C

1    struct rb_root mytree = RB_ROOT;
```

Searching for a value in a rbtree

Writing a search function for your tree is fairly straightforward: start at the root, compare each value, and follow the left or right branch as necessary.

Example:

```
Listing 5.8.21: Search function for rbtree                                          C

1   struct mytype *my_search(struct rb_root *root, char *string)
2   {
3       struct rb_node *node = root->rb_node;
4
5       while (node) {
6           struct mytype *data = container_of(node, struct mytype, node);
7           int result;
8
9           result = strcmp(string, data->keystring);
10
11          if (result < 0)
12              node = node->rb_left;
13          else if (result > 0)
14              node = node->rb_right;
15          else
16              return data;
17      }
18      return NULL;
19  }
```

Inserting data into a rbtree

Inserting data in the tree involves first searching for the place to insert the new node, then inserting the node and rebalancing ("recoloring") the tree. The search for insertion differs from the previous search by finding the location of the pointer on which to graft the new node. The new node also needs a link to its parent node for rebalancing purposes.

Example:

```
Listing 5.8.22: Insertion in rbtree                                                 C

1   int my_insert(struct rb_root *root, struct mytype *data)
2   {
3       struct rb_node **new = &(root->rb_node), *parent = NULL;
4
5       /* Figure out where to put new node */
6       while (*new) {
7           struct mytype *this = container_of(*new, struct mytype, node);
8           int result = strcmp(data->keystring, this->keystring);
9
10          parent = *new;
11          if (result < 0)
12              new = &((*new)->rb_left);
13          else if (result > 0)
14              new = &((*new)->rb_right);
15          else
16              return FALSE;
17      }
18
19      /* Add new node and rebalance tree. */
```

```
20    rb_link_node(&data->node, parent, new);
21    rb_insert_color(&data->node, root);
22
23  return TRUE;
24  }
```

Removing or replacing existing data in a rbtree

To remove an existing node from a tree, call:

Listing 5.8.23: Removal from rbtree

```c
1    void rb_erase(struct rb_node *victim, struct rb_root *tree);
```

Example:

Listing 5.8.24: Removal from rbtree – example

```c
1    struct mytype *data = mysearch(&mytree, "walrus");
2
3  if (data) {
4    rb_erase(&data->node, &mytree);
5    myfree(data);
6  }
```

To replace an existing node in a tree with a new one with the same key, call:

Listing 5.8.25: Replace node in rbtree

```c
1    void rb_replace_node(struct rb_node *old, struct rb_node *new,
2           struct rb_root *tree);
```

Replacing a node this way does not re-sort the tree: If the new node doesn't have the same key as the old node, the rbtree will probably become corrupted.

Iterating through the elements stored in a rbtree (in sort order)

Four functions are provided for iterating through a rbtree's contents in sorted order. These work on arbitrary trees, and should not need to be modified or wrapped (except for locking purposes):

Listing 5.8.26: Iterate through rbtree

```c
1    struct rb_node *rb_first(struct rb_node *tree);
2    struct rb_node *rb_last(struct rb_node *tree);
3    struct rb_node *rb_next(struct rb_node *node);
4    struct rb_node *rb_prev(struct rb_node *node);
```

To start iterating, call rb_first() or rb_last() with a pointer to the root of the tree, which will return a pointer to the node structure contained in the first or last element in the tree. To continue, fetch the next or previous node by calling rb_next() or rb_prev() on the current node. This will return NULL when there are no more nodes left.

The iterator functions return a pointer to the embedded struct rb_node, from which the containing data structure may be accessed with the container_of() macro, and individual members may be accessed directly via rb_entry(node, type, member).

Example:

Listing 5.8.27: Iterate through rbtree – example

```c
1   struct rb_node *node;
2     for (node = rb_first(&mytree); node; node = rb_next(node))
3       printk("key=%s\n", rb_entry(node, struct mytype, node)->keystring);
```

Cached rbtrees

An interesting feature of the Linux implementation of the red-black tree is caching. Because computing the leftmost (smallest) node in a red-black tree is quite a common task, the cached rbtree rb_root_cached can be used to optimize O(logN) rb_first() calls to an O(1) simple pointer fetch, avoiding potentially expensive tree iterations. The runtime overhead for maintenance is negligible, and the memory footprint is only slightly larger: a cached rbtree is simply a regular rb_root with an extra pointer to cache the leftmost node. Consequently, any occurrence of rb_root can be substituted by rb_root_cached.

5.8.9 Linux scheduling commands and API

There are a number of commands that allow users to set and change process priorities for both normal and real-time tasks.

Normal processes

The nice command allows the user to set the priority of the process to be executed:

Listing 5.8.28: Use of the nice command

```bash
1   $ nice -n 12 command
```

The renice command allows to change the priority of a running process:

Listing 5.8.29: Use of the renice command

```bash
1   $ renice -n 15 -p pid
```

Remember that nice values range from -20 to 19 and lower nice values correspond to higher priority. So, -12 has a higher priority than 12. The default nice value is 0. Regular users can set lower priorities (positive nice values).To use higher priorities (negative nice values), superuser privileges are required.

Real-time processes

There is a single command to control the real-time properties of a process, chrt. This command sets or retrieves the real-time scheduling attributes of a running process or runs the command with the given attributes. The are a number of flags that allow us to set the scheduling policy (–other, –fifo,–rr, –batch, –idle, –deadline).

For example:

Listing 5.8.30: Use of the chrt command   *Bash*

```
1    $ chrt --batch 0 pwd
```

All real-time policies require superuser privileges, for example:

Listing 5.8.31: Use of the chrt command   *Bash*

```
1    $ sudo chrt --rr 32 pwd
```

The –deadline policy only works with sporadic tasks that have actual runtime, deadline, and period attributes set via the sched_setattr system call.

5.9 Summary

In this chapter, we have introduced the concept of scheduling, the rationale behind it, and how it relates to the process life cycle and to the concept of system calls. We have discussed the different scheduling principles and criteria and covered a number of scheduling policies, both the basic policies and the more advanced policies used in the Linux kernel, including soft and hard real-time scheduling policies. Then we have applied all this basic scheduling theory in a study of the Linux scheduler, covering the actual data structures and algorithms used by the different schedulers supported by the Linux kernel, the Completely Fair Scheduler, the soft real-time scheduler, and the hard real-time scheduler.

5.10 Exercises and questions

5.10.1 Writing a scheduler

For this exercise, we suggest you start from existing code provided in the tutorial series Bare-Metal Programming on Raspberry Pi 3 on GitHub. Start from the provided cyclic executive example.

1. Create a round-robin scheduler.
2. Create a FIFO scheduler.

5.10.2 Scheduling

1. What are the reasons for having an operating systems scheduler?
2. How does scheduling relate to the process lifecycle?

5.10.3 System calls

Process	Arrival Time	Burst Time	Priority
P1	0	10	3
P2	1	1	1
P3	2	2	3
P4	3	1	4
P5	4	5	2

1. What is the rationale behind system calls?
2. What are the implications of the system call mechanism on scheduling?

5.10.4 Scheduling policies

1. What are the criteria for evaluating the suitability of a given scheduling policy?
2. Consider the following set of processes, with the arrival time and burst time given in milliseconds:

It is assumed below that a process arriving at time t is added to the Ready Queue before a scheduling decision is made.

a) Draw three Gantt charts that illustrate the execution of these processes using the following scheduling algorithms: FCFS, preemptive priority (a smaller priority number implies a higher priority), and RR (quantum = 1).

b) The best possible turnaround time for a process is its CPU burst time – i.e., that it is scheduled immediately upon arrival and runs to completion without being pre-empted. We will call the difference of the *turnaround time*, and the *CPU burst time the excess turnaround time*. Which of the algorithms results in the *minimum average excess turnaround time*?

3. Discuss the similarities and differences between the Shortest job first (SJF), Shortest remaining time first (SRTF) and Shortest elapsed time first (SETF) scheduling policies.

5.10.5 The Linux scheduler

1. How are priorities used in the Completely Fair Scheduler?

▧ Explain the use of the Red-Black tree in the Completely Fair Scheduler.

▧ Discuss the policies for soft and hard real-time scheduling in the Linux kernel.

References

[1] A. Stevenson, *Oxford dictionary of English*. Oxford University Press, USA, 2010.

[2] *ARM® Architecture Reference Manual – ARMv8, for ARMv8-A architecture profile*, Arm Ltd, 12 2017, issue: C.a. [Online]. Available: https://silver.arm.com/download/download.tm?pv=4239650&p=1343131

[3] A. Silberschatz, P. B. Galvin, and G. Gagne, *Operating system concepts essentials*. John Wiley & Sons, Inc., 2014.

[4] D. R. Smith, "A new proof of the optimality of the shortest remaining processing time discipline," *Operations Research*, vol. 26, no. 1, pp. 197–199, 1978.

[5] B. Kalyanasundaram and K. Pruhs, "Speed is as powerful as clairvoyance," J. ACM, vol. 47, no. 4, pp. 617–643, Jul. 2000. [Online]. Available: http://doi.acm.org/10.1145/347476.347479

[6] N. Navet, I. Loria, N. N. Koblenz, N. N. Koblenz, and N. N. Koblenz, "Posix 1003.1b: scheduling policies (1/2)."

[7] M. G. Harbour, "Real-time Posix: an overview," in *VVConex 93 International Conference, Moscu*. Citeseer, 1993.

[8] L. Abeni and G. Buttazzo, "Integrating multimedia applications in hard real-time systems," *Proceedings of the 19th IEEE. Real-Time Systems Symposium*, 1998, pp. 4–13.

Chapter 6

Memory management

6.1 Overview

As with other hardware resources, a machine's random access memory (RAM) is managed by the operating system on behalf of user applications. This chapter explores specific details of memory management in Linux.

What you will learn
After you have studied the material in this chapter, you will be able to:

1. Contrast the speed and size of data storage locations across the range of physical memory technologies.

2. Justify the reasons for using a virtual addressing scheme.

3. Navigate Linux page table data structures to decode a virtual address.

4. Assess the relative merits of various page replacement policies.

5. Appraise the design decisions underlying Arm hardware support for virtual memory.

6. Explain why a process must maintain its working set of data in memory.

7. Describe the operation of key kernel routines that must be invoked to maintain the virtual memory abstraction.

6.2 Physical memory

Memory is a key high-level computing component. Along with the processor, it is the main element identified in Von Neumann's original, abstract model of computer architecture from the 1940s, see Figure 6.1.

Figure 6.1: Von Neumann architecture of a computer.

RAM technology has advanced significantly since those early days, when a flat memory structure, featuring a few kilobytes of storage, would require large, specialized, analog circuits.

The sheer complexity of modern memory is mostly due to the inherent trade-off between size and speed. Small memory may be accessed rapidly, e.g., an individual register in a CPU. On the other hand, large memory has a high access latency—the worst case is often backing storage based on tape drives in a data warehouse.

Let's examine the physical memory hierarchy of a Raspberry Pi device. Figure 6.2 shows a photo of a Pi board, labeling the components that contain the physical memory (processor registers and cache in the system-on-chip package, off-chip memory in the DRAM, and flash storage in the SD card).

In terms of memory size and access speed, the diversity on the Pi is striking; there are six orders of magnitude difference in access latency from top to bottom of the hierarchy, and four orders of magnitude difference in size. The memory technology pyramid in Figure 6.3 shows precise details for a Raspberry Pi model 3B.

Figure 6.2: Raspberry Pi 2 board with labeled physical memory components; note that on more recent Pi models, the DRAM is stacked directly underneath the Broadcom system-on-chip, so it is not visible externally. Photo by author.

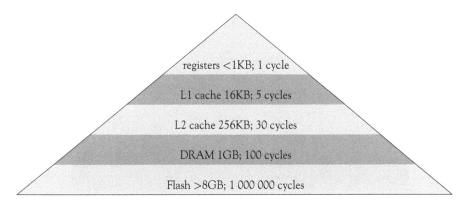

Figure 6.3: Typical access latency and size for the range of physical memory technologies in Raspberry Pi.

The OS cooperates with hardware facilities to minimize application memory access latency as much as possible. This involves ensuring cache locality and DRAM residency for application code and data. First, let's consider how the OS assists processes in organizing their allocated memory.

6.3 Virtual memory

6.3.1 Conceptual view of memory

In simplest terms, memory may be modeled as a gigantic linear array data structure. From the perspective of a C program, memory is a one-dimensional `int[ ]` or `byte[ ]`.

Each data item has an *address* (its index in the conceptual array) and a *value* (the bits stored at that address). Low-level machine instructions allow us to access data at byte, word, or multi-word granularity, where a word might be 32 or 64 bits, depending on the platform configuration. The Arm instruction set is a classic load/store architecture, with explicit instructions to read from (i.e., LDR) and write to (i.e., STR) memory.

6.3.2 Virtual addressing

In common with all modern high-level OSs, Linux uses *virtual addressing*. This is different from microcontrollers like typical Arduino and Mbed devices, which perform direct physical addressing.

In Linux, each process has its own *virtual address space*, with virtual addresses (also known as logical addresses) mapped onto physical addresses, conceptually as a one-to-one mapping.

Historically the Atlas computer, built at the University of Manchester in the 1960s, was the first machine to implement virtual memory. Figure 6.4 shows the original installation. The system was designed to map disparate memory technology onto a single address space, with address translation support in dedicated hardware.

Figure 6.4: The Atlas machine, designed at the University of Manchester, was the first system to feature virtual memory. Photo by Jim Garside.

Several key benefits are enabled by virtual memory.

Process isolation: It is impossible to trash another process' memory if the currently executing process is unable to address that memory directly. Accessing 'wild' pointers may cause a segmentation fault, but this will only impact the currently executing program, rather than the entire system.

Code relocation: Binary object files are generally loaded at the same virtual address, which is straightforward for linking and loading tools. This can ensure locality in the virtual address space, minimizing problems with memory fragmentation.

Hardware abstraction: The virtual address space provides a uniform, hardware-independent view of memory, despite physical memory resources changing when we install more RAM or modify a hosted VM configuration.

Virtual addressing requires direct, integrated hardware support in the form of a memory management unit (MMU). The MMU interposes between the processor and the memory, to translate virtual addresses (in the processor domain) to physical addresses (in the memory domain). This translation process is known as *hardware-assisted dynamic address relocation* and is supported by all modern processor families. The refined Von Neumann architecture in Figure 6.5 gives a schematic overview of the MMU's interposing role.

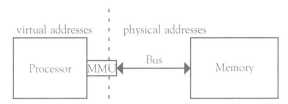

Figure 6.5: Refined Von Neumann architecture showing the Memory Management Unit (MMU).

When the OS boots up, the processor starts in a physical addressing configuration with the MMU turned off. The early stages of the kernel boot sequence initialize basic data structures for virtual memory management; then the MMU is turned on. For the Linux boot sequence on Arm, this happens in the `__turn_mmu_on` procedure in `arch/arm/kernel/head.S`.

6.3.3 Paging
The Linux virtual address space layout (for 32- and 64-bit Arm architectures) is shown in Figure 6.6. The split between user-space and kernel-space is either 3:1 or 2:2, for the 4GB address space. The default Raspberry Pi Linux kernel 32-bit configuration specifies `CONFIG_VMSPLIT_2G=y` which means a 2:2 split. The 64-bit address boundary literals in Figure 6.6 assume effective 39-bit virtual addresses; several other variants are possible.

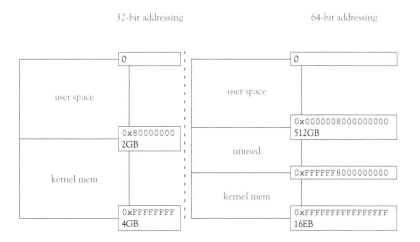

Figure 6.6: Linux virtual address space map for 32- and 64-bit architectures, lower addresses at the top.

The particular mechanism chosen to implement virtual addressing in Linux is *paging*, which supports fine-grained resource allocation and management of physical memory. In a paged memory scheme, physical memory is divided into fixed-size frames. Virtual memory is similarly divided into fixed-sized pages, where a single page has the same size as a single frame. This allows us to set up a mapping from pages to frames. The typical size of a single page in Linux is 4KB on a 32-bit Arm platform. Try `getconf PAGESIZE` on your terminal to find your system's configured page size in bytes.

The default page size is small enough to minimize fragmentation but large enough to avoid excessive overhead for per-page metadata. A page is the minimum granularity of memory that can be allocated to a user process. Larger pages are supported natively on Arm. For instance, 64KB pages and multi-MB 'huge' pages are possible. The advantage of larger pages is that fewer virtual to physical address translation mappings need to be stored. The main disadvantage comes from *internal fragmentation*, where a process is unable to use such a large amount of contiguous space effectively. Effectively, internal fragmentation means there is free memory which belongs to one process and cannot be assigned to another process. Generally, huge pages are appropriate for database systems and similar specialized data-intensive application workloads.

The next section examines the underlying mechanisms required to translate page-based virtual addresses into physical addresses.

6.4 Page tables

During normal process execution, the processors and caches operate entirely in terms of virtual addresses. As outlined above, the MMU intercepts all memory requests and translates virtual addresses into physical addresses.

The translation process relies on a mapping table, known as a *page table* which is stored in memory, see Sections 6.4.1 and 6.4.2. Dedicated MMU base registers are available to point to page tables for rapid access. An MMU cache of frequently used address mappings is maintained in the *translation look-aside buffer*, see Section 6.4.4.

Generally, the address translation is performed by the MMU hardware, transparently from the process or OS point of view. However, the OS is involved when a translation does not succeed—this causes a page fault, see Section 6.5.2. Further, when a process begins execution, the OS needs to set up the initial page table and subsequently maintain it as the virtual address space evolves.

Sometimes OS needs to operate on physical addresses directly, perhaps for device driver interactions. There are macros to convert between virtual and physical addresses, e.g., `virt_to_phys()`, but these only work for memory buffers allocated by the kernel with the `kmalloc` routine.

6.4.1 Page table structure

The page table is an in-memory data structure that translates from virtual to physical addresses. The translation happens automatically through the MMU hardware, which is directly supported by the processor. The MMU will automatically read the translation tables when necessary; this process is known as a *page table walk*. The OS simply has to maintain up-to-date mapping information in each process's page table, and refresh the page table base register each time a different process is executing.

The simplest possible structure is a *single-level* page table. For each page in the virtual address space, there is an entry in the table which contains a value corresponding to the appropriate physical address. This wastes space—a typical 32-bit 4GB address space, divided into distinct 4K pages, will need a single-level page table to contain 1M entries. Each entry consists of an address, say 4B, along with some metadata bits. However, most processes do not make use of their entire virtual address space, so many page table entries would remain unused.

This motivates the design of a *hierarchical page table*. Before we get into specific details for Linux on Arm, let's consider an idealized two-level page table. A typical 32-bit virtual address is divided into three parts:

1. A 10-bit first-level page table index.
2. A 10-bit second-level page table index.
3. A 12-bit page offset.

Given that pages are 4KB, this is a convenient subdivision. The 10 bits enable us to address 1024 32-bit word entries. Each entry can contain a single address. This means each sub-table of the page table can fit into a single page.

For unused regions of the address space, the OS can invalidate corresponding entries in the first-level page table, as a consequence of which, we do not need second-level page tables for these address ranges. This is the main space-saving for hierarchical page tables since each invalid first-level page table entry corresponds to 1024 invalid second-level page table entries—potentially saving up to 4MB of second-level page table space.

Figure 6.7 gives a schematic overview of a single virtual address translation, as handled by the MMU, using the two-level page table outlined above. Note the consecutive pair of table indexing operations, based on the P1 and P2 bitfields in the virtual address. The entry in the second-level page table contains the physical frame number, which is concatenated bitwise with the page offset to generate the actual physical address. There are spare bits in the 32-bit page table entry since the frame number will only occupy 20 bits. These remaining (low-order) bits can be used for page metadata such as access permissions, see Section 6.4.3.

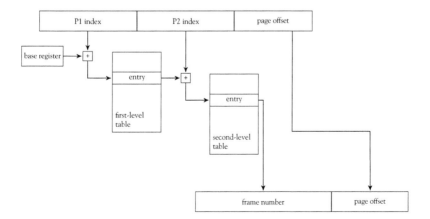

Figure 6.7: Virtual address translation via a two-level page table.

An *n*-level hierarchical page table will impose an overhead of *n* (page table) memory references for each 'actual' memory reference. There are techniques to mitigate this overhead; for instance, see Section 6.4.4.

6.4.2 Linux page tables on Arm

This section explores how the Linux model for page tables is realized on the Arm architecture. First, we examine the generic Linux page table architecture; then we review the platform-specific optimizations that are enabled for the Raspberry Pi.

Linux supports a multi-level hierarchical page table. Since kernel version 4.14, page tables can have up to five levels.

1. **PGD**, page global directory: one per process, with a base pointer stored in an MMU register, and in the process state context at current->mm.pgd.

2. **P4D**, fourth level directory: only applicable to 5-level page tables, currently not supported on Arm.

3. **PUD**, page upper directory: applicable to 4- and 5-level page tables, currently supported on AArch64.

4. **PMD**, page middle directory: intermediate level table.

5. **PTE**, page table entry: a leaf of the page table, containing multiple pages to frame translations.

With some platforms, fewer hardware page table levels are available than the Linux kernel supports. For instance, the default 32-bit Raspberry Pi Linux kernel configuration uses a two-level page table, as documented in `arch/arm/asm/pgtable-2level.h`. The PMD is defined to have a nominal size of single entry; it folds back directly onto the page global directory (PGD), which is optimized away at compile time. This unit-sized intermediate page table 'trick' is also applied to other architectures and configurations.

The two-level page table structure maps neatly onto the Arm MMU paging hardware in the Raspberry Pi Broadcom SoC, which has a two-level page table where the first level contains 4096 entries (i.e., 4 consecutive pages) and each of the second level tables has 256 entries. Each entry is a 32-bit word.

However, because the Arm MMU hardware does not provide a sufficiently rich set of page metadata for the Linux memory manager, the metadata bits for each page have to be managed in software, via page faults and software fixups. For instance, Linux requires a 'young' bit for each page. This bit tracks whether the page has been accessed recently, which is useful for page replacement policies. The 'young' bit is not supported natively on Arm.

Linux sees the abstraction of 2048 64-bit entries in the PGD, defined in the `pgtable-2level.h` with #define `PTRS_PER_PGD 2048`. Each 64-bit PGD composite entry breaks down into two 32-bit pointers to consecutive second-level blocks. Since the Arm MMU supports 256 entries in a second-level page table block, then there are 512 entries in two consecutive blocks. Thus Linux sees the abstraction of 512 32-bit entries in a logical PTE. This is defined in the `pgtable-2level.h` file with `#define PTRS_PER_PTE 512`.

These PTE blocks only occupy *half* a 4KB page. The other half is occupied by arrays of Linux per-page metadata, which is not supported natively by the Arm MMU. Effectively, the Linux PTE metadata *shadows* the Arm hardware-supported metadata and is maintained by the OS using a page fault and fixup mechanism. The relevant code is in `set_pte_ext`, which is generally implemented as an assembler intrinsic routine, for efficiency reasons. For instance, check out the assembler routine `cpu_v7_set_pte_ext` in file `arch/arm/mm/proc-v7-2level.S`. The hardware page metadata word is generally 2048 bytes ahead of the corresponding Linux shadow metadata. To find this, execute the command:

```
grep -4, 2048 *.S
```
Bash

in the `linux/arch/arm/mm/` directory. Section 6.4.3 outlines the Linux metadata that the OS maintains for each page.

Effectively, two different page table mechanisms are superimposed seamlessly onto the one-page table data structure, for both the Arm MMU and the Linux virtual memory manager. Figure 6.8 shows this page table organization as a schematic diagram.

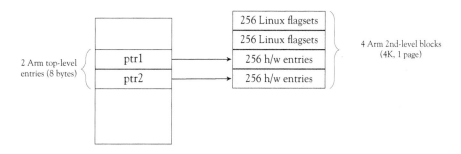

Figure 6.8: Linux page table organization fits into the Arm hardware-supported two-level paging structure, with Linux page metadata bits shadowing hardware metadata at a distance of half a page (2048 bytes).

There are several more complex variants on this virtual addressing scheme. For instance:

- 1MB sections are contiguous areas of physical memory that can be translated directly from a single PGD entry. This enables more rapid virtual address translation.

- Large Physical Address Extension (LPAE) is a scheme that enables 32-bit virtual addresses to be mapped onto 40-bit physical addresses. This permits 1TB of physical memory to be used on 32-bit Arm platforms.

6.4.3 Page metadata

To avoid confusion, note that a 'page table entry' may refer to one of two different concepts:

1. A Linux PTE, which is a leaf in the page table, containing 512 mappings from virtual to physical addresses.

2. A single mapping from a virtual to a physical address, along with corresponding metadata.

Throughout this chapter, when we mean (1), we will refer to it as a 'Linux PTE' specifically.

As well as recording the page frame number, to perform the mapping from a virtual to a physical address, a page table entry also stores appropriate metadata about the page. This includes information related to memory protection, sharing, and caching. Individual bits in the page table entry are reserved for specific information, so the OS can find attributes of pages with simple bitmask and shift operations.

Linux devotes a number of PTE bits to metadata. A typical layout is below, for the Raspberry Pi two-level pagetable (consult file `arch/arm/include/asm/pgtable-2level.h for details`).

If a process attempts to make an illegal memory access (e.g., if it tries to execute code in a non-executable page or to read data from an invalid page), then a page fault event occurs and the system traps to a page fault handler, see Section 6.5.2.

From a user perspective, the simplest way to see memory metadata is to look at the `/proc/PID/maps` file for a process. Although the information is not presented at page level, it is shown at the level of segments, which are contiguous page sequences in the virtual address space. For each segment, the permissions are listed: these might include read (r), write (w), and execute (x). A further column shows whether the memory is private (p) to this process or shared (s) between multiple processes.

Macro	Description	Bit position
L_PTE_VALID	Is this page resident in physical memory, or has it been swapped out?	0
L_PTE_YOUNG	Has data in this page been accessed recently?	1
—	4 bits associated with cache residency	2–5
L_PTE_DIRTY	Has data in this page been written, so the page needs to be flushed to disk?	6
L_PTE_RDONLY	Does this page contain read-only data?	7
L_PTE_USER	Can this page be accessed by user-mode processes?	8
L_PTE_XN	Does this page not contain executable code? (protection for buffer overflow attaches)	9
L_PTE_SHARED	Is this page shared between multiple process address spaces?	10
L_PTE_NONE	Is this page protected from unprivileged access?	11

Table 6.1: Metadata associated with each page table entry in Linux.

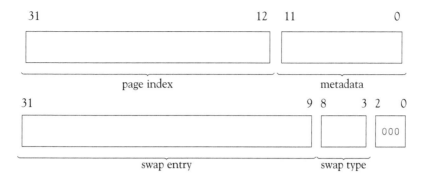

Figure 6.9: Bitmap patterns for page table entries, for a resident page to frame translation (above) and for a non-resident (swapped out) page (below).

Figure 6.10 shows an example of this memory mapping data for a single Linux process.

```
pi@raspberrypi:/home/pi $ cat /proc/23655/maps
00010000-00011000 r-xp 00000000 b3:02 42164 /home/pi/.../a.out
00020000-00021000 rw-p 00000000 b3:02 42164 /home/pi/.../a.out
76e67000-76f92000 r-xp 00000000 b3:02 1941 /lib/arm-.../libc-2.19.so
76f92000-76fa2000 ---p 0012b000 b3:02 1941 /lib/arm-.../libc-2.19.so
76fa2000-76fa4000 r--p 0012b000 b3:02 1941 /lib/arm-.../libc-2.19.so
76fa4000-76fa5000 rw-p 0012d000 b3:02 1941 /lib/arm-.../libc-2.19.so
76fa5000-76fa8000 rw-p 00000000 00:00 0
76fa8000-76fad000 r-xp 00000000 b3:02 10133 /usr/lib/.../libarmmem.so
76fad000-76fbc000 ---p 00005000 b3:02 10133 /usr/lib/.../libarmmem.so
76fbc000-76fbd000 rw-p 00004000 b3:02 10133 /usr/lib/.../libarmmem.so
76fbd000-76fdd000 r-xp 00000000 b3:02 1906 /lib/arm-.../ld-2.19.so
```

address range   access permissions   mapped file

Figure 6.10: Extract from a process memory mapping reported in /proc/PID/maps.

The binary file /proc/PID/pagemap records actual mapping data. Access to this file requires root privileges, otherwise reads return zero values or cause permission errors. The pagemap file has a 64-bit value for each page. The low 54 bits of this value correspond to the physical address or swap location of that page. Higher bits are used for page metadata. The Python code below performs a single virtual to physical address translation using this map.

Listing 6.4.1: Reading from the /proc pagemap file   *Python*

```python
1   import sys
2
3   pid = int(sys.argv[1], 10)   # specify as decimal
4   vaddr = int(sys.argv[2], 16)   # specify as hex
5
6   PAGESIZE=4096   # 4K pages
7   ENTRYSIZE=8
8
9   with open(("/proc/%d/pagemap" % pid), "rb") as f:
10      f.seek((vaddr/PAGESIZE) * ENTRYSIZE)
11      x = 0
```

```
12      for i in range(ENTRYSIZE):
13          x = (ord(f.read(1))<<(8*i)) + x # little endian
14
15      # interpret entry
16      present = (x>>63) & 1
17      swapped = (x>>62) & 1
18      file_page = (x>>61) & 1
19      soft_dirty =(x>>54) & 1
20
21      paddr = x & ((1<<32)-1)
22
23      print ("virtual address %x maps to **%d%d%d%d** %x" %
24          (vaddr, present, swapped, file_page, soft_dirty, (paddr*PAGESIZE)))
```

6.4.4 Faster translation

Since every access to main memory requires an address translation, it is helpful to cache frequently used translations to reduce overall access latency. The micro-architectural component that supports this address translation caching is known as a *translation look-aside buffer* (TLB). This is a fully associative cache that stores a small set of virtual to physical (i.e., page to frame number) mappings. Accessing data in the TLB is much quicker than a page table lookup; a TLB access may take only a single cycle, at least one order of magnitude faster than a full page table walk. Figure 6.11 shows how a TLB works. When a virtual address needs to be translated, the TLB looks up all its (*page, frame*) entries in parallel. If any page tag matches then we have a *TLB hit*. The translation succeeds with minimal overhead. On the other hand, if no entry tag matches then we have a *TLB miss*, and an expensive page table lookup is necessary.

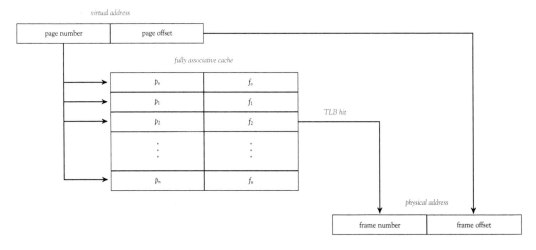

Figure 6.11 Fast virtual address lookup with a translation look-aside buffer.

Effective use of the TLB depends on the same memory access behavior as for standard caches, i.e., spatial and temporal locality of data accesses. If we can maximize TLB hits, most memory addresses will be translated without needing to access the page table in main memory. Thus, in the common case, the performance will be the same as for direct physical addressing; the TLB minimizes translation overhead.

The Arm Cortex A53 processor in the Raspberry Pi 3 features a two-level TLB. Each core has a micro-TLB, with 10 entries for instruction address lookups, and a further 10 for data address lookups. This corresponds to the Harvard architecture of the L1 cache. The main TLB is a 512 entry 4-way set associative cache. Each entry is tagged with a process-specific address space identifier (ASID) or is global for all application spaces. The hardware automatically populates and maintains the state of the TLB; although, if the OS modifies an address translation that is cached in the TLB, it is then the responsibility of the OS to invalidate this stale TLB entry.

Since the TLB caches virtual addresses, its data must be flushed when the virtual address space mapping changes, perhaps at an OS context switch. The Arm system coprocessor has a TLB Operations Register c8, which supports TLB entry invalidation. There are different options for how much to invalidate since a TLB flush is particularly expensive in terms of its impact on performance. For instance, it is not necessary to flush kernel addresses, since the kernel address space is common across all processes in the system. Each process may be associated with a distinct ASID, and only entries linked with the relevant ASID need to be invalidated on a context switch.

6.4.5 Architectural details

In the Arm architecture model, the system control coprocessor CP15 is responsible for the configuration of memory management. Translation table base registers (TTBRs) in this unit are configured to point to process-specific page tables by the OS, on a context switch. These registers are only accessible in privileged mode.

To read TTBR0 into general purpose register $r0$, we use the instruction:

```
MRC p15, 0, r0, c2, c0, 0
```

where p15 is the coprocessor, and c0 and c2 are coprocessor-specific registers. The dual MCR instruction writes from $r0$ into TTBR0, to update the page table base pointer.

Generally, Arm uses a one-page table base register for process-specific addresses (TTBR0) and devotes the other for OS kernel addresses (TTBR1). The page table control register TTBCR determines which page table base register is used for hardware page table walks; TTBCR is set when we vector into the kernel.

When the OS performs a context switch, it updates the process page table root pointer, PGD, to switch page tables. Since the on-chip caches are indexed using virtual addresses, it may be necessary to flush the cache on a context switch as well. Since this is a high-overhead operation, there are various techniques to avoid cache flush on context switch. These optimizations may require more complex cache hardware (e.g., ASIDs per cache line) or more intricate OS memory management (e.g., avoid overlaps in virtual address space ranges between concurrent processes).

6.5 Managing memory over-commitment

Since a process virtual address space may be much larger than the available physical memory, it is possible to allocate more memory than the system contains. This supports the abstraction that the system appears to have more memory than is physically installed. Recall that each process has a separate virtual address space (VAS); all VASs are mapped onto a single physical address space. This memory over-commitment is managed by the OS.

6.5.1 Swapping

When the system has more pages allocated than there are frames available in physical memory, the OS has to swap pages out of RAM and into the backing store. The Linux swap facility handles this overflow of pages. Swapping in Linux is often referred to as paging in other OS vocabularies.

Swap space is persistent storage, generally orders of magnitude slower than RAM. Typical swap space is a file system partition or a large file on the root file system. Check out cat `/proc/swaps` to inspect swap storage facilities on your Raspberry Pi Linux device. The Raspian default swap facility is a single 100MB file in `/var/swap`.

```
sudo hexdump -C /var/swap  | less                                           Bash
```

Examine to see what is stored in the swap space currently, although much of this data may be stale copies of old pages. Look for the `SWAPSPACE2` magic header near the start of the file. In general, the swap file is divided up into page-sized slots. Note that swapping is not particularly common on Raspberry Pi since access latency to SD card storage is particularly high and frequent access can cause device corruption.

In a process page table, individual entries may be marked as swapped out. The `pte_present()` macro checks whether a page is resident in memory or swapped out to disk. The bitfield layout of the page table entry for a swapped out page is shown in Figure 6.9, with distinct fields for the swap device number and the device-specific index.

A process may execute when some of its pages are not resident in memory. However, the OS needs to handle the situation when the process tries to execute a memory access from a swapped out (non-resident) page. The next section describes this OS support for page faults.

6.5.2 Handling page faults

A page fault event is a processor exception, which must be handled by an OS-installed exception handler. In Linux, the page fault handler is `do_page_fault()`, defined in `arch/arm/mm/fault.c`, which calls out to non-architecture-specific routines in `mm/memory.c`.

Figure 6.12 depicts a simplified flow graph for the page fault handling code. Initially, the handler checks whether this page is a sensible page for the process to be accessing, as opposed to a 'wild' access outside the process' mapped address space. Then there is a permissions check of the page table entry to determine whether the process is allowed to perform the requested memory operation (read, write, or execute). If either check fails, then there is a segmentation fault. If the checks pass, then the page fault handler will take appropriate remedial action, swapping in a swapped out page, reading in data from a file, performing a copy on write operation, or allocating a fresh frame for a new page.

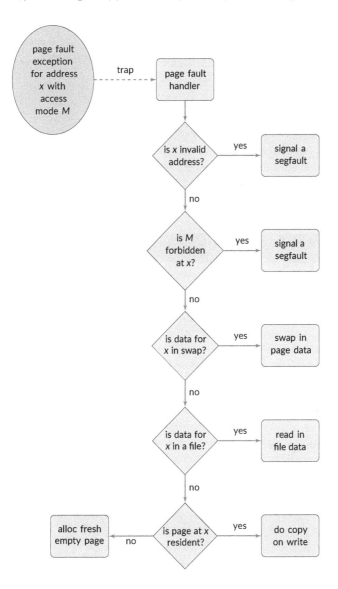

Figure 6.12: Flow chart for Linux page fault handling code.

Once the page fault has been handled, the OS restarts the faulting process at the instruction that originally caused the exception, and user-mode execution resumes, subject to process scheduling. Suppose you have just launched a process with PID 6903, you can inspect the actual page faults incurred by this process with the command:

```
ps -o min_flt,maj_flt,cmd,args 6903                                              Bash
```

Running the command without a PID integer argument lists statistics for all the user's processes. To run a program and get a total count for its page faults, use the `/usr/bin/time` command. (This may require you to install the `time` package with `sudo apt-get install time`. Note you need the full path, since `time` is also a bash built-in command). Now try `/usr/bin/time ls` and see how the output reports the number of page faults.

Note that Linux distinguishes between *minor faults* — when a page is already resident, but not mapped in this process' VAS (e.g., code shared between multiple processes), and *major faults* — when the OS has to access the persistent store and read in data from a file.

As an example, consider the C code below. It creates a multi-page array and accesses a single byte in each page. Because of *demand paging*, the pages are only mapped into the process' VAS when first accessed. As the program is executed with larger sized arrays (use the command line parameter to increase the size) the number of minor page faults increases. Try running it with an argument of 64000 (256MB sized array). Note if there is not enough memory, then the program will terminate.

```c
1   #include <stdlib.h>
2
3   /* assume 4KB page size */
4   #define PAGES 1024*4
5
6   int main(int argc, char **argv) {
7       char *p = 0;
8       int i = 0, j = 0;
9       /* n is number of pages */
10      int n = 100;
11      if (argc == 2) {
12          n = atoi(argv[1]);
13      }
14      p = (char *)malloc(PAGES*n);
15      for (i=0; i<PAGES; i++) {
16          for (j=0; j<PAGES*(n-1); j+=PAGES) {
17              p[(i+j)] = 42;
18          }
19      }
20      return 0;
21  }
```

Listing 6.5.1: Program that induces minor page faults

Now consider a similar program, but one that uses memory-mapped files, so the OS has to fetch the data from the backing store. Grab a text file, e.g., with:

```bash
curl -o alice.txt http://www.gutenberg.org/files/11/11-0.txt
```

and then compile the code shown below.

Listing 6.5.2: Program that induces major page faults   C

```c
1   #include <assert.h>
2   #include <fcntl.h>
3   #include <stdio.h>
4   #include <sys/mman.h>
5   #include <sys/stat.h>
6   #include <unistd.h>
7
8   size_t get_size(const char* filename) {
9       struct stat st;
10      stat(filename, &st);
11      return st.st_size;
12  }
13
14  int main(int argc, char** argv) {
15      int i, total = 0;
16      size_t filesize = get_size(argv[1]);
17      int fd = open(argv[1], O_RDONLY, 0);
18      char *data;
19      assert(fd != -1);
20      posix_fadvise(fd, 0, filesize, POSIX_FADV_DONTNEED);
21      data = mmap(NULL, filesize, PROT_READ, MAP_PRIVATE |
22                          MAP_NONBLOCK, fd, 0);
23      assert(data != MAP_FAILED);
24      for (i=0; i<filesize; i+=1024)
25          total += data[i];
26      printf("total = %d\n", total);
27      int rc = munmap(data, filesize);
28      assert(rc==0);
29      close(fd);
30  }
```

The first time you run this program with:

```bash
/usr/bin/time -v ./a.out alice.txt 2>&1 | grep Major
```
Bash

notice there is at least one major fault as the file is read into memory. However, if you run it immediately again, for a second time, there will be *no* major faults; the file data is already cached in memory, so the program only causes minor faults.

6.5.3 Working set size
The *working set* for a process measures the number of pages that must be resident for that process to make useful progress, i.e., to avoid constant swapping.

There are various files that track per-process memory consumption. For instance, for a process with id PID, the file `/proc/PID/statm` reports page-level memory usage. The first column shows the vmsize (the number of pages allocated in the virtual address space) , and the second column shows the resident set size (the number of pages resident in physical memory for this process). The following inequality always holds: *rss < vmsize*. The file `/proc/PID/status` shows the same information in a more readable format.

For a process to execute effectively, the RSS should be at least as large as the working set size (WSS). Linux does not measure WSS directly; however, various third-party scripts are available to estimate process WSS, e.g., consult http://www.brendangregg.com/wss.html

6.5.4 In-memory caches

Physical memory frames that are not being used to store process pages could be used effectively by the OS for other purposes, such as caching data. Linux features several kinds of in-memory caches that use these free frames.

The file system *page cache* stores page-sized chunks of files in memory, after they are first touched. The OS reads ahead, to load portions of the file into memory in anticipation of future accesses. The fadvise function allows the process to specify how the file will be accessed. The page cache is the reason why second and subsequent accesses to a file generally take much less time than the initial access.

The *swap cache* keeps track of which physical frames have been written out to a swap file. This is highly useful for pages shared between multiple processes, for example. Once a page has been written out to the swap file, then the next time the page is swapped in, the data remains in the swap file slot. If this page is not modified after regaining memory residence, and then at some later stage it needs to be swapped out again, we can avoid the writeback if it has not been modified since the last swap in. The swap file records where the page lives in swap, so we can record this in the relevant page table entry. On the other hand, if the page is modified in memory, then its swap cache entry is expunged because the page becomes dirty and must be written back. This swap cache feature may save unnecessary swap file writebacks.

The *buffer cache* is used to optimize access to block devices (see later chapter on I/O). Since read and write operations are expensive for slow block devices, the buffer cache interposes these accesses to reduce I/O latency. For instance, individual writes from a collection of processes could be batched up for a block device. A buffer cache will record blocks of data that have been read from or written to a block device.

We can use commands like `free -h` or `vmstat -S m` to inspect how the Raspberry Pi physical RAM is allocated between process pages, OS buffers, page cache, etc. Ideally, all unused frames in a system would be occupied by buffers and caches, since this is preferable to underutilizing physical RAM. Then the caches are shrunk when the process page requirements increase as more processes are admitted.

6.5.5 Page replacement policies

The *kernel swap daemon* is a background process that commences running after kernel initialization.

```
ps -eo | grep kswapd                                                    Bash
```

Invoke to see this daemon running on your Pi. The responsibility of kswapd is to swap out pages that are not currently needed. This serves to maintain a set of free frames that are available for newly allocated or swapped in pages.

Some pages are obvious candidates for swapping out; these are *clean* pages whose data is already in the backing store, e.g., executable code, other memory-mapped files, or pages in the swap cache. Such pages can be discarded without copying any data since the data is already stored elsewhere. On the other hand, *dirty* pages have been updated since they were read in from backing store; other pages (e.g., anonymous process pages) may never have been written out to the backing store. Such pages must have their data transferred to persistent storage before they can be swapped out.

It is not efficient to swap out pages if their data may be required again in the near future since the swap out operation will be followed swiftly by a swap in of the same data.

Bélády's optimal page replacement policy is a theoretical oracle that looks into the future, to select a candidate page for replacement that will not be used again, or will only be used further in the future than any other page currently resident. Since this abstraction is not implementable, Linux assumes that, if a page has not been used in the recent past, then it is unlikely to be used again in the near future. This is the principle of *temporal locality*.

Two memory manager mechanisms are used to keep track of page usage over time:

1. Each page has an associated metadata bit that may be set when the page is accessed.

2. Pages may be stored in a doubly-linked list that approximates least-recently-used (LRU) order.

Pages grow older as they are not accessed over time; old pages are ideal candidates for swapping out. Below we review several page replacement policies.

Random
The simplest page replacement algorithm does not take page age or usage into account. It simply selects a random victim page to be swapped out immediately, to make space for a new page.

Not recently used
A page is not recently used (NRU) if its access metadata bit is unset. Such a page is a good candidate for replacement. The NRU algorithm might work as follows:

1. A page p is randomly selected as a candidate.

2. If p access bit is set, go back to (1).

3. Assert p access bit is unset, and select p for replacement.

There is no guarantee of termination with NRU, since all pages may have access bits set. We assume the OS will periodically unset all bits.

Clock
The clock algorithm keeps a circular list of pages. There is a conceptual 'hand' that points to the next candidate page for replacement, see Figure 6.13. When a page replacement needs to take place, the

clock algorithm inspects the current candidate—if its access bit is set, then the access bit is unset and the clock hand advances to the next page. The first page with an unset access bit is selected as the victim to be swapped out. This is a 'second chance' algorithm.

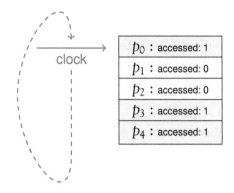

Figure 6.13: Clock page replacement algorithm.

Least recently used

A genuine least recently used (LRU) scheme either upgrades the single access bitfield to a longer, last access timestamp field for each page, or shuffles pages in a doubly-linked list to sort them in order of access time. The victim page is then easily selected as the page with the oldest timestamp, or the page at the tail of the list respectively. Both of these techniques have significant management overhead.

The Linux memory manager actually implements a variant of the LRU page replacement scheme. Pages allocated to processes are added to the head of a global active pages queue. When a page needs to be evicted, the tail of this queue is examined. If the tail page has its access bit set, then it is moved back to the head of the queue, and its access bit is unset. However, if the tail page does not have its access bit set, then it is a candidate for replacement, and it is moved to the inactive pages queue from where it may be swapped out.

The page replacement algorithm is implemented in function `do_try_to_free_pages()` in source code file `linux/mm/vmscan.c`, but be aware that this is a complex piece of code to trace.

Tuning the system

Linux has a kernel parameter called *swappiness*, which controls how aggressively the kernel swaps pages out to the backing store. The value should be an integer between 0 and 100 inclusive. Higher values are more aggressive at swapping pages from less active processes out of physical memory, which improves file-system performance (cache).

Note that, on a Raspberry Pi device, the swappiness may set at a particularly low value, since the swap file or partition is on an SD card, which has high access latency and may fail with excessive write operations.

Find your current system's swappiness value with:

```
cat /proc/sys/vm/swappiness
```
Bash

On a desktop Linux installation, the default value is generally 60. Try something like:

```
sudo sysctl -w vm.swappiness=100
```
Bash

and see whether this changes the performance of your system over time.

When the physical memory resource becomes chronically over-committed, active pages must be swapped out and swapped in again with increasing frequency. The whole system slows down drastically since no process can make progress without incurring major page faults. All the system time is spent servicing these page faults, so no useful work is achieved. The phenomenon is known as *thrashing*, and it badly affects system performance.

6.5.6 Demand paging

Linux implements *demand paging*, which means physical memory is allocated to processes in a lazy, or just-in-time, manner. A call to mmap only has an effect on the process page table; frames are not allocated to the process directly. The process is only assigned physical memory resource when it really needs it.

The Linux memory management subsystem records areas of virtual memory that are mapped in the virtual address space, but for which the physical memory has not yet been allocated. (These are zeroed-out entries in the page table.) This is the core mechanism that underlies demand paging: when the process tries to access a memory location that is in this uninitialized state, a page fault occurs, and the physical memory is directly allocated. This corresponds to the bottom left case (*alloc fresh empty page*) in Figure 6.12.

The high-level layout of a process' virtual address space is specified by the mm_struct data structure. The process' task_struct instance contains a field that points to the relevant mm_struct. The definition of mm_struct is in file include/linux/mm_types.h. It stores a linked list of vm_area_struct instances, which model *virtual memory areas* (VMAs).

The list of VMAs encapsulates a set of non-overlapping, contiguous blocks of memory. Each VMA has a start- and end-address, which are aligned with page boundaries. The vm_area_struct, also defined in include/linux/mm_types.h. has access permission flags, and prev and next pointers for the linked list abstraction. Reading from /proc/PID/maps simply traces the linked list of VMAs and prints out their metadata one-by-one, for instance, see Figure 6.10.

Each vm_area_struct also has a field for a backing file, in case this VMA is a memory-mapped file. If there is no file, this is an *anonymous* VMA which corresponds to an allocation of physical memory. When a page fault occurs for an address due to demand paging, the kernel looks up the relevant VMA data via the mm_struct pointer. Each VMA has an embedded set of function pointers wrapped in a vm_operations_struct. One of these entries points to a specific do_no_page function that implements the appropriate demand paging behavior for this block of memory: the invoked action might be allocating a fresh physical frame for an anonymous VMA, or reading data from a file pointer for a file-backed VMA.

A process may use the `madvise` API call to provide hints to the kernel about when data is likely to be needed, or what kind of access pattern will be used for a particular area of memory— sequential or random access, for instance.

6.5.7 Copy on write

When a child process is forked, it shares its parent's memory (although logically it has a distinct, isolated copy of the parent's virtual address space). The child process virtual address space maps to the same physical frames, until either parent or child tries to write some data. At that stage, a *fresh* frame is allocated dynamically for the writing process.

This copy on write mechanism is supported through duplicated page table entries between parent and child processes, page protection mechanisms, and sophisticated page fault handling, as outlined above.

Copy on write leads to efficient process forking; child page allocation is deferred until data write operations occur—pages are shared between parent and child until their data diverges through write operations.

For a simple example of copy on write activity, execute the source code below and check the measured time overheads for the buffer updates. Where the time is longest, then copy on write paging activity is taking place.

Listing 6.5.3: Measuring overhead of copy on write activity   C

```c
1    #include <errno.h>
2    #include <stdio.h>
3    #include <stdlib.h>
4    #include <time.h>
5    #include <unistd.h>
6
7    #define PAGE_SIZE 4096
8    #define NUM_PAGES 100000
9
10   void write_data(char *buffer, int size) {
11     int i;
12     static char x = 0;
13     clock_t start, end;
14     start = clock();
15     for (i=0; i<size; i+=PAGE_SIZE)
16       buffer[i] = x;
17     x++;
18     end = clock();
19     printf("time taken: %f seconds\n",
20       (double) (end-start) / CLOCKS_PER_SEC);
21   }
22
23   int main(int argc, char **argv) {
24     static char buffer[NUM_PAGES*PAGE_SIZE];
25     int res;
26
27     printf("1st test - expect high time - pages allocating\n");
28     write_data(buffer, sizeof buffer);
29
30     switch(res = fork()) {
31     case -1:
```

```
32      fprintf(stderr,
33          "Unable to fork: %s(errno=%d)\n",
34          strerror(errno), errno);
35      exit(EXIT_FAILURE);
36  case 0: /* child */
37      printf("child[%d]: 2nd test - expect high time - copy on write\n", getpid());;
38      write_data(buffer, sizeof buffer);
39      printf("child[%d]: 3rd test - expect low time - pages available\n", getpid());
40      write_data(buffer, sizeof buffer);
41      exit(EXIT_SUCCESS);
42  default: /* parent */
43      printf("parent[%d]: waiting for child[%d] to finish\n",
44        getpid(), res);
45      wait(NULL); /* child runs before parent */
46      printf("parent[%d]: 4th test - expect fairly low time - pages available"
47              "but not in processor cache\n", getpid());
48      write_data(buffer, sizeof buffer);
49      exit(EXIT_SUCCESS);
50      }
51  }
```

Copy on write is a widely used technique. For instance, check out online information about 'purely functional data structures' to see how copy on write is used to make high-level algorithms and data structures more efficient.

6.5.8 Out of memory killer

In the worst case, there is insufficient physical memory available to support all running processes. The kernel invokes a killer process (OOM-killer) at this stage, to identify a victim process to be terminated, freeing up physical memory resource. Heuristics are used to identify memory hogging processes; look at the integer value in /proc/PID/oom_score — higher numbers indicate more memory hogging processes.

It's possible to invoke the OOM-killer manually. Run this memory-hogging Python script:

Listing 6.5.4: A memory-hogging script *Python*

```python
#!/usr/bin/python
import time
megabyte = (0,) * (1024 * 1024 / 8)
data = megabyte*400
time.sleep(60)
```

and then execute these bash commands:

Listing 6.5.5: Trigger the OOM killer interactively *Bash*

```bash
sudo chmod 777 /proc/sysrq-trigger  # to allow us to trigger special events
echo "f" > /proc/sysrq-trigger  # trigger OOM killer
dmesg  # find out what happened
```

and observe the OOM-killer is triggered and kills the Python runtime. Note the gruesome "kill process or sacrifice child" log message — the OOM-killer (mm/oom_kill.c) attempts to terminate child processes rather than parents where possible, to minimize system disruption.

Check whether the OOM-killer is frequently invoked on your system with something like:

```
sudo cat /var/log/messages | grep "oom-killer"                              Bash
```

6.6 Process view of memory

A process has the abstraction of logical memory spaces, which are superimposed on the paged virtual address space as contiguous segments. The text segment contains the program code. This is generally loaded to known addresses by the runtime loader, reading data from the static ELF file. Text generally starts at a known address. For instance, invoke:

```
ld --verbose | grep start                                                   Bash
```

to find this address for your system.

Data is usually located immediately after the text. This includes statically allocated data which may be initialized (the data section) or uninitialized (the bss section). The runtime heap comes after this data. The runtime stack, which supports function evaluation, parameter passing, and scoped variables, starts near the top of memory and grows downwards.

From a process perspective, there are three ways in which the OS might add new pages to the virtual address space while the program is running:

1. `brk` or sbrk extends the program break, effectively growing the heap.

2. `mmap` allocates a new block of memory, possibly backed by a file.

3. The stack can grow down, as more functions are called in a dynamically nested scope; the stack expands on-demand, managed as part of the page fault handler.

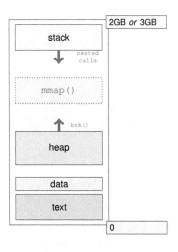

Figure 6.14: Evolution of a process's user virtual address space, dynamic changes in red, lower addresses at the bottom.

Figure 6.14 illustrates these three ways in which a process virtual address space may evolve. For a more concrete example of process interaction with memory, we can use a tool like valgrind to trace memory accesses at instruction granularity. The visualizations in Figure 6.15 show the sequence of memory accesses recorded by valgrind for an execution of the `ls` command. The precise command used to generate the trace is:

```
valgrind --tool=lackey --trace-mem=yes ls                                    Bash
```

6.7 Advanced topics

There are several memory management techniques to improve system security and defend against buffer overflow attacks. Address space layout randomization (ASLR) introduces random noise into the locations of executable code and runtime memory areas like the stack and heap. This unpredictability makes it more difficult for an attacker to vector to known code. The page metadata bit NX indicates a page is not executable. Again, this mitigates code injection attacks from user-input data.

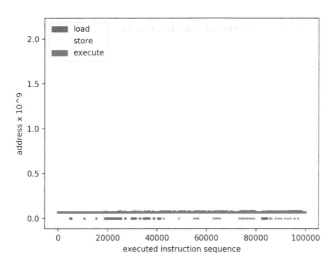

Figure 6.15: Visualizations of memory access patterns for an invocation of the ls command, shown for first 100,000 instructions; the high red/yellow line is the stack, the low blue line is the program executable text.

As single address space systems become larger, in terms of both the number of processor cores and the amount of installed physical memory, there is increasing variance in memory access latency. One reason for this is that some processor cores are located closer to particular RAM chips; perhaps a motherboard has several sockets, and integrated packages are plugged into each socket with RAM and processor cores. This arrangement is referred to as *non-uniform memory access* or NUMA.

Figure 6.16 shows an example NUMA system, based on the Cavium ThunderX2 Arm processor family. There are two NUMA regions (one per socket). Each region has tens of cores and a local bank of RAM. Physical memory is mapped to pages, as outlined above. There is a single address space, so every memory location is accessible from every core, but with different access latencies. Processor caches may hide some of the variance in memory access times, but NUMA caching protocols are complex. Writes to shared data can invalidate shared cache entries, forcing fresh data fetches from main memory.

Figure 6.16 The Isambard HPC facility uses Cavium ThunderX2 NUMA processors which support multiple sockets with a shared address space; note the distinctive memory banks surrounding each processor package. Photo by Simon McIntosh-Smith.

Linux has several schemes to optimize memory access for NUMA architectures. Memory allocation may be *interleaved*, so it is placed in a round-robin fashion across all the nodes; this ensures memory access times are uniform on average, assuming an equal distribution of probable accesses across the address space. Another allocation policy is *node-local*, which allocates memory close to the processor executing the `malloc`; this assumes the memory is likely to be accessed by threads running on cores in that same NUMA region.

You can determine whether your Linux system supports NUMA, by executing:

```
numactl --hardware                                                          Bash
```

and see how many nodes are reported. Most Arm systems (in particular, all Raspberry Pi boards) are not NUMA. However, multiple socket motherboards will become increasingly common as core counts increase, tracking Moore's law in future years.

Another memory issue that affects large-scale servers, but may soon be apparent on smaller systems is *distributed memory*. Protocols such as *remote dynamic memory access* (RDMA) enable pages to be transferred rapidly from other machines to the local machine, copying memory from a remote buffer to a local buffer with minimal OS intervention. This is useful for migration of processes or virtual machines in cloud data centers. In more general terms, *direct memory access* (DMA) is a technique for efficient copying of data between devices and memory buffers. We will cover DMA in more detail in Chapter 8 when we explore input/output. There is some additional complexity because many devices work entirely in terms of physical memory addresses since they operate outside of the processor's virtual addressing domain.

Next-generation systems may feature *non-volatile memory* (NV-RAM). Whereas conventional volatile RAM loses its data when the machine is powered down, NV-RAM persists data (like flash drives or hard disks, but with faster access times). NV-RAM is byte-addressable and offers significant new features for OSs, such as immediate restart of processes or entire systems, and full persistence for in-memory databases.

6.8 Further reading

The *Understanding the Linux Kernel textbook* has helpful chapters on memory management, disk caches, memory mapping, and swapping [1].

Gorman's comprehensive documentation on memory management in Linux [2] is a little dated (based on kernel version 2.6) but still contains plenty of relevant and valuable material, including source code commentary. It is the definitive overview of the complex virtual memory management subsystem in the Linux kernel.

Details of more recent kernel changes are available at the Linux Memory Management wiki, https://linux-mm.org.

To learn about Arm hardware support for memory management, consult Furber's Arm System-on-Chip textbook [3] for a generic overview, or the appropriate Arm architecture reference manual for specific details.

6.9 Exercises and questions

6.9.1 How much memory?

Calculate the size of your Raspberry Pi system's virtual address space in megabytes by writing a short C program.

Listing 6.9.1: Compute the size of the virtual address space
C

```c
#include <stdio.h>
#include <sys/sysinfo.h>
#include <unistd.h>

int main() {
    int pages = get_phys_pages();
    int pagesize = getpagesize();    /* in bytes */
    double ramGB = ((double)pages * (double)pagesize / 1024 / 1024 / 1024);
    printf("RAM Size %.2f GB, Page Size %d B\n", ramGB, pagesize);
    return 0;
}
```

How does the value reported compare with the system memory size stated by (a) /proc/meminfo and (b) the official system documentation? Can you account for any discrepancies?

6.9.2 Hypothetical address space

Consider a 20-bit virtual address space, with pages of size 1KB.

1. Assuming byte-addressable memory, how many bits are required for a page/frame offset?

2. How many bits does this leave for specifying the page number?

3. Assume the page index bitstring is split into two equal portions, for first-level and second-level page table indexing. How many first-level page tables should there be?

4. What is the maximum number of second-level page tables?

5. How many individual entries will there be in each page table?

6. What is the space overhead of this hierarchical page table, as opposed to a single-level page table, when all pages are mapped to frames?

7. What is the space-saving of this hierarchical page table, as opposed to a single-level page table, when only one page is mapped to a frame, i.e., there is a single entry in the page table mapping?

6.9.3 Custom memory protection

The `mprotect` library function allows you to set page-level protection (read, write, execute) for allocated memory in user space. See `man mprotect` for more details. Sketch a scenario when a developer may want to change page permissions:

1. From read/write to read-only, once a data structure has been initialized;

2. To make a page executable, once its data has been populated.

6.9.4 Inverted page tables

The simplest variant of an inverted page table contains one entry per frame. Each entry stores an address space identifier (ASID) to record which process is currently occupying this frame, along with the virtual address corresponding to this physical address. Metadata permission bits may also be stored with each entry. To look up a virtual address, it is only necessary to check whether the address is present in any table entry—by looking up all table entries at once. This *content-addressable* approach is how TLBs work since hardware support makes it possible to check all entries simultaneously.

1. What is the main problem with supporting inverted page tables entirely in software, using an in-memory data structure for the table?

2. Can you think of a more efficient solution for inverted page table storage in software?

6.9.5 How much memory?

Assume an OS is running p processes, and the platform has an n-level hierarchical page table. Each node (including leaf nodes) in the page table occupies a single page. The page size is large enough to store at least n address entries in a page table node:

1. How many pages would all the page tables occupy if each process has a single page of data in its virtual address space?

2. What is the smallest number of pages occupied by all the page tables if each process has n pages of data in its virtual address space?

3. What is the largest number of pages occupied by all the page tables if each process has n pages of data in its virtual address space?

6.9.6 Tiny virtual address space

Imagine a system with an 8-bit, byte-addressable physical address space:

1. How many bytes of memory will there be?

2. For this system, consider using a virtual addressing scheme with single-level paging. If each page contains 16 bytes, how many pages will there be?

3. In the worst case, what happens to memory access latency in a virtual addressing environments with a single-level page table, with respect to physical addressing?

4. What could be done to mitigate this worst-case memory access latency?

5. In practice, why is it unlikely that 8-bit memory would feature a virtual addressing scheme?

6.9.7 Definitions quiz

Match the following concepts with their definitions:

1. **Swap file**	1. Contains translation data and protection metadata for one or more pages.
2. **Page table entry**	2. When the OS perturbs regions of memory to ensure unpredictable addresses for key data elements.
3. **Thrashing**	3. When a system cannot make useful progress since almost every memory access requires pages to be swapped from the backing store.
4. **MMU**	4. Backing storage for pages that are not resident in memory.
5. **Address space randomization**	5. A specialized hardware unit that maintains the abstraction of virtual address spaces from the point-of-view of the processor.

References

[1] D. P. Bovet and M. Cesati, *Understanding the Linux Kernel*, 3rd ed. O'Reilly, 2005.

[2] M. Gorman, *Understanding the Linux Virtual Memory Manager*. Prentice Hall, 2004, https://www.kernel.org/doc/gorman/

[3] S. Furber, *ARM System-on-Chip Architecture*, 2nd ed. Pearson, 2000.

Chapter 7

Concurrency
and parallelism

7.1 Overview

In this chapter, we discuss how the OS supports concurrency, how the OS can assist in exploiting hardware parallelism, and how the OS support for concurrency and parallelism can be used to write parallel and concurrent programs. We look at OS support for concurrent and parallel programming via POSIX threads and present an overview of practical parallel programming techniques such as OpenMP, MPI, and OpenCL.

The exercises in this chapter focus on POSIX thread programming to explore the concepts of concurrency, shared resource access and parallelism, and programming using OpenCL to expose the student to practical parallel heterogeneous programming.

What you will learn
After you have studied the material in this chapter, you will be able to:

1. Relate definitions to the programmer's view of concurrency and parallelism.

2. Discuss programming primitives and APIs to handle concurrency and the OS and hardware support for them.

3. Use the POSIX programming API to exploit parallelism and OS and hardware support for them.

4. Compare and contrast data- and task-parallel programming models.

5. Illustrate by example the popular parallel programming APIs.

7.2 Concurrency and parallelism: definitions

To understand the implications and properties, first of all, we need clear definitions of concurrency and parallelism.

7.2.1 What is concurrency?
Concurrency means that more than one task is running concurrently (at the same time) on the system. In other words, concurrency is a property of the workload rather than the system, provided that the system has support for running more than one task at the same time. In practice, one of the key reasons to have an OS is to support concurrency through scheduling of tasks on a single shared CPU.

7.2.2 What is parallelism?
Parallelism, by contrast, can be viewed as a property of the system: when a system has more than one CPU core, it can execute several tasks in parallel, even if there is no scheduler to time-slice the tasks. If the kernel supports hardware parallelism, it will try to speed up the execution of tasks by making use of the available parallel resources.

7.2.3 Programming model view
Another way of defining the terms parallelism and concurrency is as programming models. In practical terms, *concurrent programming* is about user experience and *parallel programming* about performance.

In a concurrent program, several threads of operation are running at the same time because the user expects several actions to be happening at the same time. For example, a web browser must at least have a thread for networking, one for rendering the pages and one for user interactions (mouse clicks, keyboard input). If these threads were not concurrent, the browser would not be usable.

By contrast, in a parallel program, what happens is that the work that would be performed on a single CPU is split up and handed to multiple CPUs who execute each part in parallel. We can further distinguish between task parallelism and data parallelism. Task parallelism means that every CPU core will perform a different part of the computation; for example, the steps in an image processing pipeline. Data parallelism means that every CPU core will perform the same computation but on a different part of the data. If we run a parallel program on a single-core system, the only effect will be that it runs slower.

Because effectively parallel programs execute concurrent threads, many of the issues of concurrent programs are also encountered in parallel programming.

7.3 Concurrency

In this section, we have a closer look at concurrency: the issues arising from concurrency and the techniques to address them; support for concurrency in the hardware and the OS, and the POSIX programming API.

7.3.1 What are the issues with concurrency?

There are two factors which can lead to issues when several tasks are running concurrently: shared resources and exchange of information between tasks.

Shared resources

When concurrent tasks share a resource, then access to that resource needs to be controlled to avoid undesirable behavior. A very clear illustration of this problem is a shared section of railroad track, as shown in Figure 7.1. Clearly, uncontrolled access could lead to disaster. Therefore, points in a railway system are protected by semaphore signals. The single-track section is the shared resource as it is required by any trains traveling on the four tracks leading to it. When the signal indicates "Clear," the train can use the shared section, at which point the signal will change to "Stop." Any train wanting to use the shared section will have to wait until the train occupying it has left, and the signal is "Clear" again. We will discuss the OS equivalent in Section 7.3.3.

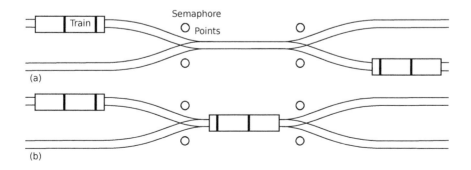

Figure 7.1: Shared railroad track section with points and semaphores.

In a computer system, there many possible shared resources: file system, IO devices, memory. Let's first consider the case of a shared file, e.g., a file in your home directory will be accessible by all processes owned by you. Slightly simplifying, when a process opens a file, the file content is read into the memory space of the process. When the process closes the file again, any changes will be written back to disk. If two or more processes access the file concurrently for writing, there is a potential for conflict: the changes made by the last process to write back to disk will overwrite all previous changes. Therefore, most editors will warn if a file was modified by another process while open in the editor.

Figure 7.2: Concurrent access to a shared file using echo and vim.

For example, in Figure 7.2, I opened a file `test_shared_access.txt` in vim (right pane), and while it was open, I modified it using echo (left pane). As you can see, when I then tried to save the file in the editor, it warned me the file had been changed.

In the case of shared files, most operating systems leave the access control to the user. In the previous example, before writing, vim checked the file on disk for changes. This is not possible for shared access to IO devices because they are controlled by the operating system. In a way, this makes access control easy because the OS can easily keep track of the processes using an IO resource. Shared access to memory is more problematic. As we have seen, memory is not normally shared between processes; each process has its own memory space. However, in a multithreaded process, the memory is shared between all threads. In this case, again, the operating system leaves the access control to the user, i.e., the programmer of the application. However, the operating system and the hardware provide support for access control. The OS uses the hardware support to implement its internal mechanisms, and these are used to implement the programmer API (e.g., POSIX pthreads).

Exchange of information

When concurrent tasks need to exchange information that is required to continue execution, there is a need to make sure that the sender either waits for the message (if it is sent late) or stores the message until needed (if it was sent early). Furthermore, if two or more tasks require information from one another, care must be taken to avoid *deadlock*, i.e., the case where all tasks are waiting for the other tasks so no tasks can continue execution. In the case of communication between threads in a multithreaded process, the communication occurs via the shared memory. For communication between processes, there are a number of possibilities, e.g., communication using shared files, operating system pipes, network sockets, operating system message queues, or even shared memory.

The issues with the exchange of information in concurrent processes can be best explained using the *producer-consumer* problem: each process is either a producer or a consumer of information. Ideally, any item of information produced by a producer would be immediately consumed by a consumer. However, in general, the rate of progress of producers and consumers is different (i.e., they are not operating synchronously). Therefore, information needs to be buffered, either by the consumer or by the producer. In practice buffering capacity is always limited (the problem is therefore also known as the *bounded buffer* problem), so at some point, it is possible that the producer will have to suspend execution until there is sufficient buffer capacity for the information to be produced. Note that in general there can be more than one buffer (e.g., it is common for each consumer to have a buffer per producer).

Effectively, the buffer is a shared resource, so in terms of access control, information exchange, and resource sharing are effectively the same problem. This is also true for synchronization: the consumer needs the information from the producer(s) in order to progress. So as long as that information is not there, the producer has to wait. This is also the case with shared resources; for example, trains have to wait until the shared section of track is free. In other words, control of access to shared resources and synchronization of the exchange of information are just two different views on the same problem. Consequently, there will be a single set of mechanisms that can be used to address this problem.

Note that if there are multiple producers and/or consumers, and a single shared resource, the problem is usually known as the *reader-writer* problem, and has to address the concurrent access to the shared resource.

7.3.2 Concurrency terminology
When discussing synchronization and shared resources, it is useful to define some additional terms and concepts.

Critical section
A critical section for a shared resource is that portion of a program which accesses the resource in such a way that multiple concurrent accesses would lead to undefined or erroneous behavior. Therefore, for a given shared resource, only one process can be executing its critical section at a time. The critical section is said to be *protected* if the access to it is controlled in such a way that the behavior is well-defined and correct.

Synchronization
In this context, by synchronization, we mean synchronization between concurrent threads of execution. When multiple processes need the exchange information, synchronization f the processes results in a well-defined sequence of interactions.

Deadlock
Deadlock is the state in which each process in a group of communicating process is waiting for a message from the other process in order to proceed with an action. Alternatively, in a group of

processes with shared resources, there will be deadlock if each process is waiting for another process to release the resource that it needs to proceed with the action.

A classic example of how the problem can occur is the so-called *dining philosophers* problem. Slightly paraphrased, the problem is as follows:

- Five philosophers sit around a round table with a bowl of noodles in front of each and a chopstick between each of them.

- Each philosopher needs two chopsticks to eat the noodles.

- Each philosopher alternately.

  - ☐ thinks for a while,

  - ☐ picks up two chopsticks,

  - ☐ eats,

  - ☐ puts down the chopsticks.

It is clear that there is potential for deadlock here because there are not enough chopsticks for all philosophers to eat at the same time. If for example, they would all first take the left chopstick, then try to take the right one (or vice-versa), there would be deadlock. So how do they ensure there is no deadlock?

Edsger Dijkstra (May 11, 1930 – Aug. 6, 2002) was a Dutch computer scientist. He did his Ph.D. research from the University of Amsterdam's Mathematical Center (1952–62). He taught and researched at the Technical University of Eindhoven from 1963 to 1973 and at the University of Texas from 1984 onwards. He was widely known for his 1959 algorithm that solves the shortest-path problem. This algorithm is still used to determine the shortest path between two points, in particular for routing of communication net-works. In the course of his research on the mutual exclusion in communications he suggested in 1962 the concept of computer semaphores. His famous letter to CACM in 1968, "Go To Statement Considered Harmful" was very influential in the development of structured programming. He received the Turing Award in 1972.

Image ©2002 Hamilton Richards

www.cs.utexas.edu/users/EWD/

7.3.3 Synchronization primitives

In 1962, the famous Dutch computer scientist Edsger Dijkstra wrote a seminal – though interestingly, technically unpublished – article titled "Over seinpalen" [1], i.e., "About Semaphores," in which he introduced the concept of *semaphores* as a mechanism to protect a shared resource. In Dijkstra's article, a semaphore *S* is a special type of shared memory, storing a non-negative integer. To access the semaphore register, Dijkstra proposes two operations, *V(S)*, which stands for "verhoog," i.e., increment, and *P(S)*, which stands for "prolaag," i.e., try to decrement. The P(S) operation will block until the value of S has been successfully decremented. Both operations must be atomic.

If the semaphore can only take the values 0 or 1, Dijkstra specifically mentions the railway analogy, where the V-operation means "free the rail track" and the P-operation "try to pass by the semaphore onto the single track", and that this is only possible if the semaphore is set to "Safe" and passing it implies setting it to "Unsafe".

Dijkstra calls a binary semaphore a *mutex* (mutual exclusion lock) [2]; a non-binary semaphore is sometimes called a *counting semaphore*. Although there is no general agreement on this definition, the definitions in the Arm Synchronization Primitives Development Article [3] agree with this:

Mutex *A variable, able to indicate the two states locked and unlocked. Attempting to lock a mutex already in the locked state blocks execution until the agent holding the mutex unlocks it. Mutexes are sometimes called locks or binary semaphores.*

Semaphore *A counter that can be atomically incremented and decremented. Attempting to decrement a semaphore that holds a value of less than 1 blocks execution until another agent increments the semaphore.*

The key requirement of Dijkstra's semaphores is the atomicity of the operation. Modern processors provide special atomic instructions that allow implementing semaphores efficiently.

7.3.4 Arm hardware support for synchronization primitives

Exclusive operations and monitors

The ARMv6 architecture introduced the Load-Exclusive and Store-Exclusive synchronization primitives, LDREX and STREX, in combination with a hardware feature called *exclusive monitor*. Quoting from the Arm Synchronization Primitives Development Article [3]:

LDREX *The LDREX instruction loads a word from memory, initializing the state of the exclusive monitor(s) to track the synchronization operation. For example, LDREX R1, [R0] performs a Load-Exclusive from the address in R0, places the value into R1 and updates the exclusive monitor(s).*

STREX *The STREX instruction performs a conditional store of a word to memory. If the exclusive monitor(s) permit the store, the operation updates the memory location and returns the value 0 in the destination register, indicating that the operation succeeded. If the exclusive monitor(s) do not permit the store, the operation does not update the memory location and returns the value 1 in the destination register. This makes it possible to implement conditional execution paths based on the success or failure of the memory operation. For example, STREX R2, R1, [R0] performs a Store-Exclusive operation to the address in R0, conditionally storing the value from R1 and indicating success or failure in R2.*

Exclusive monitors *An exclusive monitor is a simple state machine, with the possible states open and exclusive. To support synchronization between processors, a system must implement two sets of monitors, local and global (Figure 7.3). A Load-Exclusive operation updates the monitors to exclusive state. A Store-Exclusive operation accesses the monitor(s) to determine whether it can complete successfully. A Store-Exclusive can succeed only if all accessed exclusive monitors are in the exclusive state.*

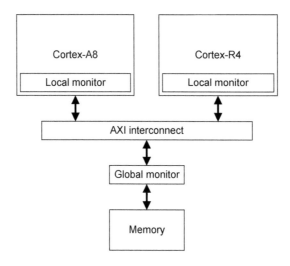

Figure 7.3: Local and global monitors in a multi-core system (from [3]).

The LDREX and STREX instructions are used by the Arm-specific Linux kernel code to implement the kernel-specific synchronization primitives which in their turn are used to implement POSIX synchronization primitives. For example, include/asm/spin lock.h implements spin lock functionality for the Arm architecture, and this is used in the non-architecture-specific implementation in include/linux/spin lock.h.

Shareability domains

In the context of cache-coherent symmetric multiprocessing (SMP), the Arm system architecture uses the concept of *shareability domains* [4], which can be the *Inner Shareable, Outer Shareable, System, or Non-shareable* , as illustrated in Figure 7.4. These domains are mainly used to restrict the range of memory barriers, as discussed in Section 7.3.5.

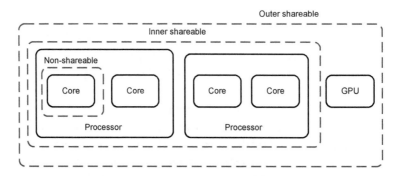

Figure 7.4: Shareability domains in an Arm manycore system, based on [5].

The architectural definition of these domains is that they enable us to define sets of observers for which the shareability makes the data transparent for accesses. The Inner domain shares both code and data, i.e., in practice a multicore system running an instance of an operating system will be in the Inner domain; the Outer domain shares data but not code, and as shown in the figure could, for example, contain a GPU, or a DSP or DMA engine. Marking a memory region as non-shareable means that the local agent (core) does not share this region at all. This domain is not typically used in SMP systems. Finally, if the domain is set to System, then an operation on it affects all agents in the system. For example, a UART interface would not normally be put in a shareable domain, so its domain would be the full system.

7.3.5 Linux kernel synchronization primitives

The Linux kernel implements a large number of synchronization primitives; we discuss here only a selection.

Atomic primitives

The Linux kernel implements a set of atomic operations know as read-modify-write (RMW) operations. These are operations where a value is read from a memory location, modified, and then written back, with the guarantee that no other write will occur to that location between the read and the write (hence the name *atomic*).

Most RMW operations in Linux fall into one of two classes: those that operate on the special `atomic_t or atomic64_t data type`, and those that operate on *bitmaps*, either stored in an unsigned long or in an array of unsigned long.

The basic set of RMW operations that are implemented individually for each architecture are known as "atomic primitives." As a kernel developer, you would use these to write architecture-independent code such as a file system or a device driver.

As these primitives work on atomic types or bitmaps, let's first have a look at these. The atomic types are defined in types.h and they are actually simply integers wrapped in a struct:

Listing 7.3.1: Linux kernel atomic types

```c
1    typedef struct {
2      int counter;
3    } atomic_t;
4
5    #ifdef CONFIG_64BIT
6    typedef struct {
7      long counter;
8    } atomic64_t;
9    #endif
```

The reason for this is that the atomic types should be defined as a signed integer but should also be opaque so that a cast to a normal C integer type will fail.

The simplest operation on atomic types are initialization, read and write, defined for the arm64 architecture in include/asm/atomic.h as:

Listing 7.3.2: Linux kernel atomic type operations (1)   C

```
1   #define ATOMIC_INIT(i)    { (i) }
2
3   #define atomic_read(v)      READ_ONCE((v)->counter)
4   #define atomic_set(v, i)    WRITE_ONCE(((v)->counter), (i))
```

The READ_ONCE and WRITE_ONCE macros are defined in include/linux/compiler.h and are not architecture-specific. Their purpose is to stop the compiler from merging or refetching reads or writes or reordering occurrences of statements using these macros. We present them here purely to show how non-trivial it is to stop a C compiler from optimizing.

Listing 7.3.3: Linux kernel atomic type operations (2)   C

```
1   #include <asm/barrier.h>
2   #define __READ_ONCE(x, check)                       \
3   ({                             \
4     union { typeof(x) __val; char __c[1]; } __u;      \
5     if (check)                   \
6         __read_once_size(&(x), __u.__c, sizeof(x));   \
7     else                         \
8         __read_once_size_nocheck(&(x), __u.__c, sizeof(x));   \
9     smp_read_barrier_depends(); /* Enforce dependency ordering from x */ \
10    __u.__val;                   \
11  })
12  #define READ_ONCE(x) __READ_ONCE(x, 1)
13
14  #define WRITE_ONCE(x, val) \
15  ({ \
16    union { typeof(x) __val; char __c[1]; } __u =  \
17      { .__val = (__force typeof(x)) (val) }; \
18    __write_once_size(&(x), __u.__c, sizeof(x));  \
19    __u.__val;                   \
20  })
```

Bitmaps are, in a way simpler, as they are simply arrays of native-size words. The Linux kernel provides the macro DECLARE_BITMAP() to make it easier to create a bitmap:

Listing 7.3.4: Linux kernel bitmap   C

```
1   #define DECLARE_BITMAP(name,bits) \
2       unsigned long name[BITS_TO_LONGS(bits)]
```

Here, BITS_TO_LONGS returns the number of words required to store the given number of bits. The most common operations on bitmaps are set_bit() and clear_bit() which for the arm64 architecture are defined in include/asm/bitops.h as:

Listing 7.3.5: Linux kernel bitmap operations (1)

```
1   #ifndef CONFIG_SMP
2   /*
3    * The __* form of bitops are non-atomic and may be reordered.
4    */
5   #define ATOMIC_BITOP(name,nr,p)              \
6     (__builtin_constant_p(nr) ? ____atomic_##name(nr, p) : _##name(nr,p))
7   #else
8   #define ATOMIC_BITOP(name,nr,p)    _##name(nr,p)
9   #endif
10
11  /*
12   * Native endian atomic definitions.
13   */
14  #define set_bit(nr,p)      ATOMIC_BITOP(set_bit,nr,p)
15  #define clear_bit(nr,p)    ATOMIC_BITOP(clear_bit,nr,p)
16  }
```

The actual atomic operations used in these macros are defined in include/asm/bitops.h as:

Listing 7.3.6: Linux kernel bitmap operations (2)

```
1   /*
2    * These functions are the basis of our bit ops.
3    *
4    * First, the atomic bitops. These use native endian.
5    */
6   static inline void ____atomic_set_bit(unsigned int bit, volatile unsigned long *p)
7   {
8     unsigned long flags;
9     unsigned long mask = BIT_MASK(bit);
10
11    p += BIT_WORD(bit);
12
13    raw_local_irq_save(flags);
14    *p |= mask;
15    raw_local_irq_restore(flags);
16  }
17
18  static inline void ____atomic_clear_bit(unsigned int bit, volatile unsigned long *p)
19  {
20    unsigned long flags;
21    unsigned long mask = BIT_MASK(bit);
22
23    p += BIT_WORD(bit);
24
25    raw_local_irq_save(flags);
26    *p &= ~mask;
27    raw_local_irq_restore(flags);
28  }
```

The interesting point here is that the atomic behavior is achieved by masking the interrupt requests and then restoring them, through the use of the architecture-independent functions `raw_local_irq_save()` and `raw_local_irq_restore()`. The architecture-specific implementation of these functions for AArch64 is also provided in include/asm/bitops.h:

Listing 7.3.7: Atomic behavior through masking interrupt requests C

```c
1   / *
2    * Aarch64 has flags for masking: Debug, Asynchronous (serror), Interrupts and
3    * FIQ exceptions, in the 'daif' register. We mask and unmask them in 'dai'
4    * order:
5    * Masking debug exceptions causes all other exceptions to be masked too/
6    * Masking SError masks irq, but not debug exceptions. Masking irqs has no
7    * side effects for other flags. Keeping to this order makes it easier for
8    * entry.S to know which exceptions should be unmasked.
9    */
10
11  / *
12   * CPU interrupt mask handling.
13   */
14  static inline unsigned long arch_local_irq_save(void)
15  {
16    unsigned long flags;
17    asm volatile(
18      "mrs %0, daif    // arch_local_irq_save\n"
19      "msr daifset, #2"
20      : "=r" (flags)
21      :
22      : "memory");
23    return flags;
24  }
25
26  / *
27   * restore saved IRQ state
28   */
29  static inline void arch_local_irq_restore(unsigned long flags)
30  {
31    asm volatile(
32      "msr daif, %0    // arch_local_irq_restore"
33      :
34      : "r" (flags)
35      : "memory");
36  }
```

Masking interrupts is a simple and effective mechanism to guarantee atomicity on a single-core processor because the only way another thread could interfere with the operation would be through an interrupt. On a multicore processor, it is in principle possible that a thread running on another core would access the same memory location. Therefore, this mechanism is not useful outside the kernel. If you use it in kernel code, it is assumed that you know what you're doing, that is also why the routines have _local_ in their name, to indicate that they only operate on interrupts for the local CPU.

A nice overview of the API for operations on atomic types can be found in the Linux kernel documentation in the files atomic_t.txt and atomic_bitops.txt. The operations can be divided into non-RMW and RMW. The former are read, set, read_acquire and set_release; the latter are arithmetic, bitwise, swap, and reference count operations. Furthermore, each of these comes in an atomic_ and atomic64_ variant, as well as variants to indicate that there is a return value or not, and that the fetched rather than the stored value is returned. Finally, they all come with relaxed, acquire, and release variants, which need a bit more explanation.

Memory operation ordering

On a symmetric multiprocessing (SMP) system, accesses to memory from different CPUs are in principle not ordered. We say that the memory operation ordering is relaxed. Very often, some degree of ordering is required. The default for the Linux kernel is to impose a strict overall order via what is called a memory barrier. Strictly speaking, a memory barrier imposes a perceived partial ordering over the memory operations on either side of the barrier. To quote from the Linux kernel documentation (memory_barriers.txt),

Such enforcement is important because the CPUs and other devices in a system can use a variety of tricks to improve performance, including reordering, deferral, and combination of memory operations; speculative loads; speculative branch prediction and various types of caching. Memory barriers are used to override or suppress these tricks, allowing the code to sanely control the interaction of multiple CPUs and/or devices.

The kernel provides the memory barriers `smp_mb {before,after}_atomic()` and in practice, the strict operation is composed of a relaxed operation preceded and followed by a barrier, for example. Thus:

Listing 7.3.8: Linux kernel atomic operation through barriers

```
1    atomic_fetch_add();
2    // is equivalent to :
3    smp_mb before_atomic();
4    atomic_fetch_add_relaxed();
5    smp_mb after_atomic();
```

Between relaxed and strictly ordered there are two other possible semantics, called *acquire* and *release*.

Acquire semantics applies to RMW operations and load operations that read from shared memory (*read-acquire*), and it prevents memory reordering of the read-acquire with any read or write operation that follows it in program order.

Release semantics applies to RMW operations and store operations that write to shared memory (*write-release*), and it prevents memory reordering of the write-release with any read or write operation that precedes it in program order.

Table 7.1 provides a summary of the possible cases.

Type of operation		Ordering
Non-RMW operations		Unordered
RMW operations		
RMW operations	That have no return value	Unordered
	That have a return value	Fully ordered
	That have an explicit ordering	
	{operation name}_relaxed	Unordered
	{operation name}_acquire	RMW read is an ACQUIRE
	{operation name}_release	RMW write is a RELEASE

Table 7.1: Memory operation ordering semantics.

Memory barriers
The memory barriers `smp_mb {before,after}_atomic()` are not the only types of barrier provided by the Linux kernel. We can distinguish the following types [6]:

General barrier
A general barrier (`barrier()` from include/linux/compiler.h) has no effect at runtime; it only serves as an instruction to the compiler to prevent reordering of memory accesses from one side of this statement to the other. For the gcc compiler, this is implemented in the kernel code as

```c
1   #define barrier() __asm__ __volatile__("": : :"memory")
```
Listing 7.3.9: Linux kernel general barrier

Mandatory barriers
To enforce memory consistency on a full system level, you can use mandatory barriers. This is most common when communicating with external memory-mapped peripherals. The kernel mandatory barriers are guaranteed to expand to at least a general barrier, independent of the target architecture.

The Linux kernel has three basic mandatory CPU memory barriers:

GENERAL mb() A full system memory barrier. All memory operations before the mb() in the instruction stream will be committed before any operations after the mb() are committed. This ordering will be visible to all bus masters in the system. It will also ensure the order in which accesses from a single processor reaches slave devices.

WRITE wmb() Like mb(), but only guarantees ordering between read accesses: all read operations before an rmb() will be committed before any read operations after the rmb().

READ rmb() Like mb(), but only guarantees ordering between write accesses: all write operations before a wmb() will be committed before any write operations after the wmb(). [6]

For the Arm AArch64 architecture, these barriers are implemented in arm64/include/asm/barrier.h as: with the dsb() macro implemented in arm/include/asm/barrier.h as:

```c
1   #define mb() dsb(sy)
2   #define rmb() dsb(ld)
3   #define wmb() dsb(st)
```
Listing 7.3.10: Arm implementation of kernel memory barriers (1)

with the dsb() macro implemented in arm/include/asm/barrier.h as:

```c
1   #define isb(option) __asm__ __volatile__ ("isb " #option : : : "memory")
2   #define dsb(option) __asm__ __volatile__ ("dsb " #option : : : "memory")
3   #define dmb(option) __asm__ __volatile__ ("dmb " #option : : : "memory")
```
Listing 7.3.11: Arm implementation of kernel memory barriers (2)

Here, DMB, DSB, and ISB are respectively Data Memory Barrier, Data Synchronization Barrier, and Instruction Synchronization Barrier instructions [7]. In particular, DSB acts as a special kind of memory barrier. No instruction occurring in the program order after this instruction executes until this instruction has completed. The DSB instruction completes when all explicit memory accesses before this instruction have completed (and all cache, branch predictor and TLB maintenance operations before this instruction have completed).

The argument SY indicates a full system DSB operation; LD is as DSB operation that waits only for loads to complete and ST is a DSB operation that waits only for stores to complete.

SMP conditional barriers
The SMP conditional barriers are used to ensure a consistent view of memory between different cores within a cache-coherent SMP system. When compiling a kernel without CONFIG_SMP, SMP barriers are converted into plain general (i.e., compiler) barriers. Note that this means that SMP barriers cannot replace a mandatory barrier, but a mandatory barrier can replace an SMP barrier.

The Linux kernel has three basic SMP conditional CPU memory barriers:

GENERAL smp_mb() *Similar to mb(), but only guarantees ordering between cores/processors within an SMP system. All memory accesses before the smp_mb() will be visible to all cores within the SMP system before any accesses after the smp_mb().*

WRITE smp_wmb() *Like smp_mb(), but only guarantees ordering between read accesses.*

READ smp_rmb() *Like smp_mb(), but only guarantees ordering between write accesses.* [6]

The SMP barriers are implemented in include/asm-generic/barrier.h as:

Listing 7.3.12: Linux kernel SMP barriers

```c
#ifdef CONFIG_SMP
#ifndef smp_mb
#define smp_mb() __smp_mb()
#endif
#ifndef smp_rmb
#define smp_rmb() __smp_rmb()
#endif
#ifndef smp_wmb
#define smp_wmb() __smp_wmb()
#endif
#endif
```

For the Arm AArch64 architecture, the SMP barriers are implemented in arm64/include/asm/barrier.h as:

Listing 7.3.13: Arm implementation of kernel SMP barriers   C

```
1    #define __smp_mb() dmb(ish)
2    #define __smp_rmb() dmb(ishld)
3    #define __smp_wmb() dmb(ishst)
```

---

with the dmb() macro defined above.

DMB is the Data Memory Barrier instruction. It ensures that all explicit memory accesses that appear in program order before the DMB instruction are observed before any explicit memory accesses that appear in program order after the DMB instruction. It does not affect the ordering of any other instructions executing on the processor.

The argument ISH restricts a DMB operation to the inner shareable domain; ISHLD is a DMB operation that waits only for loads to complete, and is restricted to inner shareable domain; ISHST is a DMB operation that waits only for stores to complete, and is restricted to the inner shareable domain. Recall that the "inner shareable domain" is in practice the memory space of the hardware (SMP system) controlled by the Linux kernel.

Implicit barriers

Instead of explicit barriers, it is possible to use locking constructs available within the kernel that act as implicit SMP barriers (similar to pthread synchronization operations in user space, see Section 7.3.6). Because in practice a large number of device drivers do not use the required barriers, the kernel I/O accessor macros for the Arm architecture (readb(), iowrite32() etc.) act as explicit memory barriers when the kernel is compiled with CONFIG_ARM_DMA_MEM_BUFFERABLE, for example in arm/include/asm/io.h:

Listing 7.3.14: Kernel I/O accessor macros for Arm as explicit memory barriers   C

```
1    #ifdef CONFIG_ARM_DMA_MEM_BUFFERABLE
2    #include <asm/barrier.h>
3    #define __iormb() rmb()
4    #define __iowmb() wmb()
5    #else
6    #define __iormb() do { } while (0)
7    #define __iowmb() do { } while (0)
8    #endif
```

(the Linux kernel code uses do { } while (0) as an architecture-independent no-op).

Spin locks

Spin locks are the simplest form of locking. Essentially, the task trying to acquire the lock goes into a loop doing nothing until it gets the lock, in pseudocode:

Listing 7.3.15: Spin lock pseudocode   C

```
1    while (! has_lock ) {
2    // try to get the lock
3    }
```

Spin locks have the obvious drawback of occupying the CPU while waiting. If the wait is long, another task should get the CPU; in other words, the task trying to obtain the lock should be put to sleep. However, for the cases where it is not desirable to put a task to sleep, or if the user knows the wait will be short, the kernel provides spin locks, also known as busy-wait locks (kernel/locking/spin lock.c).

The spin lock functionality for SMP systems is implemented as a macro which creates a lock function for a given operation (e.g., read or write). Essentially, the implementation is a forever loop with a conditional break. First, preemption is disabled, then the function tries to atomically acquire the lock, and exits the loop if it succeeded; otherwise, it re-enables preemption and calls the architecture-specific relax operation, which effectively is an efficient way of doing a no-op, and it performs another iteration of the loop and tries again.

Listing 7.3.16: Linux kernel SMP lock-building macro   C

```
1    #define BUILD_LOCK_OPS(op, locktype)                      \
2    void __lockfunc __raw_##op##_lock(locktype##_t *lock)    \
3    {                                                         \
4        for (;;) {                                            \
5            preempt_disable();                                \
6            if (likely(do_raw_##op##_trylock(lock)))          \
7                break;                                        \
8            preempt_enable();                                 \
9                                                              \
10           arch_##op##_relax(&lock->raw_lock);               \
11       }                                                     \
12   }
```

For uniprocessor systems (include/linux/spin lock_api_up.h), the spin lock is much simpler:

Listing 7.3.17: Linux kernel uniprocessor spin lock   C

```
1    #define ___LOCK(lock) \
2      do { __acquire(lock); (void)(lock); } while (0)
3
4    #define __LOCK(lock) \
5      do { preempt_disable(); ___LOCK(lock); } while (0)
6
7    // ...
8    #define _raw_spin_lock(lock)                        __LOCK(lock)
```

In other words, the code just disables preemption; there is no actual spin lock. The references to the lock variable are there only to suppress compiler warnings.

Futexes

As discussed in Section 7.3.3, a mutex is a binary semaphore. A futex is a *"fast user-space mutex,"* a Linux-specific implementation of mutexes optimized for performance for the case when there is no contention for resources.

A futex (implemented in kernel/futex.c is identified by a user-space address which can be shared between processes or threads. A basic futex has semaphore semantics: it is a 4-byte integer counter that can be incremented and decremented only atomically; processes can wait for the value to become positive. Processes can share this integer using *mmap(2)*, via shared memory segments, or – if they are threads – because they share memory space.

As the name suggests, futex operation occurs entirely in user space *for the non-contended case.* The kernel is only involved to handle the contended case. If the lock is already owned and another process tries to acquire it then the lock is marked with a value that says, "waiter pending," and the `sys_futex(FUTEX_WAIT)` syscall is used to wait for the other process to release it. The kernel creates a 'futex queue' internally so that it can, later on, match up the waiter with the waker – without them having to know about each other. When the owner thread releases the futex, it notices (via the variable value) that there were waiter(s) pending, and does the `sys_futex(FUTEX_WAKE)` syscall to wake them up. Once all waiters have taken and released the lock, the futex is again back to the uncontended state. At that point there is no in-kernel state associated with it, i.e., the kernel has no memory of the futex at that address. This method makes futexes very lightweight and scalable.

Originally futexes, as described above, were used to implement POSIX pthread mutexes. However, the current design is slightly more complicated due to the need to handle crashes. The problem is that when a process crashes, it can't clean up the mutex, but the kernel can't do it either because it has no memory of the futex. The changes required to address this issue are described in the kernel documentation in robust-futexes.txt.

Kernel mutexes

The Linux kernel also has its own mutex implementation (mutex.h), which is intended for kernel-use only (whereas the futex is designed for use by user-space programs). As usual, the kernel documentation (mutex-design.txt) is the canonical reference. Here we summarize the key points of the implementation. The mutex consists of the following struct:

```c
Listing 7.3.18: Linux kernel mutex struct                                    C

1    struct mutex {
2        atomic_long_t owner;
3        spin_lock_t wait_lock;
4        struct optimistic_spin_queue osq; /* Spinner MCS lock */
5        struct list_head wait_list;
6    };
```

The kernel mutex uses a three-state atomic counter to represent the different possible transitions that can occur during the lifetime of a lock: 1: unlocked; 0: locked, no waiters; <0: locked, with potential waiters

In its most basic form, it also includes a wait-queue and a spin lock that serializes access to it. CONFIG_SMP systems can also include a pointer to the lock task owner as well as a spinner MCS lock (see the kernel documentation).

When acquiring a mutex, there are three possible paths that can be taken, depending on the state of the lock:

1. Fastpath: tries to atomically acquire the lock by decrementing the counter. If it was already taken by another task, it goes to the next possible path. This logic is architecture-specific but typically requires only a few instructions.

2. Midpath: aka optimistic spinning, tries to spin for acquisition while the lock owner is running, and there are no other tasks ready to run that have higher priority (need_resched). The rationale is that if the lock owner is running, it is likely to release the lock soon.

3. Slowpath: if the lock is still unable to be acquired, the task is added to the wait queue and sleeps until woken up by the unlock path. Under normal circumstances, it blocks as `TASK_-UNINTERRUPTIBLE`.

While formally kernel mutexes are sleepable locks, it is the midpath that makes this lock attractive, because busy-waiting for a few cycles has a lower overhead than putting a task on the wait queue.

Semaphores

Semaphores (include/linux/semaphore.h) are also locks with blocking wait (sleep), they are a generalized version of mutexes. Where a mutex can only have values 0 or 1, a semaphore can hold an integer count, i.e., a semaphore may be acquired `count` times before sleeping. If the `count` is zero, there may be tasks waiting on the `wait_list`. The spin lock controls access to the other members of the semaphore. Unlike the mutex above, the semaphore always sleeps.

Listing 7.3.19: Linux kernel semaphore struct   *C*

```
1    struct semaphore {
2        raw_spin_lock_t lock;
3        unsigned int count;
4        struct list_head wait_list;
5    };
```

The supported operations on the semaphore (see kernel/locking/semaphore.c) are *down* (attempt to acquire the semaphore, i.e., the *P* operation) and *up* (release the semaphore, the *V* operation). Both of these have a number of variants, but we focus here on the basic versions.

As long as the count is positive, down() simply decrements the counter:

Listing 7.3.20: Linux kernel semaphore down() operation (1)

```c
1   void down(struct semaphore *sem) {
2     unsigned long flags;
3
4     raw_spin_lock_irqsave(&sem->lock, flags);
5     if (likely(sem->count > 0))
6       sem->count--;
7     else
8       __down(sem);
9     raw_spin_unlock_irqrestore(&sem->lock, flags);
10  }
```

If no more tasks are allowed to acquire the semaphore, calling *down()* will put the task to sleep until the semaphore is released. This functionality is implemented in *down()* which simply calls *down_common (sem,*TASK_UNINTERRUPTIBLE,MAX_SCHEDULE_TIMEOUT). The variable `state` refers to the state of the current running process, as discussed in Chapter 5. The function adds the current process to the semaphore's wait list and goes into a loop. The trick here is that specifying a timeout value of MAX_SCHEDULE_TIMEOUT on *schedule_timeout()* will call *schedule()* without a bound on the timeout. So this will simply put the current task to sleep. The return value will be MAX_SCHEDULE_TIMEOUT.

Listing 7.3.21: Linux kernel semaphore down() operation (2)

```c
1   / *
2    * Because this function is inlined, the 'state' parameter will be
3    * constant, and thus optimized away by the compiler. Likewise the
4    * 'timeout' parameter for the cases without timeouts.
5    */
6   static inline int __sched __down_common(struct semaphore *sem, long state,
7                       long timeout)
8   {
9     struct semaphore_waiter waiter;
10
11    list_add_tail(&waiter.list, &sem->wait_list);
12    waiter.task = current;
13    waiter.up = false;
14
15    for (;;) {
16      if (signal_pending_state(state, current))
17        goto interrupted;
18      if (unlikely(timeout <= 0))
19        goto timed_out;
20        __set_current_state(state);
21      raw_spin_unlock_irq(&sem->lock);
22      timeout = schedule_timeout(timeout);
23      raw_spin_lock_irq(&sem->lock);
24      if (waiter.up)
25        return 0;
26    }
27
28   timed_out:
29     list_del(&waiter.list);
```

```
30    return -ETIME;
31
32 interrupted:
33    list_del(&waiter.list);
34    return -EINTR;
35 }
```

The up() function is much simpler. It checks if there are no waiters, if so increments count, if not wakes up the waiter at the head of the queue (using_up()).

Listing 7.3.22: Linux kernel sempahore up() operation (1)

```c
1  void up(struct semaphore *sem) {
2    unsigned long flags;
3
4    raw_spin_lock_irqsave(&sem->lock, flags);
5    if (likely(list_empty(&sem->wait_list)))
6      sem->count++;
7    else
8      __up(sem);
9    raw_spin_unlock_irqrestore(&sem->lock, flags);
10 }
```

Listing 7.3.23: Linux kernel semaphore up() operation (2)

```c
1  static noinline void __sched __up(struct semaphore *sem)
2  {
3    struct semaphore_waiter *waiter = list_first_entry(&sem->wait_list,
4            struct semaphore_waiter, list);
5    list_del(&waiter->list);
6    waiter->up = true;
7    wake_up_process(waiter->task);
8  }
```

7.3.6 POSIX synchronization primitives

Unless you are a kernel or device driver programmer, you would not use the Linux kernel synchronization primitives directly. Instead, for userspace code, you would use the synchronization primitives provided by the POSIX API. These are implemented using the kernel primitives discussed above. The most important POSIX synchronization primitives are mutexes, semaphores, spin lock, and condition variables. The majority of the API is defined in <pthread.h>, with most of the types in <sys/types.h>. The actual implementation for Linux is the GNU C library glibc source code for, see glibc.

Mutexes

POSIX mutexes are defined as an opaque type pthread_mutex_t (effectively a small integer). The API is small and simple:

```c
Listing 7.3.24: POSIX mutex API                                                    C

1    //To create mutex:
2    pthread_mutex_t lock = PTHREAD_MUTEX_INITIALIZER;
3    // or
4    int pthread_mutex_init(pthread_mutex_t *mutex, const pthread_mutexattr_t *attr)
5
6    // To destroy a mutex:
7    int pthread_mutex_destroy(pthread_mutex_t *mutex);
8
9    //To lock/unlock the mutex:
10   int pthread_mutex_lock(pthread_mutex_t *lock);
11   int pthread_mutex_unlock(pthread_mutex_t *lock);
```

Semaphores

POSIX semaphores (defined in <semaphore.h>) are counting semaphores as introduced above, i.e., the block on an attempt to decrement them when the counter is zero. The Linux man page sem_-overview(7) provides a good overview. The semaphore is defined using the opaque type semt_t. The P and V operations are called sem_wait() and sem_post():

```c
Listing 7.3.25: POSIX semaphore API                                                C

1    // Separate header file, not in <pthread.h>
2    #include <semaphore.h>
3    // V operation
4    int sem_post(sem_t *sem);
5    // P operation
6    int sem_wait(sem_t *sem);
7    // Variants
8    int sem_trywait(sem_t *sem);
9    int sem_timedwait(sem_t *sem, const struct timespec *abs_timeout);
```

The *sem_wait()* variant *sem_trywait()* returns an error if the decrement cannot be immediately performed instead of blocking. The variant *sem_timedwait()* allows to set a timeout on the waiting time. If the timeout expires while the semaphore is still blocked, an error is returned.

POSIX semaphores come in two forms: named semaphores and unnamed semaphores.

Named semaphores

A named semaphore is identified by a name of the form "/somename," i.e., a null-terminated string consisting of an initial slash, followed by one or more characters, none of which are slashes. Two processes can operate on the same named semaphore by passing the same name to *sem_open()*. The API consists of three functions. The *sem_open()* function creates a new named semaphore or opens an existing named semaphore. When a process has finished using the semaphore, it can use *sem_close()* to close the semaphore. When all processes have finished using the semaphore, it can be removed from the system using *sem_unlink()*.

Listing 7.3.26: POSIX named semaphore API   C

```c
1  sem_t *sem_open(const char *name, int oflag);
2  int sem_close(sem_t *sem);
3  int sem_unlink(const char *name);
```

Unnamed semaphores (memory-based semaphores)

An unnamed semaphore is placed in a region of memory that is shared between multiple threads or processes. The API consists of three functions. An unnamed semaphore must be initialized using *sem_init()*. When the semaphore is no longer required, the semaphore should be destroyed using *sem_destroy()*.

Listing 7.3.27: POSIX unnamed semaphore API   C

```c
1  int sem_init(sem_t *sem, int pshared, unsigned int value);
2  int sem_destroy(sem_t *sem);
```

Spin locks

POSIX spin locks are defined as an opaque type *pthread_spin lock_t* (effectively a small integer). The API consists of calls to initialize, destroy, lock, and unlock a spin lock. The trylock call tries to obtain the lock and returns an error when it fails, rather than blocking.

Listing 7.3.28: POSIX spin lock API   C

```c
1  // To create a spin lock
2  int   pthread_spin_init(pthread_spin lock_t *, int);
3  // To destroy a spin lock
4  int   pthread_spin_destroy(pthread_spin lock_t *);
5  // Get the lock
6  int   pthread_spin_lock(pthread_spin lock_t *);
7  int   pthread_spin_trylock(pthread_spin lock_t *);
8  // Release the lock
9  int   pthread_spin_unlock(pthread_spin lock_t *);
```

Condition variables

Finally, the POSIX pthread API provides a more advanced locking construct called a condition variable. Condition variables allow threads to synchronize based upon the actual value of data. Without condition variables, the program would need to use polling to check if the condition is met, similar to a spin lock. A condition variable allows the thread to wait until a condition is satisfied, without polling. A condition variable is always used in conjunction with a mutex lock.

Below is a typical example of the use of condition variables. The code implements the basic operations for a thread-safe queue using an ordinary queue (*Queue_t* with methods *enqueue()*, *dequeue()* and *empty()* and an attribute status), a mutex lock and a condition variable. The *wait_- for_data()* function blocks on the queue as long as it is empty. The lock protects the queue *q*, and the *pthread_cond_wait()* call blocks until *pthread_cond_signal()* is called, in *enqueue_data()*.

Note that the call to *pthread_cond_wait()* automatically and atomically unlocks the associated mutex; the mutex is automatically and atomically unlocked when receiving a signal.

The *dequeue_data()* method similarly protects the access to the queue with a mutex and uses the condition variable to block until the queue is non-empty. The functions *init()*, and *clean_up()* are used to create and destroy the mutex and condition variable.

Listing 7.3.29: POSIX condition variable API   C

```c
1   pthread_mutex_t q_lock;
2   pthread_cond_t q_cond;
3
4   void init(pthread_mutex_t* q_lock_ptr,q_cond_ptr) {
5       pthread_mutex_init(q_lock_ptr,NULL);
6       pthread_cond_init(q_cond_ptr,NULL);
7   }
8
9   void wait_for_data(Queue_t* q) {
10      pthread_mutex_lock(&q_lock);
11      while(q->empty()) {
12          pthread_cond_wait(&q_cond, &q_lock);
13      }
14      q->status=1;
15  pthread_mutex_unlock(&q_lock);
16  }
17
18  void enqueue_data(Data_t* data, Queue_t* q) {
19      pthread_mutex_lock(&q_lock);
20      bool was_empty = (q->status==0);
21      q->enqueue(data);
22      q->status=1;
23      pthread_mutex_unlock(&q_lock);
24      if (was_empty)
25          pthread_cond_signal(&q_cond);
26  }
27
28  Data_t* dequeue_data(Queue_t* q) {
29      pthread_mutex_lock(&RXlock);
30      while(q->empty()) {
31          pthread_cond_wait(&RXcond, &RXlock);
32      }
33      Data_t* t_elt=q->front();
34      q->pop_front();
35      if (q->empty()) q->status=0;
36      pthread_mutex_unlock(&RXlock);
37      return t_elt;
38  }
39
40
41  void clean_up(pthread_mutex_t* q_lock_ptr,q_cond_ptr) {
42      pthread_mutex_destroy(q_lock_ptr);
43      pthread_cond_destroy(q_cond_ptr);
44  }
```

There is an additional API call *pthread_cond_broadcast()*. The difference with pthread_cond_- signal() is that the broadcast call unlocks all threads blocked on the condition variable, whereas the signal only unlocks one thread.

POSIX condition variables are implemented in glibc for linux using futexes. The implementation is quite complex. The source code (nptl/pthread_cond_wait.c) contains an in-depth discussion of the issues and design decisions. However, essentially, the implementation can be written in Python pseudocode as follows:

Listing 7.3.30: POSIX condition variable pseudocode *Python*

```python
1   def Condition(lock):
2       lock = Lock()
3       waitQueue = ThreadQueue()
4
5       def wait():
6           DisableInterrupts()
7           lock.release()
8           waitQueue.sleep()
9           lock.acquire()
10          RestoreInterrupts()
11
12      def signal():
13          DisableInterrupts()
14          waitQueue.wake()
15          RestoreInterrupts()
16
17      def broadcast():
18          DisableInterrupts()
19          waitQueue.wake-all()
20          RestoreInterrupts()
```

7.4 Parallelism

In this section, we look at the hardware parallelism offered by modern architectures, the implications for the OS and the programming support. For clarity, we will refer to one of several parallel hardware execution units as a "compute unit." For example, in the Arm system shown in Figure 7.5, there would be four quad-core A72 clusters paired with four quad-core A53 clusters, so a total of 32 compute units.

7.4.1 What are the challenges with parallelism?

The main challenge in exploiting parallelism is in a way similar to scheduling: we want to use all parallel hardware threads in the most efficient way. From the OS perspective, this means control over the threads to run on each compute unit. But whereas scheduling of threads/processes means multiplexing in time, parallelism effectively means the placement of tasks in space. The Linux kernel has for a long time supported symmetric multiprocessing (SMP), which means an architecture where multiple identical compute units are connected to a single shared memory, typically via a hierarchy of fully-shared, partially-shared and/or per-compute-unit caches. The kernel simply manages a scheduling queue per core.

With the advent of systems like Arm's big.LITTLE (of which the system in Figure 7.5 is an example, with "big" A72 cores and "little" A53 cores), this model is no longer adequate, because tasks will spend a much longer time running if they are scheduled on a "little" core than on a "big" core. Therefore efforts have been started towards "global task scheduling" or "Heterogeneous multiprocessing" (HMP), which require modifications of the scheduler in the Linux kernel.

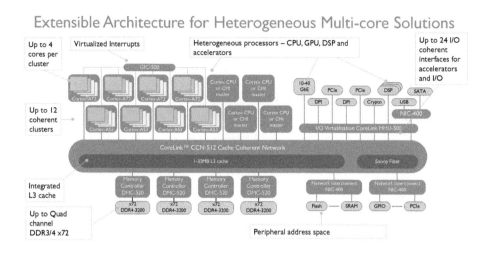

Figure 7.5: Extensible Architecture for Heterogeneous Multi-core Solutions (from ARM Tech Forum talk by Brian Jeff, September 2015).

Apart from these issues, there is also the issue of the control the user has over the placement of tasks: ideally, the programmer should be able to decide on which compute unit a task should run. This feature is known as "thread pinning" and supported by a POSIX API, and we will see how it is implemented. Finally, parallel tasks on a shared memory system effectively communicate via the memory, which means that multiple concurrent accesses to the main memory are possible. This poses challenges for cache coherency and TLB management, which are topics of Chapter 6, "Memory management." But even ignoring caches, communication effectively means that the issues discussed under the previous Section on concurrency have to be addressed in parallel programs as well. The main challenge is to ensure that there is no unnecessary sequentialization of tasks, while at the same time guaranteeing that the resulting behavior is correct.

7.4.2 Arm hardware support for parallelism

When a processor comprises multiple processing cores, the hardware must be designed to support parallel processing on all cores. Apart from supporting cache-coherent shared memory and the features to support concurrency as discussed above, there are a few other ways in which Arm multicore processors support parallel programming. The first is through SIMD (Single Instruction Multiple Data) instructions, also known as vector processing. This type of parallelism does not require intervention from the OS as it is instruction-based per-core parallelism, i.e., it is handled by the compiler. The Arm Cortex-A53 MPCore Processor used in the Raspberry Pi 3 supports "Advanced SIMD" extensions, as discussed in [8].

Next, the handling of interrupts must also be multi-core-aware. The Arm Generic Interrupt Controller Architecture [9] provides support for software control the delivery of hardware interrupts to a particular processing element ("Targeted distribution model") as well as to a one PE out of a given set ("1 of N model"); and to control the delivery of software interrupts to multiple PEs ("Targeted list model").

Then we have support for processor affinity through the Multiprocessor Affinity Register, MPIDR. This feature allows the OS to identify the PE on which a thread is to be scheduled.

Finally, there are two hint instructions [10] to improve multiprocessing, YIELD, and SEV. Software with a multithreading capability can use a YIELD instruction to indicate to the PE that it is performing a task, for example, a spin-lock, that could be swapped out to improve overall system performance. The PE can use this hint to suspend and resume multiple software threads if it supports the capability. The Send Event (SEV) hint instruction causes an event to be signaled to all PEs in the multiprocessor system (as opposed to SEVL, which only signals to the local PE). The receipt of a singled SEV or SEVL event by a PE sets the Event Register on that PE. The Event Register can be used by the Wait For Event (WFE) instruction. If the Event Register is set, the instruction clears the register and completes immediately; if it is clear, the PE can suspend execution and enter a low-power state. It remains in that state until and SEV instruction is executed by any of the PEs in the system.

7.4.3 Linux kernel support for parallelism

As mentioned above, the Linux kernel supports parallelism through symmetric multiprocessing (SMP) (ever since kernel version 2.0). What this means is that every compute unit runs a separate scheduler, and there are mechanisms to move tasks between scheduling queues on different compute units.

SMP boot process

The boot process is, therefore extended from the boot sequence discussed in Chapter 2, as illustrated in Figure 7.6. Essentially, the kernel boots on a primary CPU and when all common initialization is finished, the primary CPU sends interrupt requests to the other cores which result in running *secondary_start_kernel()* (defined in arm/kernel/smp.c).

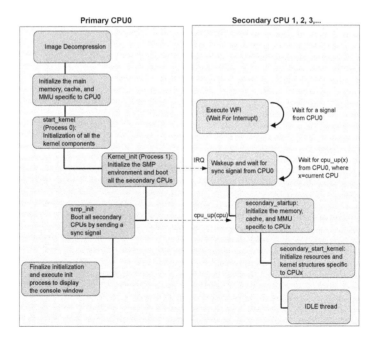

Figure 7.6: Booting flowchart for the ARM Linux Kernel on SMP systems (from [11]).

Load balancing

The main mechanism to support parallelism in the Linux kernel is automatic load balancing, which aims to improve the performance of SMP systems by offloading tasks from busy CPUs to less busy or idle ones. The Linux scheduler regularly checks how the task load is spread throughout the system and performs load balancing if necessary [12].

To support load balancing, the scheduler supports the concepts of *scheduling domains* and *groups* (defined in include/linux/sched/topology.h). Scheduling domains allow the grouping one or more processors hierarchically for purposes load balancing. Each domain must contain one or more groups, such that the domain consists of the union of the CPUs in all groups. Balancing within a domain occurs between groups. The load of a group is defined as the sum of the load of each of its member CPUs, and only when the load of a group becomes unbalanced are tasks moved between groups. The groups are exposed to the user via two different mechanisms. The first is autogroups, an implicit mechanism in the sense that if it is enabled in the kernel (in /proc/sys/kernel/sched_autogroup_ enabled), all members of an autogroup are placed in the same kernel scheduler group. The second mechanism is called control groups or *cgroups* (see cgroups(7)). These are not the same as the scheduling task groups, but a way of grouping processes and control the resource utilization (including CPU scheduling) at the level of the cgroup rather than at individual process level.

Processor affinity control
The functionality used to move tasks between CPUs is exposed to the user using a kernel API defined in include/linux/sched.h. This API consists of two calls (see sched_setaffinity(2)), *sched_ - setaffinity()* and *sched_getaffinity()*.

Listing 7.4.1: Linux processor affinity control

```c
#define _GNU_SOURCE
#include <sched.h>

int sched_setaffinity(pid_t pid, size_t cpusetsize,
                      const cpu_set_t *mask);

int sched_getaffinity(pid_t pid, size_t cpusetsize,
                      cpu_set_t *mask);
```

These calls control the thread's CPU affinity mask, which determines the set of CPUs on which it can be run. On multicore systems, this can be used to control the placement of threads. This allows user-space applications to take control over the load balancing instead of the scheduler. Usually, a programmer will not use the kernel API but the corresponding POSIX thread API (Section 7.6.1), which is implemented using the kernel API.

7.5 Data-parallel and task-parallel programming models
7.5.1 Data parallel programming
Data parallelism means that every compute unit will perform the same computation but on a different part of the data. This is a very common parallel programming model, supported for example by CPU cores with SIMD vector instructions, manycore systems, and GPGPUs.

Full data parallelism: *map*
Purely in terms of performance, in an ideal data-parallel program, the threads working on different sections of the data would not interact at all. This type of problems is known as "embarrassingly

parallel." In computational terms (especially in the context of functional programming) this pattern is known as a *map*, a term which has become well-known through the popularity of map-reduce frameworks. In principle, a *map* operation can be executed on all elements of a data set in parallel, so given unlimited parallelism, the complexity is *O(1)*. In practice, parallelism is never unlimited, and in terms of implementation of the map in programming languages, you cannot assume any parallelism, for example, Python's `map` function does not operate in parallel. However, we use the term here to refer to the computational pattern that allows full data parallelism.

Reduction

On the opposite side of the performance spectrum, we have purely sequential computations, i.e., where it is not possible at all to perform even part of the computation in parallel. In computational terms, this is the case for non-associative reduction operations. Reduction (the second part in map-reduce) means a computation which combines all elements of a data set to produce its final result. In functional programming, reductions are also known as *folds*. In Python, the corresponding function is `reduce`. Unless a reduction operation is *associative*, it cannot be parallelized and will have linear time complexity *O(N)* for a data set of N elements.

Associativity

In formal terms, a function of two arguments is associative if and only if

```
f(f(x,y),z)=f(x,(f(y,z))
```

For example, addition and multiplication are associative:

```
x+y+z=(x+y)+z=x+(y+z)
```

but division and modulo are not:

```
(x/y)/z≠x/(y/z)
```

Binary tree-based parallel reduction

In practice, many of the common operations on sets are associative: sum, product, min, max, concatenation, comparison, ...

If the reduction operation is associative, the computation can still be parallelized, not using a map pattern but through a binary tree-based parallelization (tree-based fold). For example, to sum 8 numbers, we can perform 4 pairwise sums in parallel, then sum the 4 results in two parallel operations, and then compute the final sum.

```
1+2+3+4+5+6+7+8
= 3+7+11+15
= 10+26
= 36
```

Another example is merge sort, where the list to be sorted is split into as many chunks as there are threads, then each chunk is sorted in parallel, and the chunks are merged pairwise. Whereas sequential merge sort is *O(N log N)*, if there are at least half as many threads as elements to sort, then the sorting can be done in *O(log N)*.

In general, for a data set of size N, with unlimited parallelism, an associative operation can be reduced in *O(log N)* steps.

7.5.2 Task parallel programming

Instead of parallelizing the computation by performing the same operation on different parts of the data, we can also perform different computations in parallel. For example, we can split a Sobel filter for edge detection in a vertical and horizontal part and perform these in parallel on the image data. In practice, this approach is particularly effective if the input data is a stream, e.g., frames from a video, as in that case, we can create a pipeline which performs different operations in parallel on different frames. Figure 7.7 shows the complete task graph for a Sobel edge detection pipeline [13]. In this example, if a node has a fan-out of more than one, copies of the frame are sent to each downstream node. In general, of course, a node could send different data to each of its downstream nodes.

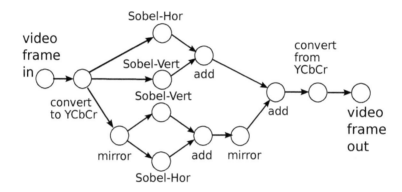

Figure 7.7: Task graph for a Sobel edge detection pipeline.

7.6 Practical parallel programming frameworks

7.6.1 POSIX Threads (pthreads)

We have already covered the POSIX synchronization primitives in Section 7.3.6, but we did not discuss the API for creating and managing threads. The POSIX thread (*pthreads*) API provides data types and API calls to manage threads and control their attributes. A good overview can be found in pthreads(7). The thread is represented by an opaque type *pthread_t* which represents the thread ID (i.e., it is a small integer). Each thread has a number of attributes managed via the opaque type pthread_attr_t, which is accessed via a separate set of API calls.

The most important thread management calls are *pthread_create()*, *pthread_join()* and *pthread_- exit()*. The *pthread_create()* call takes a pointer to the subroutine to be called in the thread and a pointer to its arguments. Inside the thread, *pthread_exit()* can be called to terminate the calling thread. The *pthread_join()* call waits for the thread indicated by its first argument to terminate, if that thread is in a joinable state (see below). If that thread called *pthread_exit()* with a non-NULL argument, then this argument will be available as the second argument in *pthread_join()*.

Listing 7.6.1: POSIX pthread API: create and join   *C*

```c
1   #include <pthread.h>
2
3   int pthread_create(
4       pthread_t *thread, const pthread_attr_t *attr,
5       void *(*start_routine)(void*), void *arg);
6
7   int pthread_join(pthread_t thread, void **value_ptr);
8
9   // inside the thread
10      int pthread_exit(void *retval)
```

Another convenient call is pthread_self(), it simply returns the thread ID of the caller:

Listing 7.6.2: POSIX pthread API: self   *C*

```c
1   pthread_t pthread_self(void);
```

In many cases, it is not necessary to specify the thread attributes, but we can use the attributes for example to control the processor affinity or the detached state of the thread, i.e., if a thread is joinable or detached. Detached means that you know you will not use pthread_join() to wait for it, so on exit the thread's resources will be released immediately.

The attribute is created and destroyed using the following calls:

Listing 7.6.3: POSIX pthread API: init and destroy   *C*

```c
1   int pthread_attr_init(pthread_attr_t *attr);
2   int pthread_attr_destroy(pthread_attr_t *attr);
```

For example, to set or get the affinity, we can use the following calls:

Listing 7.6.4: POSIX pthread API: affinity   *C*

```c
1   #define _GNU_SOURCE
2   int pthread_attr_setaffinity_np(pthread_attr_t *attr,
3     size_t cpusetsize, const cpu_set_t *cpuset);
4
5   int pthread_attr_getaffinity_np(pthread_attr_t
6     *attr, size_t cpusetsize, cpu_set_t *cpuset);
```

Similar, if we want to get or set the detach state we can use:

Listing 7.6.5: POSIX pthread API: attributes   *C*

```c
1   int pthread_attr_setdetachstate(pthread_attr_t *attr, int detachstate);
2   int pthread_attr_getdetachstate(const pthread_attr_t *attr, int *detachstate);
```

There are many more API calls both to manage the threads and the attributes, see the man page pthreads(7) for more details.

Below is an example of typical use of pthreads to create a number of identical worker threads to perform work in parallel.

Listing 7.6.6: POSIX pthread API example   C

```c
1    #include <pthread.h>
2
3    struct thread_info {      /* Used as argument to thread_start() */
4        pthread_t thread_id;           /* ID returned by pthread_create() */
5        // Any other field you might need
6        // ...
7    };
8
9    // This is the worker which will run in each thread
10   void* thread_start(void *vtinfo) {
11       struct thread_info *tinfo = vtinfo;
12       // do work
13       // ...
14       pthread_exit(NULL); // no return value
15   }
16
17   int main(int argc, char *argv[]) {
18       int st;
19       struct thread_info *tinfo;
20       unsigned int num_threads = NTH; // macro
21
22       /* Allocate memory for pthread_create() arguments */
23       tinfo = calloc(num_threads, sizeof(struct thread_info));
24       if (tinfo == NULL)
25           handle_error("calloc");
26
27       /* Create threads (attr is NULL) */
28       for (unsigned int tnum = 0; tnum < num_threads; tnum++) {
29           // Here you would populate other fields in tinfo
30           st = pthread_create(&tinfo[tnum].thread_id, NULL,
31                   &thread_start, &tinfo[tnum]);
32       if (st != 0)
33           handle_error_en(st, "pthread_create");
34       }
35
36       /* Now join with each thread */
37       for (unsigned int tnum = 0; tnum < num_threads; tnum++) {
38           st = pthread_join(tinfo[tnum].thread_id, NULL);
39           if (st != 0)
40               handle_error_en(st, "pthread_join");
41       }
42
43       // do something with the results if required
44       // ...
45
46       free(tinfo);
47   exit(EXIT_SUCCESS);
48   }
```

In this program, we create num_threads threads by calling *pthread_create()* in a for-loop (line 28). Each thread is provided with a struct thread_info which contains the arguments for that thread.

Each thread takes a function pointer `&thread_start` to the subroutine that will run in the thread. The `thread_info` struct could, for example, contain a pointer to a large array, and each thread would work on a portion of that array. As these threads are joinable (this is the default) we wait on them by calling *pthread_join()* in a loop (line 37). Because the threads work on shared memory, the results of the work done in parallel will be available in the main routine when all threads have been joined.

7.6.2 OpenMP

OpenMP is the de-facto standard for shared-memory parallel programming. It is based on a set of compiler directives or *pragmas*, combined with a programming API to specify parallel regions, data scope, synchronization, etc.. OpenMP is a portable parallel programming approach, and the specification supports C, C++, and Fortran. It has been historically used for data-parallel programming through its compiler directives. Since version 3.0, OpenMP also supports task parallelism [14]. It is now widely used in both task and data parallel scenarios. Since OpenMP is a language enhancement, every new construct requires compiler support. Therefore, its functionality is not as extensive as library-based models. Moreover, although OpenMP provides the user with a high level of abstraction, the onus is still on the programmer to ensure proper synchronization.

A typical example of OpenMP usage is the parallelization of a for-loop, as shown in the following code snippet:

Listing 7.6.7: OpenMP example

```c
1    #include <omp.h>
2    // ...
3    #pragma omp parallel \
4    shared(collection,vocabulary) \
2    private(docsz_min,docsz_max,docsz_mean)
6    {
7    // ...
8        #pragma omp for
9        for (unsigned int docid = 1; docid<NDOCS; docid++) {
10       // ...
11       }
12   }
```

The `#pragma omp for` directive will instruct the compiler to parallelize the loop (using POSIX threads), treating it effectively as a *map*. The shared() and private() clauses in the #pragma omp parallel directive let the programmer identify which variables are to be treated as shared by all threads or private (per-thread). However, this clause does not regulate access to the variables, so we require some kind of access control. OpenMP provides a number of directives to control access to sections of code, the most important of which correspond to concepts introduced earlier:

#pragma omp critical indicates a critical section, i.e., it specifies a region of code that must be executed by only one thread at a time.

#pragma omp atomic indicates that a specific memory location must be updated atomically, rather than letting multiple threads attempt to write to it. Essentially, this directive provides a single-statement critical section.

#pragma omp barrier indicates a memory barrier; a thread will wait at that point until all other threads have reached that barrier. Then, all threads resume parallel execution of the code following after the barrier.

For a full description of all directive-based OpenMP synchronization constructs, see the OpenMP specification [15]. In some cases, the directive-based approach might not be suitable. Therefore OpenMP also provides an API for synchronization, similar to the POSIX API. The following snippet illustrates the use of locks to protect a critical section.

Listing 7.6.8: OpenMP lock example

```c
1    omp_lock_t writelock;
2    #pragma omp parallel \
3    shared(collection,vocabulary) \
4    private(docsz_min,docsz_max,docsz_mean)
5    {
6        omp_init_lock(&writelock);
7      #pragma omp for
8      for (unsigned int docid = 1; docid<NDOCS; docid++) {
9          // ...
10         omp_set_lock(&writelock);
11         // shared access
12         // ...
13         omp_unset_lock(&writelock);
14     }
15     omp_destroy_lock(&writelock);
16 }
```

7.6.3 Message passing interface (MPI)

The Message Passing Interface (commonly known under its acronym MPI) [16] is an API specification designed for high-performance computing. Since MPI provides a distributed memory model for parallel programming, its main targets have been clusters and multiprocessor machines. The *message passing* model means that tasks do not share any memory. Instead, every task has its own private memory, and any communication between tasks is via the exchange of messages.

In MPI, the two basic routines for sending and receiving messages are `MPI_Send` and `MPI_- Recv`:

Listing 7.6.9: MPI send and receive API

```c
1    int MPI_Send(const void *buf, int count, MPI_Datatype datatype, int dest, int tag,
2            MPI_Comm comm)
3    int MPI_Recv(void *buf, int count, MPI_Datatype datatype, int source, int tag,
4            MPI_Comm comm, MPI_Status *status)
```

The buffer `buf` contains the data to send or receive, the `count` its size in multiples of the specified `datatype`. Further arguments are the destination (for send) or source (for receive). These are usually called ranks, i.e. "a sender with rank X sends to a receiver with rank Y." The two remaining fields, tag, and communicator, require a bit more detail.

The *communicator* is essentially an object describing a group of processes that can communicate with one another. For simple problems, the default communicator `MPI_COMM_WORLD` can be used, but custom communicators allow, for example, collective communication between subsets of all processes. An important point is that the rank of a process is specific to the communicator being used, i.e., the same process will typically have different ranks in different communicators.

The *tag* is an arbitrary integer that is used for matching of point-to-point messages like send and receive: if a sender sends a message to a given destination with rank `dest` with a communicator `comm` and a tag `tag`, then the receiver must match all of these specifications in order to receive the message, i.e., it must specify `comm` as its communicator, `tag` for its tag (or the special wildcard `MPI_ANY_TAG`), and the rank of the sender as the `source` (or the special wildcard `MPI_ANY_-SOURCE`).

The MPI specification has evolved considerably since its initial release in 1994. For example, MPI-1 already provided point-to-point and collective message communication. Messages could contain either primitive or derived data types in packed or unpacked data content. MPI-2 added dynamic process creation, one-sided communication, remote memory access, and parallel I/O.

Since there are lots of MPI implementations with emphasizes on different aspects of high-performance computing, Open MPI [17], an MPI-2 implementation, evolved to combine these technologies and resources with the main focus on the components concepts. The specification is very extensive, with almost 400 API calls.

MPI is portable, and in general, an MPI program can run on both shared memory and distributed memory systems. However, for performance reasons and due to the distributed nature of the model, there might exist multiple copies of the global data in a shared memory machine, resulting in an increased memory requirement. Message buffers also introduce the overhead of MPI on shared-memory platforms [18]. Furthermore, because the API is both low level and very extensive, MPI programming, especially for performance, tends to be complicated.

7.6.4 OpenCL

OpenCL is an open standard for parallel computing using heterogeneous architectures [19]. Arm provides an implementation as part of the Compute Library One of the main objectives of OpenCL is to increase portability across different platforms and devices, e.g., GPUs, multicore processors, and other accelerators such as FPGAs, as well as across operating systems. OpenCL provides an abstract platform model and an abstract device model [20]. The platform (Figure 7.8) consists of a *host* and a number of *compute devices*.

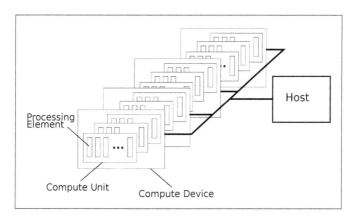

Figure 7.8: OpenCL platform model (from [20]).

Each compute device (Figure 7.9) consists of a number of compute units which each comprise a number of processing elements. All compute units can access the shared *compute device memory* (which consists of a *global* and a *constant* memory), optionally via a shared cache; each compute unit has *local* memory accessible by all processing elements, and *private* memory per processing element.

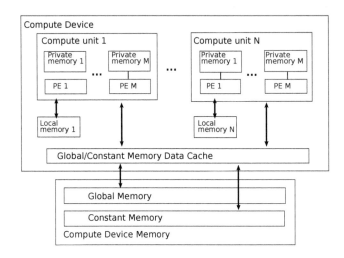

Figure 7.9: OpenCL device model (from [20]).

The programming framework of OpenCL consists of an API for controlling the operation of the devices and transfer of data and programs between the host memory and the device memory, and a language for writing *kernels* (the programs running on the devices) based on C99, with the following restrictions: no function pointers; no recursion; no variable-length arrays; no irreducible control flow. Furthermore, as it is assumed that memory space of the compute device is not under control of the host OS and that it does not run its own OS, system calls are not supported either. These restrictions originate from the nature of typical OpenCL devices, in particular, GPUs.

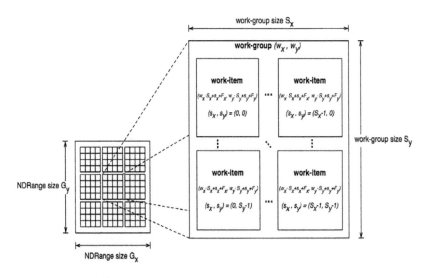

Figure 7.10: NDRanges, work-groups and work-items (from [20]).

Although OpenCL supports task-parallel programming, its main model is data parallelism. To divide a data space over the compute units and processing elements, OpenCL provides the concepts of the n-dimensional range (NDRange), work-groups and work-items, as illustrated in Figure 7.10 for a 2-D space. The NDRange specifies how many threads will be used to process the data set. Note that this can be larger than the actual number of hardware threads, in which case OpenCL will schedule the threads on the available hardware. The NDRange can be further split into a global range and a local range. To illustrate this usage, consider a 1-D case for a device with 16 compute units which each have 128 threads, and we want to map exactly one hardware thread per element in the NDRange. In that case, the global NDRange will be 16*128 and the local NDRange 128. Now assume that the data to be processed is an array of 64M words, then we have to process 32,768 elements per hardware thread. We can use the global NDRange index and global size to identify which portion of the array a thread must process, as shown in the following code snippet:

Listing 7.6.10: OpenCL example

```c
1   // aSize is the size of array, i.e. 64M
2   __kernel square(__global float* a, __global float a_squared, const int aSize) {
3
4       int gl_id = get_global_id(0); // 0 .. 16*128-1
5       int gSize = get_global_size(0); // 16*128
6   // alternatively
7       int n_groups = get_num_groups(0); // 16
8       int l_id = get_local_id(0); // 0 .. 127
9       int gr_id = get_group_id(0); // 0 .. 15
10
11      int wSize = aSize/gSize; // 32,768
12
13      int start = gl_id*wSize;
14      int stop = (gl_id+1)*wSize;
15      for (int idx = start; idx<stop; idx++) {
16          a_squared[idx]=a[idx]*a[idx];
17      }
18  }
```

Alternatively we could use the local NDRange index, group index and number of workgroups, the relationship is as follows:

```
work_group_size = global_size/number_of_work_groups
```

```
global_id = work_group_id*work_group_size+local_id
```

The OpenCL host API is quite large and fine-grained; we refer the reader to the specification [20]. We have created a library called oclWrapper[1] to simplify OpenCL host code for the most common scenarios. Using this wrapper, typically a program looks like this:

```
Listing 7.6.11: OpenCL wrapper example                                              C

1    // Create wrapper for default device and single kernel
2    OclWrapper ocl(srcfilename,kernelname,opts);
3
4    // Create read and write buffers
5    cl::Buffer rbuf = ocl.makeReadBuffer(sz);
6    cl::Buffer wbuf = ocl.makeWriteBuffer(sz);
7
8    // Transfer input data to device
9    ocl.writeBuffer(rbuf,sz,warray);
10
11   // Set up index space
12   ocl.enqueueNDRange(globalrange, localrange);
13
14   // Run kernel
15   ocl.runKernel(wbuf,rbuf ).wait();
16
17   // Read output data from device
18   ocl.readBuffer(wbuf,sz,rarray);
```

First, we create an instance of the OclWrapper class, which is our abstraction for the OpenCL host API. The constructor takes the kernel file name, kernel name and some options, e.g., to specify which device to use. Then we create buffers, these are objects used by OpenCL to manage the transfer of data between host and device. Then we transfer the input data for the device (via what in OpenCL is called the *read buffer*). Then we set up the NDRange index space, and run the kernel. Finally, we read the output data (through what OpenCL calls the *write buffer*).

7.6.5 Intel threading building blocks (TBB)

Intel threading building blocks (TBB) is an open-source, object-oriented C++ template library for parallel programming originally developed by Intel [21, 22]. It is not specific to the Intel CPU architecture and works well on the Arm architecture[2], because it is implemented using the POSIX pthread API. Intel TBB contains several templates for parallel algorithms, such as `parallel_for` and `parallel_reduce`. It also contains useful parallel data structures, such as `concurrent_vector` and `concurrent_queue`. Other important features of the Intel TBB are its scalable memory allocator as well as its primitives for synchronization and atomic operations.

TBB abstracts the low-level threading details. However, the tasking comes along with an overhead. Conversion of the legacy code to TBB requires restructuring certain parts of the program to fit the TBB templates. Moreover, there is a significant overhead associated with the sequential execution of a TBB program, i.e., with a single thread [23].

---

[1] https://github.com/wimvanderbauwhede/OpenCLIntegration

[2] There is currently no tbb package in Raspbian for the Raspberry Pi 3. However, it is easy to build tbb from source, using the following command: make tbb CXXFLAGS="-DTBB_USE_GCC_BUILTINS=1 -D TBB_64BIT_- ATOMICS=0"

A *task* is the central unit of execution in TBB, which is scheduled by the library's runtime engine. One of the advantages of TBB over OpenMP is that it does not require specific compiler support. TBB is based entirely on runtime libraries.

7.6.6 MapReduce

MapReduce, originally developed by Google [24], has become a very popular model for processing large data sets, especially on large clusters (cloud computing). The processing consists of partitioning the dataset to be processed and defining *map* and *reduce* functions. The map functionality is responsible for parallel processing of a large volume of data and generating intermediate key-value pairs. The role of the reduce functionality is to merge all the intermediate values with the same intermediate key.

Because of its simplicity, MapReduce has quickly gained in popularity. The partitioning, communication and message passing, and scheduling across different nodes are all handled by the runtime system so that the user only has to express the MapReduce semantics. However, its use is limited to scenarios where the dataset can be operated on in embarrassingly parallel fashion. The MapReduce specification does not assume a shared or distributed memory model. Although most of the implementations have been on large clusters, there has been work on optimizing it for multicores [25]. Popular implementations of the MapReduce model are Spark and Hadoop.

7.7 Summary

In this chapter, we have introduced the concepts of concurrency and parallelism, explained the difference between them and looked at why both are essential in modern computer systems. We have studied at how the Arm hardware architecture and the Linux kernel handle and support concurrency and parallelism. In particular, we have discussed the synchronization primitives in the kernel (atomic operations, locks, semaphores, barriers, etc.) and how they rely on hardware features; we have also looked at the kernel support for parallelism, in particular in terms of the scheduler and the control over the placement of threads.

We have introduced the data-parallel and task-parallel programming models and briefly discussed a number of popular practical parallel programming frameworks.

7.8 Exercises and questions

1. Implement a solution to the dining philosophers problem in C using the POSIX threads API.

2. Create a system of N threads that communicate via static arrays of size N defined in each thread, using condition variables and mutexes.

3. Write a data-parallel program that produces the sum of the squares of all values in an array, using pthreads and using OpenMP.

7.8.1 Concurrency: synchronization of tasks

1. What is a critical section? When is it important for a task to enter a critical section?

2. Could a task be pre-empted while executing its critical section?

3. What is the difference between a semaphore and a mutex?

4. What is a spin lock, and what are its properties, advantages and disadvantages?

5. Sketch the operations required for two tasks using semaphores to perform mutual exclusion of a critical section, including semaphore initialization.

6. Sketch the operations required to synchronize two tasks, including semaphore initialization.

7. Specify the possible order of the code executed by two tasks synchronized using semaphores, running on a uniprocessor system.

8. What Pthreads concept is provided to enable meeting such synchronization requirements? Sketch how a typical task uses this concept in pseudocode.

9. Sketch the pseudocode for the typical use of POSIX condition variables and mutexes to implement a thread-safe queue.

10. Explain the concept of shareability domains in the Arm system architecture

7.8.2 Parallelism

1. Discuss the hardware support for parallelism in Arm multicore processors.

2. What is processor affinity, and how can controlling it benefit your parallel program?

3. Given unlimited parallelism, what is the big-O complexity for a merge sort? And what is it given limited parallelism?

4. Explain the OpenCL model of data-parallelism.

5. When would you call pthread_exit() instead of exit()?

References

[1] E. W. Dijkstra, "Over seinpalen," 1962, circulated privately. [Online].
Available: http://www.cs.utexas.edu/users/EWD/ewd00xx/EWD74.PDF

[2] ——, "A tutorial on the split binary semaphore," Mar. 1979, circulated privately. [Online].
Available: http://www.cs.utexas.edu/users/EWD/ewd07xx/EWD703.PDF

[3] *Arm Synchronization Primitives Development Article*, Arm Ltd, 8 2009, issue A. [Online].
Available: http://infocenter.arm.com/help/index.jsp?topic=/com.arm.doc.dht0008a/index.html

[4] L. Lindholm, "Memory access ordering part 2 - memory access ordering in the Arm Architecture," 2013. [Online].
Available: https://community.arm.com/processors/b/blog/posts/memory-access-ordering-part-3---memory-access-ordering-in-the-arm-architecture

[5] *Arm Cortex-A Series - Programmer's Guide for ARMv8-A - Version: 1.0*, Arm Ltd, 3 2015, issue A. [Online].
Available: http://infocenter.arm.com/help/topic/com.arm.doc.den0024a/DEN0024A_v8_architecture_PG.pdf

[6] L. Lindholm, "Memory access ordering part 2 - barriers and the Linux kernel,", 2013. [Online].
Available: https://community.arm.com/processors/b/blog/posts/memory-access-ordering-part-2---barriers-and-the-linux-kernel

[7] *Arm Compiler Version 6.01 armasm Reference Guide*, Arm Ltd, 12 2014, issue B. [Online].
Available: http://infocenter.arm.com/help/topic/com.arm.doc.dui0802b/ARMCT_armasm_reference_guide_v6_01_DUI0802B_en.pdf

[8] *ARM® Cortex®-A53 MPCore Processor Advanced SIMD and Floating-point Extension Technical Reference Manual Revision: r0p4*, Arm Ltd, 1 2016, revision: G. [Online].
Available: http://infocenter.arm.com/help/topic/com.arm.doc.ddi0502g/DDI0502G_cortex_a53_fpu_trm.pdf

[9] *Arm Generic Interrupt Controller Architecture Specification GIC architecture version 3.0 and version 4.0*, Arm Ltd, 8 2017, issue D. [Online]. Available: https://silver.arm.com/download/download.tm?pv=1438864

[10] *ARM® Architecture Reference Manual – ARMv8, for ARMv8-A architecture profile*, Arm Ltd, 12 2017, issue: C.a. [Online].
Available: https://silver.arm.com/download/download.tm?pv=4239650&p=1343131

[11] *Migrating a software application from ARMv5 to ARMv7-A/R Version: 1.0 Application Note 425*, Arm Ltd, 7 2014, issue A. [Online]. Available: http://infocenter.arm.com/help/topic/com.arm.doc.dai0425/DAI0425_migrating_an_application_from_ARMv5_to_ARMv7_AR.pdf

[12] G. Lim, C. Min, and Y. Eom, "Load-balancing for improving user responsiveness on multicore embedded systems," in *Proceedings of the Linux Symposium*, 2012, pp. 25–33.

[13] W. Vanderbauwhede and S. W. Nabi, "A high-level language for programming a NoC-based dynamic reconfiguration infrastructure," in *2010 Conference on Design and Architectures for Signal and Image Processing* (DASIP), Oct 2010, pp. 7–14.

[14] E. Ayguadé, N. Copty, A. Duran, J. Hoeflinger, Y. Lin, F. Massaioli, X. Teruel, P. Unnikrishnan, and G. Zhang, "The design of OpenMP tasks," *Parallel and Distributed Systems, IEEE Transactions on*, vol. 20, no. 3, pp. 404–418, 2009.

[15] *OpenMP Application Programming Interface Version 4.5*, OpenMP Architecture Review Board, 11 2015. [Online]. Available: http://www.openmp.org/wp-content/uploads/openmp-4.5.pdf

[16] W. Gropp, E. Lusk, and A. Skjellum, *Using MPI: portable parallel programming with the message-passing interface*. MIT Press, 1999, vol. 1.

[17] E. Gabriel, G. E. Fagg, G. Bosilca, T. Angskun, J. J. Dongarra, J. M. Squyres, V. Sahay, P. Kambadur, B. Barrett, A. Lumsdaine *et al.*, "Open MPI: Goals, concept, and design of a next-generation MPI implementation," in *Recent Advances in Parallel Virtual Machine and Message Passing Interface*. Springer, 2004, pp. 97–104.

[18] H. Jin, D. Jespersen, P. Mehrotra, R. Biswas, L. Huang, and B. Chapman, "High-performance computing using MPI and OpenMP on multi-core parallel systems," *Parallel Computing*, vol. 37, no. 9, pp. 562–575, 2011.

[19] J. E. Stone, D. Gohara, and G. Shi, "OpenCL: A parallel programming standard for heterogeneous computing systems," *Computing in science & engineering*, vol. 12, no. 3, p. 66, 2010.

[20] *The OpenCL Specification Version: 2.2*, Khronos OpenCL Working Group, 5 2017. [Online]. Available: https://www.khronos.org/registry/OpenCL/specs/opencl-2.2.pdf

[21] J. Reinders, *Intel threading building blocks: outfitting C++ for multi-core processor parallelism*. O'Reilly Media, Inc., 2007.

[22] Intel, "Threading building blocks," 2015, https://www.threadingbuildingblocks.org/

[23] L. T. Chen and D. Bairagi, "Developing parallel programs–a discussion of popular models," Technical report, Oracle Corporation, Tech. Rep., 2010.

[24] J. Dean and S. Ghemawat, "Mapreduce: simplified data processing on large clusters," *Communications of the ACM*, vol. 51, no. 1, pp. 107–113, 2008.

[25] Y. Mao, R. Morris, and M. F. Kaashoek, "Optimizing mapreduce for multicore architectures," in *Computer Science and Artificial Intelligence Laboratory, Massachusetts Institute of Technology, Tech. Rep.* Citeseer.

Chapter 8

Input/output

8.1 Overview

While the conceptual von Neumann architecture only presents processor and memory as computer components, in fact, there is a wide variety of devices that users hook up to computers. These devices facilitate input and output (IO) to enable the computer system to interact with the real world. This chapter explores the OS structures and mechanisms that are used to communicate with such devices and to control them.

What you will learn
After you have studied the material in this chapter, you will be able to:

1. Sketch the hardware organization and datapaths supporting device interaction.

2. Comprehend the rationale for the distinctive Linux approach to supporting devices.

3. Implement simple device driver and interrupt handler routines.

4. Justify the need for direct-memory access for certain classes of devices.

5. Identify buffering strategies in various parts of the system.

6. Appreciate the requirement to minimize expensive block memory copy operations between data regions.

8.2 The device zoo

A vast variety of devices may be connected to your Raspberry Pi, using a range of connection ports and protocols.

Modern devices vary wildly in size, price, bandwidth, and purpose. Input devices receive information from the outside world, digitize it, and enable it to be processed as data on the computer. In terms of input devices, a push-button (perhaps attached to the Raspberry Pi GPIO pins) is a simple input device, with a binary {0, 1} value. A high-resolution USB webcam is a more complex input device, with a large pixel array of inputs to be sampled. Output devices take data from the machine and represent this, or respond to it in some way. A simple output device is an LED, which is either on or off. The green on-board activity LED may be turned on or off with a simple shell command, as shown below.

Listing 8.2.1: Controlling the on-board LED   *Bash*

```
1    ## these commands must be executed withroot privileges
2    # turn on the green LED
3    echo 1 >/sys/class/leds/led0/brightness
4    # turn off the green LED
5    echo 0 >/sys/class/leds/led0/brightness
```

A more complex output device might be a printer, connected via USB, which is capable of producing pages of text and graphics at high-speed. Figure 8.1 shows an indoor environmental sensor node at the University of Glasgow, with a range of input and output devices attached to a Raspberry Pi.

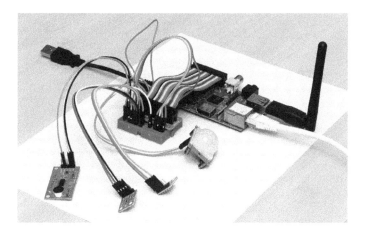

Figure 8.1: Raspberry Pi sensor node deployed at the University of Glasgow. Photo by Kristian Hentschel.

8.2.1 Inspect your devices

It is possible to inspect some of the devices that are attached to your Raspberry Pi. The `lsusb` command will display information about devices that are connected to your Pi over USB. Observe that each device has a unique ID. Also notice that the Ethernet adapter is connected via USB, which is the reason for slow network performance on Raspberry Pi.

The `lsblk` command will display information about block devices, which are generally, storage devices, connected to your Pi. Figure 8.2 shows the reported block devices on a Raspberry Pi 3 with an 8GB SD card. File system mount points for each partition are given. Note that `sda1` and `mmcblk0` alias to the same physical device. The next chapter covers file systems, presenting a more in-depth study of block storage facilities in Linux.

```
pi@raspberrypi:~ $ lsblk
NAME          MAJ:MIN RM  SIZE RO TYPE MOUNTPOINT
sda             8:0    1  7.5G  0 disk
└─sda1          8:1    1  7.5G  0 part
mmcblk0       179:0    0  7.4G  0 disk
├─mmcblk0p2   179:2    0  7.4G  0 part /
└─mmcblk0p1   179:1    0   41M  0 part /boot
```

Figure 8.2: Typical output from the lsblk command.

8.2.2 Device classes

Look at the `/proc/devices` file to see devices that are registered on your system. This file shows that Linux distinguishes between two fundamental classes of devices: *character* and *block* devices.

A character device transfers data at byte granularity in arbitrary quantities. Data is accessed as a stream of bytes, like a file, although it may not be possible to `seek` to a new position in the stream.

Example character devices include /dev/tty, which is the current interactive terminal and /dev/watchdog, which is a countdown timer.

A block device transfers data in fixed-size chunks called blocks. These large data transfers may be buffered by the OS. A block device supports a file system that can be mounted, as described in Chapter 9. Example block devices include storage media like a RAM disk or an SD card (which may be known as /dev/mmcblk0 on your system).

Other classes of device include *network* devices, which operate on packets of data, generally exchanged with remote nodes. See Chapter 10 for more details.

8.2.3 Trivial device driver

To present the typical Linux approach to devices, this section implements a trivial character device driver. A driver is a kernel module that provides a set of functions enabling the device to be mapped to a file abstraction. Once the module is loaded, we can add a device file for it and interact with the device via the file.

The C code below implements the trivial device driver as a kernel module. This is a character-level device that returns a string of characters when it is read. In homage to the inimitable Douglas Adams, our device is called 'The Meaning of Life,' and it supplies an infinite stream of * characters, which have decimal value 42 in ASCII or UTF8 encoding.

The key Linux API call is register_chrdev, which allows us to provide a `struct` of file operations to implement interaction with the device. The only operation we define is read, which returns the * characters. The registration function returns an `int`, which is the numeric identifier the Linux kernel assigns to this device.

We use this identifier to 'attach' the driver to a device file, via the `mknod` command. See the bash code below for full details of how to compile and load the kernel module, attach the driver to a device file, then read some data.

The stream of characters appears fairly slowly when we cat the device file. This is because our code is highly inefficient; we use the `copy_to_user` call to transfer a single character at a time from kernel space to user space.

Listing 8.2.2: Example device driver C

```
1    #include <linux/cdev.h>
2    #include <linux/errno.h>
3    #include <linux/fs.h>
4    #include <linux/init.h>
5    #include <linux/kernel.h>
6    #include <linux/module.h>
7    #include <linux/uaccess.h>
8
9    MODULE_LICENSE("GPL");
10   MODULE_DESCRIPTION("Example char device driver");
11   MODULE_VERSION("0.42");
```

```
12
13   static const char *fortytwo = "*";
14
15   static ssize_t device_file_read(struct file *file_ptr,
16              char __user *user_buffer,
17              size_t count,
18              loff_t *position) {
19     int i = count;
20     while (i--)
21       if( copy_to_user(user_buffer, fortytwo, 1) != 0 )
22         return -EFAULT;
23     return count;
24   }
25
26   static struct file_operations driver_fops = {
27     .owner  = THIS_MODULE,
28     .read   = device_file_read,
29   };
30
31   static int device_file_major_number = 0;
32   static const char device_name[] = "The-Meaning-Of-Life";
33
34   static int register_device(void) {
35     int result = 0;
36     result = register_chrdev(0, device_name, &driver_fops);
37     if( result < 0 ) {
38       printk(KERN_WARNING "The-Meaning-Of-Life: "
39             "unable to register character device, error code %i", result);
40       return result;
41     }
42     device_file_major_number = result;
43     return 0;
44   }
45
46   static void unregister_device(void) {
47     if(device_file_major_number != 0)
48       unregister_chrdev(device_file_major_number, device_name);
49   }
50
51   static int simple_driver_init(void) {
52     int result = register_device();
53     return result;
54   }
55
56   static void simple_driver_exit(void) {
57     unregister_device();
58   }
59
60   module_init(simple_driver_init);
61   module_exit(simple_driver_exit);
```

Listing 8.2.3: Using the new device

```
1   sudo make -C /lib/modules/`uname -r`/build M=`pwd` modules
2   sudo insmod meaningoflife.ko
3   DEVNUM=`cat /proc/devices | grep Meaning | cut -d' ' -f 1`
4   sudo mknod /dev/meaning c $DEVNUM 0
5   cat /dev/meaning
6   ^C
```

8.3 Connecting devices

8.3.1 Bus architecture

Since the Raspberry Pi is built around a commercial system-on-chip solution, which is also used for mobile phone devices, it has a rich set of direct IO connections. Figure 8.3 presents this IO connectivity at an abstract level.

Some connections are point-to-point, such as the UART (universal asynchronous transmitter/receiver) for direct device to device communication. Others allow multiple devices to share a bus, i.e., signals travel along shared wires and are directed to the appropriate device. The I²C bus supports over 1000 devices; these share data, clock and power wires, with each device having a unique address to direct message packets.

Some IO interfaces are principally for output, such as HDMI for video output to screen. Other interfaces are for input, such as the CSI (Camera Serial Interface) for digital cameras. Many interfaces, like the Ethernet network connection, are *bidirectional* in that they support both input and output.

Generally, IO is encoded as digital signals. A small number of interfaces use analog signals, such as the audio-out port. The GPIO signals are all digital; unlike Arduino devices, the Raspberry Pi does not include a built-in analog-to-digital converter.

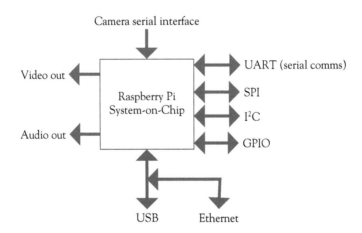

Figure 8.3: IO architectural diagram for Raspberry Pi.

In terms of bandwidth, low bandwidth connections (like those on the right-hand side of SoC in Figure 8.3) operate around 10kbps. High bandwidth connections (like those at the bottom of SoC in Figure 8.3) operate around 100Mbps. One peculiarity of the Raspberry Pi architecture is that the ethernet piggybacks onto the USB interface, which sometimes restricts network bandwidth.

More conventional, larger computers may have higher performance buses such as PCI Express. These are useful for powerful devices such as graphics cards that need to process and transfer bulk data extremely rapidly.

8.4 Communicating with Devices

8.4.1 Device Abstractions

From user space, devices generally appear like files, and processes interact with devices using standard file API calls like `open` and `read`. Some devices support special commands, accessed using the generic `ioctl` system call on Linux. We use `ioctl` for device-specific commands that cannot be mapped easily onto the file API.

A simple example involves the console. It is possible to set the status LEDs for an attached keyboard using ioctl calls. The Python script below flashes the scroll lock on then off for two seconds. Try this on your Raspberry Pi with a USB keyboard attached.

Listing 8.4.1: Flash Keyboard LEDs with ioctl   *Python*

```python
1   import fcntl
2   import os
3   import time
4
5   KDSETLED = 0x4b32
6   SCROLL_LED = 0x01
7   NUMLK_LED = 0x02
8   CAPSLK_LED = 0x04
9   RESET_ALL = 0x08
10
11  console_fd = os.open('/dev/console', os.O_NOCTTY)
12  fcntl.ioctl(console_fd, KDSETLED, SCROLL_LED)
13  time.sleep(2)
14  fcntl.ioctl(console_fd, KDSETLED, 0)
15  time.sleep(2)
16  fcntl.ioctl(console_fd, KDSETLED, RESET_ALL)
```

From kernel space in Linux on Arm, devices are memory-mapped. The kernel device handling code writes to memory addresses to issue commands to devices and uses memory accesses to transfer data between device and machine memory.

8.4.2 Blocking versus non-blocking IO

From user space, when you issue an IO command, it may return immediately (non-blocking), or it may wait (blocking) until the operation completes when all the data is transferred. The key problem with blocking is that IO can be slow, so waiting for IO to complete may take a long time. The thread that initiated the blocking IO is unable to do any other useful work while it is waiting.

On the other hand, a non-blocking IO call returns immediately, performing as much data transfer as is currently possible with the specified device. If no data transfer can be performed, an error status code is returned.

In terms of Unix file descriptor flags, the `O_NONBLOCK` flag indicates that an open file should support non-blocking IO calls. We illustrate this in the source code below, by reading bytes from the `/dev/random` device. This device generates cryptographically secure random noise, seeded by interactions with the outside world such as human interface events and network package arrival times.

If there is insufficient entropy in the system, then reads to /dev/random can block waiting for more random interactions to occur. Execute the Python script shown below for several times; see how long it takes to complete. You might be able to speed up execution by moving and clicking your USB mouse if it is connected to your Raspberry Pi.

Listing 8.4.2: Reading data from /dev/random   Python

```python
1   import os
2
3   r = os.open('/dev/random', os.O_RDONLY)
4   x = os.read(r, 100)
5   print('read %d bytes' % len(x))
6   if len(x) > 0:
7       print(ord(x[len(x)-1]))
```

The script drains randomness from the system; we top up the randomness with user events like mouse movement. When there is little randomness, the call to read blocks, waiting for data from /dev/random.

Now modify the Python script to make read operations to be non-blocking. Do this by changing the flags in the open call to be os.O_RDONLY | os.O_NONBLOCK. When we execute the script again, it always returns immediately. If there is no random data available, then it reports an OSError.

8.4.3 Managing IO interactions
There are three general approaches to interacting with IO devices, in terms of structuring a 'conversation' or communication session:

1. Polling;

2. Interrupts;

3. Direct memory access (DMA).

The particular approach is generally implemented at device driver level; it is not directly visible to the end-user. Rather, the approach is a design decision made by the manufacturer of the hardware device in collaboration with the developer of the software driver.

Subsequent paragraphs explain the three mechanisms and their relative merits. The idea is that a device has the information we want to fetch into memory, and we need to manage this data transfer.

(Alternatively, the device may require the information we have in memory, and we need to handle this transfer.)

The cartoon illustration in Figure 8.4 presents an analogy to compare the different approaches. The customer (on the left-hand side) is like a CPU requesting data; the delivery depot (on the right-hand side) is like a device; the package delivery is like the data transfer from device to CPU. In each of the three cases, this transfer is coordinated differently.

Figure 8.4: Parcel delivery analogy for IO transfer mechanisms. Image owned by the author.

Polling

Device polling is active querying of the hardware status by the client process, i.e., the device driver. This is used for low-level interactions with simple hardware. Generally, there is a device status flag or word and the process continually fetches this status data in a busy/wait loop. The pseudo-code below demonstrates the polling mechanism.

Listing 8.4.3: Typical device polling code

```c
1   while (num_bytes) {
2     while (device_not_ready())
3       busy_wait();
4     if (device_ready()) {
5       transfer_byte_of_data();
6       num_bytes--;
7     }
8   }
```

Software support for polling is straightforward, as outlined above. It is also easy to implement the appropriate hardware. However, polling may be inefficient in terms of wasted CPU cycles during the busy/wait loops, particularly when there is a significant disparity in speed between CPU and device.

Interrupts

Imagine your phone is ringing right now. You stop reading this book to answer the call. You have been interrupted! That's precisely how IO interrupts work. Normal process execution is temporarily paused, and the system deals with the IO event before resuming the task that was interrupted.

Interrupt handlers are like system event handlers. A handler routine may be registered for a particular interrupt. When the interrupt occurs (physically, when a pin on the processor goes high) the system changes mode and vectors to the interrupt handler.

Section 8.5 explains the details regarding how to define and install an interrupt handler in Linux. This is probably the most common way to deal with IO device interaction.

Direct memory access

The motivation underlying direct memory access (DMA) is to minimize processor involvement in IO data transfer. For polling and interrupts (collectively known as *programmed* IO) the processor explicitly receives each word of data from the device and writes it to a local memory buffer, or vice versa for data transfer to the device.

With DMA, the processor merely initiates the transfer of a large block of memory, then receives a notification (via an interrupt) when the entire transfer is completed. This reduces context switching overhead from being linear in the data transfer size to a small, constant cost.

The key complexity of DMA is that the hardware device must be much more intelligent since it needs to interface directly with the memory controller to copy data into the relevant buffer. DMA is most useful for high-bandwidth devices such as GPUs and hard disk controllers, not for smaller-scale embedded systems.

The Raspberry Pi has 16 DMA channels, which may be used for high-bandwidth access to IO peripherals. Various open-source libraries exploit this facility.

8.5 Interrupt handlers

There are three kinds of events that are managed by the OS using the handler pattern. These are:

1. *Hardware interrupts*, which are triggered by external devices.

2. *Processor exceptions*, which occur when undefined operations (like divide-by-zero) are executed.

3. *Software interrupts*, which take place when user code issues a Linux system call, encoded as an Arm SWI instruction.

This section focuses on hardware interrupts, but the mechanisms are similar for all three kinds of events.

Interrupt-driven IO can be more efficient than polling, given relative speed disparity between processor and IO device. A context switch occurs (from user mode to kernel mode) only when an interrupt is generated, indicating there is IO activity to be serviced by the processor. There is minimal busy-waiting with interrupts. Figure 8.5 presents a sequence diagram to show the interactions between CPU and device for interrupt-driven programmed IO.

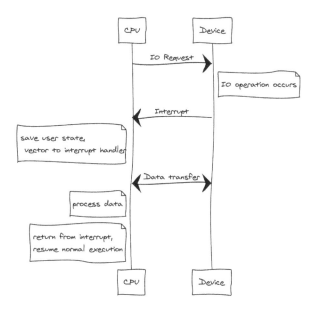

Figure 8.5: Sequence Diagram to show communication between CPU and Device during Interrupt-Driven IO.

8.5.1 Specific interrupt handling details

Look at the `/proc/interrupts` file on your Raspberry Pi. This lists the statistics for how many interrupts have been seen by the system. Figure 8.6 shows an example from a Raspberry Pi 2 Model B that has been running for several hours. Each interrupt has an integer identifier (left-most column), a count of how many times it has been handled by CPU0 (second left column) and other CPUs (in subsequent columns), and a name for the event that device that triggered the interrupt (right-most column). The `timer` and `dwc_otg` devices are likely to have the highest interrupt counts.

```
pi@raspberrypi:~ $ cat /proc/interrupts
           CPU0       CPU1       CPU2       CPU3
 16:          0          0          0          0  bcm2836-timer   0 Edge      arch_timer
 17:    1660858     400858     135168     300908  bcm2836-timer   1 Edge      arch_timer
 21:          0          0          0          0  bcm2836-pmu     9 Edge      arm-pmu
 23:        827          0          0          0  ARMCTRL-level   1 Edge      3f00b880.mailbox
 24:          2          0          0          0  ARMCTRL-level   2 Edge      VCHIQ doorbell
 46:          0          0          0          0  ARMCTRL-level  48 Edge      bcm2708_fb dma
 48:          0          0          0          0  ARMCTRL-level  50 Edge      DMA IRQ
 50:       7104          0          0          0  ARMCTRL-level  52 Edge      DMA IRQ
 59:          0          0          0          0  ARMCTRL-level  61 Edge      bcm2835-auxirq
 62:   11561063          0          0          0  ARMCTRL-level  64 Edge      dwc_otg, dwc_otg_
pcd, dwc_otg_hcd:usb1
 86:       3144          0          0          0  ARMCTRL-level  88 Edge      mmc0
 87:        522          0          0          0  ARMCTRL-level  89 Edge      uart-pl011
FIQ:              usb_fiq
IPI0:         0          0          0          0  CPU wakeup interrupts
IPI1:         0          0          0          0  Timer broadcast interrupts
IPI2:     43651     166514      69965      85015  Rescheduling interrupts
IPI3:         9          9          7        134  Function call interrupts
IPI4:         0          0          0          0  CPU stop interrupts
IPI5:    168688      58562       9321      63935  IRQ work interrupts
IPI6:         0          0          0          0  completion interrupts
Err:          0
```

Figure 8.6: Sample /proc/interrupts file.

Interrupt handlers, also known as interrupt service routines, are generally registered during system boot time, or when a module is dynamically loaded into the kernel. An interrupt handler is registered with the `request_irq()` function, from `include/linux/interrupt.h`. Required parameters include the interrupt number, the handler function, and the associated device name. An interrupt handler is unregistered with the `free_irq()` function.

In a multi-processor system, interrupt handlers should be registered for all processors, and interrupts should be distributed evenly. Check `/proc/interrupts` to verify this if you have a multicore Raspberry Pi board.

It is conceivable that, while the system is servicing one interrupt, another interrupt may arrive concurrently. Some interrupt handlers may be interrupted, i.e., they are re-entrant. Others may not be interrupted. It is possible to disable interrupts while an interrupt handler is executing, using a function like `local_irq_disable()` to prevent cascading interruption.

8.5.2 Install an interrupt handler

The C code below implements a trivial interrupt handler for USB interrupt events. This is a shared interrupt line, so multiple handlers may be registered for the same interrupt id. Check the `/proc/interrupts` file to identify the appropriate integer interrupt number on your Pi, and modify the source code `INTERRUPT_ID` definition accordingly.

Listing 8.5.1: Trivial interrupt handler

```c
1   /* ih.c */
2
3   #include <linux/interrupt.h>
4   #include <linux/module.h>
5
6   MODULE_LICENSE("GPL");
7   MODULE_DESCRIPTION("Example interrupt handler");
8   MODULE_VERSION("0.01");
9
10  #define INTERRUPT_ID 62    /* this is dwc_otg interrupt id on my pi */
11
12  static int count = 0;   /* interrupt count */
13  static char* dev = "unique name";
14
15  static irqreturn_t custom_interrupt(int irq, void *dev_id) {
16    if (count++%100==0)
17      printk("My custom interrupt handler called");
18    return IRQ_HANDLED;
19  }
20
21  static int simple_driver_init(void) {
22    int result = 0;
23    result = request_irq(INTERRUPT_ID, custom_interrupt, IRQF_SHARED,
24                         "custom-handler", (void *)&dev);
25    if (result < 0) {
26      printk(KERN_ERR "Custom handler: cannot register IRQ %d\n", INTERRUPT_ID);
27      return -EIO;
28    }
29    return result;
30  }
31
32  static void simple_driver_exit(void) {
33    free_irq(INTERRUPT_ID, (void *)&dev);
34  }
35
36  module_init(simple_driver_init);
37  module_exit(simple_driver_exit);
```

Compile this module as `ih.ko`, then install it with `sudo insmod ih.ko`. Then check dmesg to see whether the module installed successfully and whether custom interrupt handler messages are being reported in the kernel log. You can also look at `/proc/interrupts` to see whether your handler is registered against the appropriate interrupt. Finally, execute `sudo rmmod ih` to uninstall the module.

A useful 'real' interrupt handler example is in `linux/drivers/char/sysrq.c`, which handles the magic SysRq key combinations to recover from Linux system freezes. This code is well worth a careful inspection.

8.6 Efficient IO

One of the issues that makes `IO` slow is the constant need for context switches. When IO occurs, kernel-level activity must take place. User-invoked system calls will vector into the kernel, so too do interrupts generated by the hardware. Switching into the kernel takes time, switching processor mode and saving user context. DMA minimizes kernel interventions in IO, which is why it is so much more efficient.

Another inefficiency in IO is excessive memory copying. Recall from our simple device driver example that we used the `copy_to_user` function call, to transfer data from kernel memory to user memory. The problem is that user code cannot access data stored in kernel memory.

The technique of *buffering* improves performance. The objective is to batch small units of data into a larger unit and process this in bulk. Buffering quantizes data processing. Effectively, a buffer is a temporary storage location for data being transferred from one place to another.

The technique of *spooling* is useful for contended resources. A spool is like a queue; jobs wait in the queue until they are ready. The canonical example is the printer spooler, but the technique also applies to other slow peripheral devices. There may be multiple producers and a single consumer, with the producers writing each job to the spooler much faster than the consumer can perform that job. These techniques are used to accelerate IO by avoiding the need for processes to wait for slow IO devices.

8.7 Further reading

For a user-friendly introduction to interfacing devices with your Raspberry Pi, check out Molloy's highly practical textbook [1] with its companion website. There are lots of ideas for simple projects involving small-scale hardware components, building up to a Linux kernel module implementation task.

The *Linux Device Drivers* textbook from O'Reilly presents a comprehensive view of IO and the Linux approach to device drivers [2]. The book is available online for free. Although it is fairly old, dealing with Linux kernel version 2.6, the concept coverage is wide-ranging and still highly relevant.

8.8 Exercises and questions

8.8.1 How many interrupts?

Produce a simple script that parses the /proc/interrupts file and monitor the number of interrupts per second. Why might it be sensible to check the file at minute intervals and divide by 60 to get the per-second interrupt rate?

8.8.2 Comparative complexity
Draw a table with the following rows and columns:

	low / med / high
Device driver implementation complexity.	
Device hardware complexity.	
Typical device cost.	
Typical device speed.	

Fill in this table for the following devices, estimating the relative costs and complexities for each device:

1. USB mouse;

2. Depth-sensing USB camera;

3. SATA disk controller;

4. Scrolling LED text display screen.

8.8.3 Roll your own Interrupt Handler
Develop a more interesting interrupt handler, based on the trivial example in Section 8.5.2. See whether you can write a handler for a different interrupt event. Search online for helpful tutorials.

8.8.4 Morse Code LED Device
Imagine an LED that has a character device driver in Linux, so that when you write characters to the device, the LED flashes the corresponding letters in Morse code.

You could choose to use your scroll lock key or Pi on-board status LED, as outlined in this chapter. Alternatively, you might attach an external LED component to the GPIO pins.

You will need to implement a device driver with a definition for the `write` function, but you could use the trivial character device driver from Section 8.2.3 as a template. You want the rate of Morse code flashing to be readable, but it would be nice to allow the `write` operations to return while the Morse code message is being (slowly) broadcast. What would you do if another `write` request occurs while the first message is still in progress?

References

[1] D. Molloy, *Exploring Raspberry Pi: Interfacing to the Real World with Embedded Linux*. Wiley, 2016.

[2] J. Corbet, A. Rubini, and G. Kroah-Hartman, *Linux Device Drivers*, 3rd ed. O'Reilly, 2005, https://www.oreilly.com/openbook/linuxdrive3/book/

Chapter 9

Persistent storage

9.1 Overview

Where does data go when your machine is powered down? Volatile data, stored in RAM, will be lost; however, data saved on persistent storage media is retained for future execution. A file system is a key OS component that supports the consolidation of persistent data into discrete, manageable units called files.

The Linux design philosophy is often summarized as, 'Everything is a file.' All kinds of OS entities, including processes, devices, pipes, and sockets, may be treated as files. For this reason, it is important to have a good understanding of the Linux file system since it underpins the entire OS.

What you will learn

After you have studied the material in this chapter, you will be able to:

1. Illustrate the directed acyclic graph nature of the Linux file system.

2. Appreciate how the user-visible file system maps onto OS-level file system concepts and primitives.

3. Explain how file system directories work, to index and locate file contents.

4. Analyze the trade-offs involved in different file system design decisions, with reference to particular implementations such as FAT and ext4.

5. Understand the need for file system consistency and integrity, identifying approaches to preserve or repair this integrity.

6. Identify appropriate techniques for file system operations on a range of modern persistent storage media.

9.2 User perspective on the file system

9.2.1 What is a file?

A file is a collection of data that is logically related; it somehow 'belongs' together. A file is a fine-grained container for data; conceptually, it is the smallest discrete unit of data in a file system. Regular files may contain textual data (read with utilities like `cat` or `less`) or binary data (read with utilities like `hexdump` or `strings`). The `file` command will report details about a single file. It uses the built-in `stat` file system call to determine basic information about the target file, and then it checks a set of 'magic' heuristics to guess the actual type of the file based on its contents.

Other utilities infer the type of a file from its extension (the letters after the dot in the filename). However, this is not always a reliable guide to the file type, since the extension is simply a part of the filename and can be modified by users.

In Linux, everything is a file (at least, everything appears to be a file). In simplest terms, this means everything is addressable via a name in the file system, and these names can be the target of file system calls such as `stat`. Entities that aren't actually regular files have distinct types. For instance, if you execute `ls  -l` in a directory, you will see the first character on each line specifies the distinct type. For directories, this is d, for character devices, it is c, and for symbolic links it is l. The full set of types is specified in `/usr/include/arm-linux/sys/stat.h` — look at this header file and search for `Test macros for file types`.

9.2.2 How are multiple files organized?

Collections of files can be grouped together into *directories*, sometimes called *folders*. A directory contains files, including other directories. The file system abstraction is a skeuomorphism, designed to resemble the familiar paper filing cabinet, as shown in Figure 9.1. Each file corresponds to a paper document; a directory corresponds to a card folder; the entire file system corresponds to the filing cabinet.

Figure 9.1: Traditional filing cabinet containing folders with paper documents. Photo by author.

Linux has a single, top-level *root* directory, denoted as /, which is the ancestor directory of all other elements in the file system. We might assume this rooted, hierarchical arrangement leads to a tree-based structure, and this is often the graphical depiction of the hierarchy, e.g., in the Midnight Commander file manager layout shown in Figure 9.2.

```
   Left       File     Command     Options     Right
 ┌───────── Directory tree ─────────┐┌<- ...rm-linux-gnueabihf/sys -.[^]>┐
 │  ┌─ usr                          ││ .n    Name      │ Size │Modify time│
 │  │  ├─ bin                       ││/..              │UP--DIR│Apr 10  2017│
 │  │  ├─ games                     ││ acct.h          │   3319│Jan 15  2017│
 │  │  ├─ include                   ││ auxv.h          │   1282│Jan 15  2017│
 │  │  │  ├─ X11                     ││ bitypes.h       │     86│Jan 15  2017│
 │  │  │  ├─ arm-linux-gnueabihf     ││ cdefs.h         │  14503│Jan 15  2017│
 │  │  │  │  ├─ asm                  ││ dir.h           │    921│Jan 15  2017│
 │  │  │  │  ├─ bits                 ││ elf.h           │    944│Jan 15  2017│
 │  │  │  │  ├─ c++                  ││ epoll.h         │   4448│Jan 15  2017│
 │  │  │  │  ├─ gnu                  ││ errno.h         │     19│Jan 15  2017│
 │  │  │  │  └─ sys                  ││ eventfd.h       │   1390│Jan 15  2017│
 │  │  │  ├─ arpa                    ││ fanotify.h      │   1291│Jan 15  2017│
 │  │  │  ├─ asm-generic             ││ fcntl.h         │     19│Jan 15  2017│
 │  │  │  ├─ c++                     ││ file.h          │   1721│Jan 15  2017│
 │  │  │  ├─ freetype2               ││ fsuid.h         │   1187│Jan 15  2017│
 │                                  ││                                   │
 │/usr/include/arm--nux-gnueabihf/sys││ UP--DIR                          │
 └───────────────────────────────────┘└─────────────── 4459M/7392M (60%) ─┘
Hint: Bring text back from the dead with C-y.
pi@raspberrypi:/usr/include/arm-linux-gnueabihf/sys $ ▊               [^]
 1Help  2Re~an 3Fo~et 4Dynamc 5Copy  6Re~ov 7      8Rmdir 9PullDn10Quit
```

Figure 9.2: Midnight commander file manager shows a directory hierarchy as a tree.

However, files can belong to multiple directories due to *hard links*. For example, consider this sequence of commands:

Listing 9.2.1: File creation example	*Bash*

```
1    cd /tmp
2    mkdir a; mkdir b
3    echo hello > a/thefile.txt
4    ln a/thefile.txt b/samefile.txt
```

where /tmp/a/thefile.txt and /tmp/b/samefile.txt are actually the same file. Try editing one of them, and then viewing the other. You will observe that the changes are carried over; also that the two filenames have common metadata when viewed with `ls -l`. Maybe filenames should be considered more like *pointers* to files, rather than the actual file themselves. This leads to a graph-like structure, see Figure 9.3. However, if you try to remove one of the files, e.g., `rm/tmp/a/thefile.txt`, then the link is removed, but the file is still present. It can be accessed via the other link.

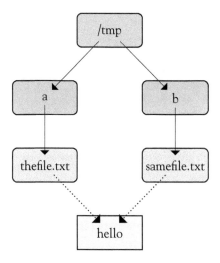

Figure 9.3: Graphical view of multiple linked files that map to the same underlying data.

Note that files can belong to multiple directories, (i.e., have multiple hard links) but directories cannot have extra links. For example, try to do `ln /tmp/a /tmp/b/another_a` and notice the error that occurs. Additional hard links for directories are not allowed. This is because we want to prevent cycles into the directory hierarchy. If we consider a link to be a directed edge in the directory graph, then we want to enforce a directed acyclic graph. If the only nodes that can have multiple incoming edges are regular files (i.e., nodes with no successors), then it is impossible to introduce cycles into the graph.

Directory cycles are undesirable since they make it more complex to traverse the directory hierarchy. Also, it is possible to create cycles of 'garbage' directories that are unreachable from the root directory.

There is a further restriction on hard links created with the `ln` command: such links cannot span across different devices. Although Linux presents the abstraction of a unified directory namespace with a single root directory, actually multiple devices (disks and partitions) may be incorporated into this unified namespace. Because of the way in which hard links are encoded (see later section on inodes) Linux only supports hard links within a single device.

Soft links or *symbolic links* (abbreviated as symlinks) are much more flexible. These are textual pointers to paths in the file system. Use `ln -s` to set up a symlink. These links can be cyclical and can span multiple devices, unlike hard links. The key property of symlinks is that they are merely strings, like the filenames and paths you use for interactive commands on the terminal. The symlink strings are not verified and may be 'dangling' links to non-existent files or directories.

9.3 Operations on files

There is a standard set of file-related actions that every Unix-derived OS must support, known as the POSIX library functions for files and directories.

First, to operate on the data stored in a file, it is necessary to `open` the file, acquiring a file descriptor which is an integer identifier. The OS maintains a table of open files across the whole system; use the `lsof` command to list currently open files.

When we open a file, we state our usage intentions: are we only reading? or writing? or appending to the end of a file? These intentions are checked against relevant file permissions. The operation fails, and an error returned (which the programmer must check) if there is a permission violation.

This file descriptor should be `closed` when the process has finished operating on the file data. Too many open file descriptors can cause problems for OS. There are strict limits imposed on the number of open files, for performance reasons, to avoid kernel denial-of-service style attacks.

The `ulimit -n` command will display the open file limit for a single process. On your Raspberry Pi, this might be set to 1024.

You can check that this limit is enforced with a simple Python script that repeatedly opens files and retains the file descriptors:

Listing 9.3.1: Open many files in rapid succession *Python*

```python
1    i = 0
2    files = []
3    while True:
4        files.append(open("file"+str(i)+".txt", "w+"))
5        i += 1
```

Notice this fails before creating 1024 files; some files are already open (such as the Python interpreter and standard input, output and error streams).

There is also a system-wide open file limit, `cat /proc/sys/fs/file-max` to inspect this value. The file `/proc/sys/fs/file-nr` shows the current number of open files across the whole system.

Once a process has acquired a file descriptor, as a result of a successful open call, it is possible to operate on that file's data content. This may involve reading data from or writing data to the file. There is the implicit notion of a *position* within a file, tracking where the pointer associated with the file descriptor is 'at.' The pointer is implicitly at the beginning of the file with open (unless we specify append mode when it starts at the end). As we read and write bytes of data, we advance the pointer. We can reset the pointer to an arbitrary position in the file with the lseek call. It is also possible to change the size of an open file with the truncate call. Figure 9.4 shows the state transitions of a file descriptor as these calls occur.

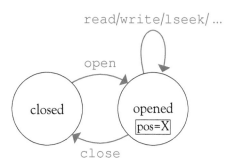

Figure 9.4: State machine diagram showing sequence of file system calls (in red) for a single file.

File metadata updates, such as name, ownership, and permissions, are atomic. There is no need to open the file for these operations; file system calls simply use the name of the file.

9.4 Operations on directories

Although directories appear to be like files, they are opened with a distinct API call opendir, to allow a program to iterate through the directory contents.

Directory modification operations are atomic, from the programmer perspective. Operations like moving, copying, or deleting files have file system API calls, but these require string filename paths rather than open file descriptors. Note that all the standard bash file manipulation commands like mv and rm have API equivalents for programmatic use.

In the same way, metadata updates can be performed programmatically, and appear to be atomic. Again, these operations require string filename paths.

9.5 Keeping track of open files

For each process, the Linux kernel maintains a table to track files that have been opened by that process. The integer file descriptor associated with the open file, also known as a *handle*, corresponds to an index into this per-process table. The table is called files_struct, defined in include/linux/fdtable.h; it is a field of the task_struct process control block.

Each entry in the files_struct table has a pointer to a struct file object, which is defined in include/linux/fs.h. These objects reside in the system-wide file table, defined in fs/file_ `table.c`. The `struct file` data structure maintains the current file position within the open file, the permissions for accessing the file, and a pointer to a `dentry` object.

The `dentry` (short for 'directory entry') encodes the filename in the directory hierarchy and links the name with the location of the file on a device, represented as an inode (see Section 9.10). This data structure is defined in `include/linux/dcache.h`.

A single process may have multiple file descriptors, corresponding to multiple entries in the `files_struct` table, that point to the same system-wide `struct file` object. This is possible with the `dup` system call that creates a fresh copy of a file descriptor.

Multiple processes may have their own distinct file descriptors, in their own `files_struct` table, that point to the same system-wide `struct file` object. This is possible because the per-process state is cloned when a new process is forked, so the forked process will inherit open file descriptors from its parent process.

In both the above situations, there is a *single* file offset. This means that if the file offset is modified via one of the aliased file descriptors, then the offset is also changed for the other(s).

It is also possible that different entries in the system-wide file table might point to the same directory entry. This happens if multiple processes open the same file, or even if a single process opens the same file several times. In these cases, each distinct `struct file` has its own associated file offset.

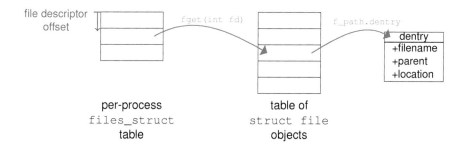

Figure 9.5: Open files are tracked in a per-process file table (left), which contains pointers into the system-wide file table (center), which references directory location information to access the underlying file contents.

9.6 Concurrent access to files

The previous section introduced the notion of multiple processes accessing the same open file. In general, multiple readers are straightforward. If each reading process has a distinct file descriptor mapping onto a distinct `struct file`, then each reader has its own unique position in the file.

Although Linux permits concurrent writing processes, there may be problems and inconsistencies. If a file is opened with the `O_APPEND` flag set, then the OS guarantees that writes will always safely append even with multiple writers. The issue here is that, while the two processes may append their writes to the file in the correct order, this data may be interleaved between the processes.

It is possible to lock a file to prevent concurrent access by multiple processes. There are various ways to perform file-based locking. The C code below demonstrates the use of `lockf`, which relies on the underlying `fcntl` system call.

Listing 9.6.1: Lock the log.txt file for single writer access   C

```c
1    #include <stdio.h>
2    #include <stdlib.h>
3    #include <string.h>
4    #include <sys/file.h>
5    #include <unistd.h>
6
7    /* takes a single integer command-line
8     * parameter, specifying how long to
9     * sleep after each write operation
10   */
11     int main(int argc, char **argv) {
12
13       int t = atoi(argv[1]);
14       int i;
15       char msg[30];
16
17       int fd = open("log.txt",   O_WRONLY|O_CREAT|O_APPEND, 0666);
18       if(fd == -1){
19         perror("unable to open file");
20         exit(1);
21       }
22       /* lock the open file */
23       if (lockf(fd, F_LOCK, 0) == -1) {
24         perror("unable to lock file");
25         exit(1);
26       }
27
28       for (i=0; i<10; i++) {
29         sprintf(msg, "sleeping for %d seconds\n", t);
30         write(fd, msg, strlen(msg));
31         sleep(t);
32       }
33
34       /* unlock file */
35       if (lockf(fd, F_ULOCK, 0) == -1) {
36         perror("unable to unlock file");
37         exit(1);
38       }
39       close(fd);
40       return 0;
41     }
```

If a particular file is already locked, then a subsequent call to `lockf` blocks until that file has been unlocked. Try compiling this C code, then running two instances of the executable concurrently to observe what happens—the first process should complete all its writes to the log before the second process is allowed to write anything.

Note that this kind of file-based locking on Linux is only *advisory*. Processes may 'ignore' file locks entirely and proceed to read from or write to open files without respecting locks.

9.7 File metadata

Metadata describes the properties of each file. There is a standard set of attributes that the Linux file system supports directly, so these items are recorded for all files.

This includes user-centric metadata, such as the textual name and type of the file. The type is conventionally encoded as part of the name, a suffix after the final period character in the name. Particular file system formats may impose restrictions on names, such as their length or permitted characters.

The file name is a human-friendly label for the user to specify the file of interest. However, the file system maintains a unique numeric identifier for each file, which is used internally. It is the case that multiple names may actually map to the same file (i.e., the same numeric id) in the directed acyclic graph directory structure of Linux, as explained in Section 9.2.2.

The size of the file is specified in bytes, i.e., its length. The file occupies some number of blocks on a device, but these blocks may not be full if the file size is not a precise multiple of the block size. Unlike null-terminated C-style strings, there is no explicit end-of-file (EOF) marker. Instead, we must use the length of the file to determine when we reach the end of its data.

File access permissions metadata is supported in Linux. Each file has an owner (generally the creator of the file, although the chown command can modify the owner). Each file has a group (to which the owner may or may not belong; note the chgrp command can modify the group). The owner and group are encoded as integer identifiers, which may be looked up in the relevant tables in /etc/passwd and /etc/group files.

For permissions, there are nine bits of metadata, three each for the owner, the group, and everyone else. Each triple of bits (from most significant to least significant bit) encodes read, write and execute permission respectively. Figure 9.6 illustrates these permission bits. This metadata can be set using the chmod command, followed by three octal numbers for the three triplets. More advanced capabilities and fine-grained permissions are supported by the SElinux system.

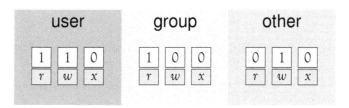

Figure 9.6: The 9-bit permissions bitstring is part of each file's metadata—in this example, the owner can read and write to the file, all other users can only read the file.

Timestamp fields record creation time, most recent edit time, and most recent access time for each file. These are recorded as seconds since 1970, the start of the Unix epoch. Since they are signed 32-bit integers, the maximum timestamp that can be encoded is some time on 19 January 2038.

Recent Linux patches have extended the timestamp fields to 64 bits, with support for nanosecond granularity and a longer maximum date.

The most important administrative metadata is the actual *location* of the file data on the disk. The precise details depend on the specific nature of the file system implementation, which we will cover in later sections.

Sometimes extra metadata is supported by graphical file managers like Nautilus (for Gnome) or Dolphin (for KDE). These might include per-file application associations or graphical icons).

For specific kinds of files, application-specific metadata may be included within the file itself, e.g., MP3 audio files include id3 tags for artist and title, PDF files include page counts. While this is not natively supported within the Linux file system, it might be parsed and rendered by custom file managers, e.g., see Figure 9.7.

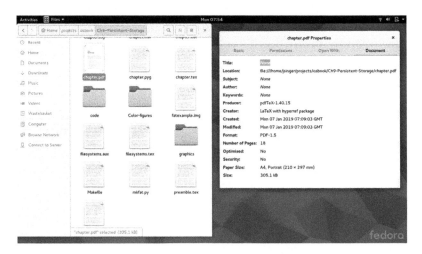

Figure 9.7: Nautilus file manager parses and displays custom metadata for a PDF file.

9.8 Block-structured storage

A file system is an abstraction built on top of a secondary storage facility such as a hard disk or, on a Raspberry Pi, an SD card.

Typical file systems depend on persistent, block-structured, random access storage.

- *Persistent* means the data is preserved when the machine is powered off.

- *Block-structured* means the storage is divided into fixed-size units, known as blocks. Each block may be accessed via a unique logical block address (LBA).

- *Random access* means the blocks may be accessed in any order, as opposed to constraining access to a fixed sequential order (which would be the case for magnetic tape storage, for instance).

While magnetic hard disks have physical geometries, and data is stored in locations based on tracks (circular strips on the disk) and sectors (sub-divisions of tracks), more recent storage media such as solid-state storage do not replicate these layouts. In this presentation, we will deal in terms of logical blocks; which is an abstraction that can be supported by all modern storage media.

So, a storage device consists of identically sized blocks, each with a logical address. This is similar to pages in RAM (see Chapter 6) only blocks are persistent. Often the block size is the same as the memory page size, to facilitate efficient in-memory caching of disk accesses.

We can examine the block size and the number of blocks for the Raspbian OS image installed on your Raspberry Pi SD card. In a terminal, type

Listing 9.8.1: Simple stat command *Bash*

```
1   stat -fc %s /
```

to show the block size (in bytes) of your file system. This should be 4096, i.e., 4KB. To see the details of free and used blocks in your file system, type

Listing 9.8.2: Another simple stat command *Bash*

```
1   stat -f /
```

and you should get a data dump like that shown in Figure 9.8. This displays the space occupied by metadata (the inodes) and by actual file data (the data blocks).

```
pi@raspberrypi:~ $ stat -f .
  File: "."
    ID: bd03be475161956d Namelen: 255      Type: ext2/ext3
Block size: 4096        Fundamental block size: 4096
Blocks: Total: 1892430    Free: 1224468    Available: 1141056
Inodes: Total: 451232     Free: 350901
pi@raspberrypi:~ $
```

Figure 9.8: Output from the stat command, showing file system block usage.

A block is the smallest granular unit of storage that can be allocated to a file. So a file containing just 10 bytes of data, e.g., hi.txt in the example below, actually occupies 4K on disk.

Listing 9.8.3: Different ways to measure file size *Bash*

```
1 echo "hello you!" > hi.txt
2 ls -l hi.txt # shows actual data size
3 du -h hi.txt # shows data block usage
```

This wasted space is internal fragmentation overhead, caused by fixed block sizes. The 4K block size is generally a good trade-off value for general purpose file systems.

This section has outlined block-structured storage at the device level; we present more details on devices in the chapter covering IO. Next, we will explore how to build a logical file system on top of these low-level storage facilities.

9.9 Constructing a logical file system

Given this block-based storage scheme, how do we build a high-level file system on top?

Some blocks must be dedicated to indexing, allowing us to associate block addresses with high-level files and directories. Other blocks will be used to store user data, the contents of files. As outlined above, the smallest space a file can occupy is a single block. Depending on the block size and the average file size, this may cause internal fragmentation, where space is allocated to a file but unused by that files.

A file system architect makes decisions about how to arrange sets of blocks for large files. There are trade-offs to consider, such as avoiding space fragmentation and minimizing file access latency. Possible strategies include:

- **Contiguous** blocks: a large file occupies a single sequence of consecutive blocks. This is efficient when there is lots of space, but can lead to external fragmentation problems (i.e., awkwardly sized, unusable holes) when files are deleted, or files need to grow in size.

- **Indexed** blocks: a large file occupies a set of blocks scattered all over the disk, with an accompanying index to maintain block ordering. This reduces locality of disk access and requires a large index overhead (like page tables for virtual memory). However, there are no external fragmentation issues.

- **Linked** blocks: a large file is a linked list of blocks, which may be scattered across the disk. There is no fragmentation issue and no requirement for a complex index. However, it is now inefficient to access the file contents in anything other than a linear sequence from the beginning.

Every concrete file system format incorporates such design decisions. First, we consider an abstraction that allows Linux to handle multiple file systems in a scalable way.

9.9.1 Virtual file system

There are many concrete file systems, such as ext4 and FAT, which are reviewed later in this chapter. These implementations have radically different approaches to organizing persistent data as files on disks, reflecting diverse design decisions. In general, an OS must support a wide range of file systems, to enable compatibility and flexibility.

The Linux *virtual file system* (VFS) is a kernel abstraction layer. The key idea is that the VFS defines a common file system API that all concrete file systems must implement. The VFS acts as a proxy layer, in terms of software design patterns. All file-related system calls are directed to the VFS, and then it redirects each call to the appropriate concrete underlying file system.

Linux presents the abstraction of a unified file system, with a single root directory from which all other files and directories are reachable. In fact, the VFS integrates a number of diverse file systems, which are incorporated into the unified directory hierarchy at different mount points. Inspect /etc/mtab to see the currently mounted file systems, their concrete file system types, and their locations within the unified hierarchy.

The pseudo-file /proc/filesystems maintains a list of file systems that are supported in your Linux kernel. Note that the nodev flag indicates the file system is not associated with a physical device. Instead, the pseudo-files on such file systems are synthesized from in-memory data structures, maintained by the kernel.

A concrete file system is registered with the VFS via the register_filesystem call. The supplied argument is a file_system_type, which provides a name, a function pointer to fetch the superblock of the file system and a next pointer. All file_system_type instances are organized as a linked list. The global variable file_systems in fs/filesystems.c points to the head of this linked list.

The superblock, in this context, is an in-memory data structure that contains key file system metadata. There is one superblock instance corresponding to each mounted device. Some of this data comes from disk (where there may be a file system block also called the superblock). Other information, in particular, the vector of function pointers named struct super_operations, is populated from the concrete file system code base directly. See the listing below for details of the function pointers that will be filled in by file system-specific implementations.

Listing 9.9.1: Vector of file system operations, from include/linux/fs.

```c
1   struct super_operations {
2     struct inode *(*alloc_inode)(struct super_block *sb);
3     void (*destroy_inode)(struct inode *);
4     void (*dirty_inode) (struct inode *, int flags);
5     int (*write_inode) (struct inode *, struct writeback_control *wbc);
6     int (*drop_inode) (struct inode *);
7     void (*evict_inode) (struct inode *);
8     void (*put_super) (struct super_block *);
9     int (*sync_fs)(struct super_block *sb, int wait);
10    int (*freeze_super) (struct super_block *);
11    int (*freeze_fs) (struct super_block *);
12    int (*thaw_super) (struct super_block *);
13    int (*unfreeze_fs) (struct super_block *);
14    int (*statfs) (struct dentry *, struct kstatfs *);
15    int (*remount_fs) (struct super_block *, int *, char *);
16    void (*umount_begin) (struct super_block *);
17    int (*show_options)(struct seq_file *, struct dentry *);
18    int (*show_devname)(struct seq_file *, struct dentry *);
19    int (*show_path)(struct seq_file *, struct dentry *);
20    int (*show_stats)(struct seq_file *, struct dentry *);
21    // ...
22  };
```

When a device is mounted, the file system is incorporated into the VFS file hierarchy at the specified location, using location specified in the superblock, which is read via the appropriate function pointer, as specified in the named file system's `file_system_type`. The `mount` system call performs this task, specifying the device to be mounted, the appropriate concrete file system type, and the directory path at which the file system should be mounted. Try inserting a USB stick in your Raspberry Pi and mounting it manually. Use `strace` to trace system call execution. You may need to disable auto-mounting temporarily; also use dmesg to find out the path of the device corresponding to your USB stick.

Listing 9.9.2: Mounting a USB stick   *Bash*

```
1    sudo strace mount /dev/sda1 /mnt 2>&1 | grep mount
```

The superblock handles VFS interactions for an entire file system. Individual files are handled using structures called inodes and dentries, which are introduced in subsequent sections.

9.10 Inodes

The *inode* (which stands for index node) is a core data structure that underpins Linux file systems. There is one inode per entity (e.g., file or directory) in a file system. You can study the definition of `struct inode` in the VFS source code at `linux/fs.h`. A simplified class diagram view of the inode data structure is shown in Figure 9.9.

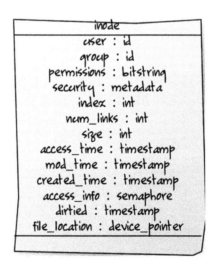

Figure 9.9: Class diagram representation of the inode data structure.

Each inode stores all the metadata associated with a file, including on-device location information for the file data. Typical metadata items (e.g., owner identity, file size, and permissions) are stored directly in the struct. Extended metadata (such as access control lists for enhanced security) are stored externally, with pointers in the inode structure.

As outlined so far, the inode is a VFS-level, in-memory data structure. Other Unix OSs refer to these structures as vnodes. Concrete file systems may have specialized versions of the inode. For instance, compare the VFS `struct inode` definition in `include/linux/fs.h` with the ext4 variants `struct ext4_inode` and `struct ext4_inode_info` in `fs/ext4/ext4.h`.

As well as being an in-memory data structure, the inode data is serialized to disk for persistent storage. Generally, when a native Linux file system is created, a dedicated contiguous portion of the block storage is reserved for inodes. Each inode is a fixed size, so there is a known limit on the number of inodes (which implies a maximum number of files). Often the inode table is at the start of the device. Each inode associated with the device has a unique index number, which refers to its entry in the inode table. You can inspect the inode number for each file with the `ls -i` command. Look at the inode numbers for files in your home directory:

Listing 9.10.1: Inspecting inode numbers for new files   *Bash*

```
1  cd ~
2  ls -i
3  echo "hello" > foo
4  echo "hello again" > bar
5  ls -i foo bar
```

Note the large integer value associated with each file. Generally, newly created files will receive consecutive inode numbers, as you might be able to see with the newly created foo and bar files (presuming you do not already have files with these names in your home directory).

9.10.1 Multiple links, single inode
As outlined above, a file name is really just a pointer (a hard link) to an inode. Multiple file names (from different paths in the file system) may map onto the same inode. The `num_links` field in the inode keeps track of how many file names refer to this inode; effectively this is a reference count.

The reference count is incremented with an `ln` command and decremented with a corresponding rm command. When the reference count reaches zero, the inode is *orphaned* and may be deleted by the OS, freeing up this slot in the table for fresh metadata associated with a new file.

Note that the inode does not contain links back to the filenames that are associated with this inode. That info is stored in the directories, separately. The inode simply keeps a count of the number of live links (valid filenames) that reference it.

9.10.2 Directories
A directory, in abstract terms, is a key/value store or a dictionary. It associates file system entity names (which are strings) onto inode numbers (which are integers). An entity name might refer to a file or a directory. There is a system-imposed limit on the length of an entity name, which is set to 255 (8-bit) characters). Use `getconf NAME_MAX /` to confirm this. If you try to create a file name longer than this limit, you will fail with a `File name too long` error.

VFS does not impose a maximum number of entries in a single directory. The only limit on directory entries is that each entry requires an inode, and there is a fixed number of inodes on the file system. (Use `df -i` to inspect the number of free inodes, labeled as `IFree`.)

In every directory, there are two distinguished entries, namely `.` (pronounced 'dot') and `..` (pronounced 'dot dot').

- `.` refers to the directory itself, i.e., it is a self-edge in the reference graph. The command `cd .` is effectively a null operation.

- `..` refers to the parent directory. The command `cd ..` allows us to traverse up the directory hierarchy to the root directory, /. Note that the parent of the root directory is the root directory itself, i.e., root's parent is also a self-edge in the reference graph.

Each process has a current working directory (cwd). For instance, you can discover the working directory of a bash process with the `pwd` command, or the working directory of an arbitrary process with PID n by executing the command `readlink /proc/n/cwd`. Relative path names (i.e., those not starting with the root directory /) are interpreted relative to the process's current working directory.

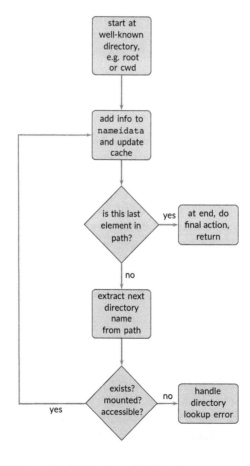

Figure 9.10: Simplified flow chart for Linux directory path lookup, based on code in fs/namei.c

Absolute path names (i.e., those starting with the root directory /) are based on a path to a file that starts from the root directory of the VFS file system. Note that paths may span multiple concrete file systems since these are mounted at various offsets from the VFS root.

One of the key facilities provided by the directory is to map from a filename string to an inode number. The algorithm presented in Figure 9.10 is a high-level overview of this translation process. You may invoke this behavior on the command line by using the `namei` utility with a filename string argument.

Translation of filename strings to inode numbers is an expensive activity. A data structure called a directory entry (dentry) stores this mapping. The `struct dentry` definition is in `include/linux/dcache.h`. VFS features a dentry entry cache (dcache) for frequently used translations. This cache is described in detail in the kernel documentation, see `Documentation/filesystems/vfs.txt`, along with other VFS structures and mechanisms.

9.11 ext4

The extended file system is the native file system format for Linux. The current incarnation is ext4, although it has much in common with the earlier versions ext2 and ext3.

Look at file `/etc/fstab`, which shows the file systems that are mounted (i.e., reachable from the root directory) as part of the OS boot sequence. On your Raspbian system, the default file system is formatted as ext4 and mounted directly at the root directory.

9.11.1 Layout on disk

The way a file system is laid out on a disk (or a disk partition) is known as its format. For any format, the first block is always the boot block. This may contain executable code, in the event that this disk is used as a boot device. Generally, this boot code sequence is very short and jumps to another location for larger, more complex booting behavior.

Immediately after the boot block, ext4 has a number of block groups. Each block group is identical in size and structure; a single block group is illustrated in Figure 9.11.

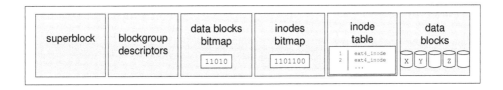

Figure 9.11: Schematic diagram showing the structure of an ext4 block group on disk.

The first two elements of a block group are at fixed offsets from the start of the block group. The superblock records high-level file system metadata, such as the overall size of the file system, the size of each block, number of blocks per block group, device pointers to important areas, and timestamps for most recent mount and write operations. The `struct ext4_super_block` is defined in `fs/ext4/ext4.h`. Note the superblock only occupies a single block on disk. This on-disk superblock is distinct from the VFS in-memory superblock structure outlined in Section 9.9.1, although some data is shared between them.

Ideally, the superblock is duplicated at the start of each block group. This provides redundancy in case of disk corruption. If there are many block groups, then the superblock is only sparsely duplicated at the start of every nth block group.

The block group descriptor table is global; i.e., it covers all blocks. There is one entry in the table for each block group, which is a `struct ext4_group_desc` as defined in the `ext4.h` header. Figure 9.12 presents this data structure as a UML class diagram. Again, the block group descriptor table is duplicated across multiple block groups for redundancy, like the superblock.

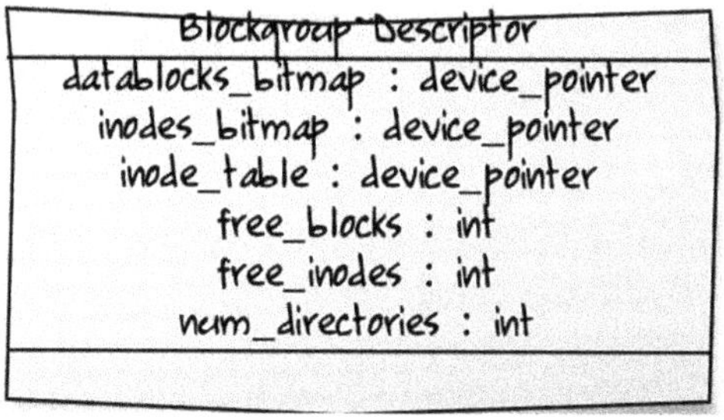

Figure 9.12: Class diagram representation of a block group descriptor.

All other file system structures are pointed to by the block group descriptor. The block and inode bitmaps use one bit to denote each data block and inode, respectively. A bit is set to 1 if the corresponding entity is used, or 0 if free. These bitmaps may be cached in memory for access speed. The inode table has one entry, a `struct ext4_inode`, per file. This table is statically allocated, as outlined in Section 9.10, so there is a fixed limit on the number of files. Special inode table entries are at well-known slots; generally, inode 2 is the root directory for the file system.

The data blocks region of the block group is the largest; these blocks actually store file data content. Generally, all blocks belonging to a file will be located in a single block group, for the locality.

You can inspect all the details of your ext4 file system on your Raspberry Pi with a command like:

Listing 9.11.1: Inspect ext4 file system *Bash*

```
1 sudo dumpe2fs -h /dev/mmcblk0p2 # for default Raspbian image on SD card
```

9.11.2 Indexing data blocks

As noted above, there are two different data structures for an inode. The generic VFS `struct inode` may be converted into a specific `ext4_inode` with a macro call, `EXT4_I(inode)`.

The key additional information is the location pointer for the data blocks that comprise the file content. Actually, an ext4 inode support three different techniques for encoding data location, unioned over its 60 bytes for physical location information. Look at `fs/ext4/ext4.h` and find the relevant `i_block[EXT4_N_BLOCKS]` field in `struct ext4_inode`.

The first approach is direct inline data storage. If the file contents are smaller than 60 bytes, they can be stored directly in the inode itself. This generally only happens for symlinks with short pathnames, although it can be used for other short files. (You may need to enable the `inline_data` feature when you format the ext4 file system.) This is the only way actual file data is stored in the inode table section of the file system.

The second approach is the traditional Unix hierarchical block map structure. This is the same as in earlier ext2 and ext3 file systems. The 60 bytes of location data are split into 15 4-byte pointers to logical block addresses. The first 12 pointers are direct pointers to the first 12 blocks of the file data. The next pointer is a single indirect pointer; it points to a block containing a table of pointers to subsequent data blocks for the file. Conventionally, the block size is 4KB, and each pointer is 4B, so it is possible to have 1K pointers in the single indirect block. The next pointer is to a double indirect pointer, and the final pointer is to a triple indirect pointer. In total, this allows us to address over 1 billion blocks, making for a maximum file size of over 4TB. Figure 9.13 illustrates this structure schematically, showing pointers for up to the second level of indirection. Note that the tables of pointers, for indirect blocks, are stored in data blocks, rather than in the inode table.

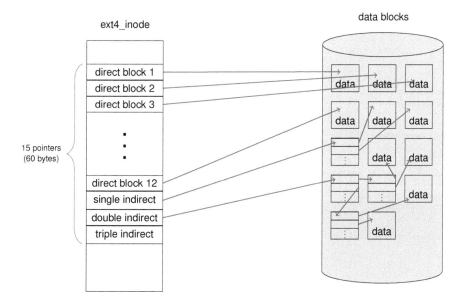

Figure 9.13: Schematic diagram of ext4 map indirection scheme for data block locations.

This multi-level indirection scheme has several benefits. There are the advantages of direct block addressing, for short files or the first few blocks of a long file. There is the advantage of hierarchical metadata, like multi-level page tables, to avoid wasted space for medium size files. There is the advantage of indirection, to avoid bloating inodes directly, for very large files. Check out `fs/ext4/indirect.c` for further implementation details.

The third approach, which is new in ext4, involves extents. An extent is a contiguous area of storage reserved for a file (or a part of a file, since a file may consist of multiple extents). An extent is characterized by a starting block number, a length measured in blocks, then the logical block address corresponding to the starting block number. See `struct ext4_extent` in `fs/ext4/ext4_extents.h` for details.

The chief benefit of an extent-based file system is a reduction in meta-data. Whereas a block map system requires a metadata entry (a block location) for every block, each extent only records a single logical block address for a contiguous run of blocks. It is good practice to make file data as contiguous as possible, to improve access times.

The 60 bytes of an `ext4_inode` may be used to store a 12-byte extent header followed by an array of up to four 12-byte extent structures.

If there are more than four extents in the file, then the extent data can be arranged as a multi-level N-ary tree, up to five levels. Extent data spills out from the inode into data blocks. A data block storing extent data begins with an `ext4_extent_header` which states how many extent entries there are in this block and the tree depth. The entries follow in an array layout. If the tree depth is 0, then the entries are leaf nodes, i.e., `ext4_extent` entries pointing directly to extents of data blocks on disk. If the tree depth is greater than 0, then the entries are index nodes, i.e., `ext4_extent_idx` entries, pointing to further blocks of extent data. These structures are all defined in `fs/ext4/ext4_extents.h`. Figure 9.14 gives an example, with a two-level extent tree. This is similar to the indirect block addressing used in the previous approach.

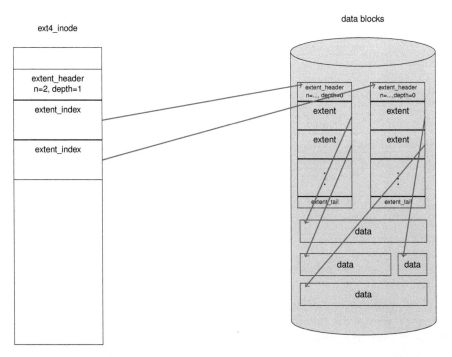

Figure 9.14: Schematic diagram of ext4 extents scheme for data block locations.

9.11.3 Journaling

The ext4 file system supports a journal, a dedicated log file that records each change that is to occur to the file system. The journal tracks whether a change has started, is in progress, or has completed. An append-only log file like this is vital when complex file system operations may be scheduled, which would cause file system corruption if they start but do not complete, e.g., due to power failure. The log may be consulted on system restart to recover the file system to a consistent state, either replaying or undoing the partial actions.

Transaction records are added to the log rapidly and atomically. The journal file is effectively a circular buffer, so older entries are overwritten when it fills up. Examine the file `/proc/fs/jbd2/<partition>/info` to see statistics about the number of transaction entries in the log.

9.11.4 Checksumming

A checksum is a bit-level error detection mechanism. This is highly useful for persistent storage, where there is a possibility of data corruption.

The most popular algorithm is CRC32c, which generates a 32-bit checksum for an arbitrary size input byte array. The CRC32c algorithm may be implemented efficiently in software, although some Arm CPUs have a built-in instruction to perform the calculation directly.

The ext4 file system supports CRC32c checksums for metadata. Try the following grep command to explore fields that have checksums attached:

Listing 9.11.2: Find checksum fields   *Bash*

```
1    cd linux/fs/ext4/
2    grep crc *.h
```

Some checksums are embedded in top-level file system metadata. These include checksum fields in the superblock and the block group descriptor, although each 32-bit value may be split across two 16-bit fields in these structures. Checksums are ideal when there are redundant copies of such metadata. If superblock corruption is detected, then the metadata can easily be restored by cloning a reserve copy.

Each block group bitmap that tracks free inodes or data blocks also has a checksum to ensure its integrity. Further, there are checksums for individual file metadata. Each inode has its own checksum field. There are checksums for some data location metadata (extent trees) and extended attributes.

Some file systems like btrfs and zfs store checksums for all blocks, including data blocks. On the other hand, ext4 only supports checksums for file system metadata.

9.11.5 Encryption

Encryption involves protecting data by means of a secret key, usually a text string. The data appears to be gibberish without this key. Encryption is used for portable devices or scenarios where untrusted individuals can access the file system. Data security is particularly important for corporate organizations, given recent developments in data protection legislation.

The ext4 file system supports encryption of empty directories, which can then have files added to them. The file names and contents are encrypted. The `e4crypt` utility is an appropriate tool to handle ext4 encrypted directories.

Note that ext4 encryption is not supported on Raspbian kernels by default. Encryption requires the following configuration:

1. The kernel build option `EXT4_ENCRYPTION` must be set.

2. The target ext4 partition must have encryption enabled.

There are alternative, single-file encryption tools. For instance, zip archives can be encrypted with a passphrase. In general, the `gpg` command-line tool allows single file payloads to be encrypted.

Lower-level encryption techniques on Linux include `dm-crypt` which operates at the block device level.

9.12 FAT

The File Allocation Table (FAT) file system is named after its characteristic indexing data structure. Originally, FAT was a DOS-based file system used for floppy disks. Although it is not 'native' to Linux, it is well-supported since FAT is ubiquitous in removable storage media such as USB flash drives and SD cards. Due to its simplicity and long history, FAT is highly compatible with other mainstream and commercial OSs, as well as hardware devices such as digital cameras. For SD cards, the default format is FAT. Observe that your Raspberry Pi SD card has a FAT partition for booting.

Listing 9.12.1: A Raspberry Pi SD card has a FAT partition *Bash*

```
1   cat /etc/mtab | grep fat
```

The key idea behind the FAT format is that a file consists of a linked list of sequential data blocks. A directory entry for a file simply needs a pointer to the first data block, along with some associated metadata. Rather than storing the data block pointers inline, where they might easily be corrupted, the FAT system has a distinct table of block pointers near the start of the on-disk file system. This is the file allocation table (FAT). Often the FAT may be duplicated for fault tolerance.

Given a fixed number of data blocks on a FAT file system, say N, then the file allocation table should have N entries, for a one-to-one correspondence between table entries and data blocks.

- If the data block is used as a part of a file, then the corresponding table entry contains the pointer to the next block.

- If this is the last block of the file, the table entry contains an end of file marker.

There are other special-purpose values for FAT entries, as listed in Figure 9.15. All entries have the same fixed length, as specified by the FAT variant. FAT12 has 12-bit entries, FAT16 has 16-bit, FAT32 has 32-bit.

entry	meaning	FAT16 value
0	free block	0x0000
1	temporarily non-free	0x0001
2 → (MAXWORD - 16)	next block pointer	
MAXWORD - 15 → MAXWORD - 9	reserved values	0xFFF6
MAXWORD - 8	bad block	0xFFF7
MAXWORD - 7 → MAXWORD	end of file marker	0xFFF8 → 0xFFFF

Figure 9.15: FAT entry values and their interpretation.

In FAT systems, a directory is a special type of file that consists of multiple entries. Each directory entry occupies 32 bytes and encodes the name and other metadata of a file (although not as rich as an inode, generally) along with the FAT index of the first block of file data.

In earlier FAT formats (i.e., 12 and 16) the root directory occupies the special root directory region. It is statically sized when the file system is created, so there is a limited number of entries in the root directory. For FAT32, the root directory is a general file in the data region so it can be resized dynamically.

Figure 9.16 shows how the various regions of the FAT file system are laid out on a device. The initial reserved block is for boot code. The FAT is a fixed size, depending on the number of blocks available in the data region. Each FAT entry is n bytes long, for the FAT-n variant of the file system, where n may be 12, 16 or 32. For FAT12 and FAT16, as shown in the diagram, the root directory is a distinct, fixed-size region. This is followed by the data region, which contains all other directories and files.

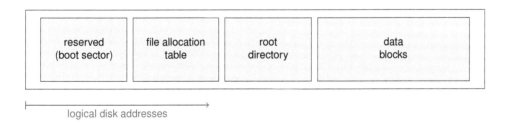

Figure 9.16: Schematic diagram showing regions for a FAT format disk image.

9.12.1 Advantages of FAT

Due to the linked list nature of files, they must be accessed sequentially by chasing pointers from the start of the file. Since the pointers are all close together (in the FAT, rather than inline in the data blocks) they have high spatial locality. The FAT is often cached in RAM, so it is efficient to access and traverse.

FAT is a simple file system in terms of implementation complexity. Its simplicity, along with its longevity, explain its widespread deployment.

9.12.2 Construct a Mini File System using FAT

The best way to understand how a file system works is to construct one for yourself. In this practical section, we will programmatically build a disk image for a simple FAT16 file system, then mount the image file on a Raspberry Pi system and interact with it.

The Python program shown below will create a blank file system image. Read through this source code to understand the metadata details required for specifying a FAT file system.

Listing 9.12.2: Programmatically create a FAT disk image *Python*

```python
# create a binary file
f = open('fatexample.img', 'wb')

### BOOT SECTOR, 512B
# first 3 bytes of boot sector are 'magic value'
f.write( bytearray([0xeb, 0x3c, 0x90]) )

# next 8 bytes are manufacturer name, in ASCII
f.write( 'TEXTBOOK'.encode('ascii') )

# next 2 bytes are bytes per block - 512 is standard
# this is in little endian format - so 0x200 is 0x00, 0x02
f.write( bytearray([0x00, 0x02]) )

# next byte, number of blocks per allocation unit - say 1
# An allocation unit == A cluster in FAT terminology
f.write( bytearray([0x01]) )

# next two bytes, number of reserved blocks -
# say 1 for boot sector only
f.write( bytearray([0x01, 0x00]) )

# next byte, number of File Allocation tables - can have multiple
# tables for redundancy - we'll stick with 1 for now
f.write( bytearray([0x01]) )

# next two bytes, number of root directory entries - including blanks
# let's say 16 files for now, so root dir is contained in single block
f.write( bytearray([0x10, 0x00]) )

# next two bytes, number of blocks in the entire disk - we want a 4 MB disk,
# so need 8192 0.5K blocks == 2^13 == 0x00 0x20
f.write( bytearray([0x00, 0x20]) )

# single byte media descriptor - magic value 0xf8
f.write( bytearray([0xf8]) )

# next two bytes, number of blocks for FAT
# FAT16 needs two bytes per block, we have 8192 blocks on disk
# 512 bytes per block - i.e. can store FAT metadata for 256 blocks in
# a single block, so need 8192/256 blocks == 2^13/2^8 == 2^5 == 32
f.write( bytearray([0x20, 0x00]) )
```

Listing 9.12.3: Continuation of FAT disk image creation   *Python*

```
1    # next 8 bytes are legacy values, can all be 0
2    f.write( bytearray([0,0,0,0,0,0,0,0]) )
3
4    # next 4 bytes are total number of blocks in entire disk -
5    # ONLY if it overflows earlier 2 byte entry otherwise 0s
6    f.write( bytearray([0x00, 0x00, 0x00, 0x00]) )
7
8    # next 2 bytes are legacy values
9    f.write( bytearray([0x80,0]) )
10
11   # magic value 29 - for FAT16 extended signature
12   f.write( bytearray([0x29]) )
13
14   # next 4 bytes are volume serial number (unique id)
15   f.write( bytearray([0x41,0x42,0x43,0x44]) )
16
17   # next 11 bytes are volume label (name) - pad with trailing spaces
18   f.write( "TEST_DISK ".encode('ascii'))
19
20   # next 8 bytes are file system identifier - pad with trailing spaces
21   f.write( "FAT16  ".encode('ascii'))
22
23
24   # pad with '\0'
25   for i in range(0,0x1c0):
26      f.write( bytearray([0]) )
27
28   # end of boot sector magic marker
29   f.write( bytearray([0x55, 0xaa]) )
30
31
32   ## FILE ALLOCATION TABLE
33   # each entry needs 2 bytes for FAT16
34   # We need 8192 entries (== 32 blocks of 512B)
35
36   # (a) first two entries are magic values 0xf8 0xff
37   f.write( bytearray([0xf8, 0xff, 0xff, 0xff]) )
38
39   # (b) subsequent 8190 FAT entries should be 0x00
40   f.write( bytearray([0x00,0x00]*8190) )
41
42   ## ROOT DIRECTORY AREA
43   # There are 16 files in the root directory
44   # Each file entry occupies 32 bytes - we just no entries for now - all zeros.
45   # Root directory takes 16*32 bytes == 512B == 1 block
46   f.write( bytearray([0x00]*512) )
47
48   ## DATA REGION
49   # create 8192 blank blocks, each containing 512 bytes of zero values
50   for i in range(8192):
51      f.write( bytearray([0x00]*512) )
52
53   ## All done - finally close file
54   f.close()
```

Listing 9.12.4: Interacting with the FAT disk image *Bash*

```
1    # Step 1: mount the file system
2    sudo mount -t vfat -o loop fatexample.img /mnt
3    # Step 2: add a multiple block file
4    sudo dd if=/usr/share/dict/words of=/mnt/words.txt count=5 bs=512
5    # Step 3: unmount the file system
6    umount /mnt
7    # Step 4: hexdump the file to find the new file's cluster addresses
8    hexdump -x fatexample.img |less
```

Inspect the FAT data, which starts at address 0x200 in the file; after the initial magic vales, subsequent entries are sequential cluster numbers, finishing with an end-of-cluster marker.

Because the FAT file system we created is initially blank, the newly allocated file is stored in consecutive clusters on the disk. Over time, as a FAT file system becomes more used and fragmented, files may not be consecutive.

*								
00001f0	0000	0000	0000	0000	0000	0000	0000	aa55
0000200	fff8	ffff	0000	0004	0005	0006	0007	ffff
0000210	0000	0000	0000	0000	0000	0000	0000	0000
*								

When free data blocks are required, the system scans through the FAT to find the index numbers of blocks that are marked as free and uses these for fresh file data.

If the Python code above is too long to attempt, you could also use the `mkfs` tool to create a blank FAT16 disk image, as shown below.

Listing 9.12.5: Automatically create a FAT image *Bash*

```
1    sudo apt-get install dosfstools  # for manipulating FAT images
2    dd if=/dev/zero of=./fat.img bs=512 count=8192  # blank image
3    mkfs.fat -f 1 -F 16 -i 41424344 -M 0xF8 -n TEST_DISK \
4      -r 32 -R 1 -s 1 -S 512 ./fat.img
```

9.13 Latency reduction techniques

To minimize the overhead of accessing persistent storage, which can have relatively high latency, Linux maintains an in-memory cache of blocks recently read from or written to secondary storage. This is known as the *buffer cache*. It is sized to occupy free RAM, so it grows and shrinks as other processes require more or less memory. The contents of the buffer cache are flushed to disk at regular intervals, to ensure consistency.

Another technique to reduce latency is the use of a RAM disk. This involves dedicating a portion of memory to be handled explicitly as part of the file system. It makes sense for transient files (e.g., those resident in /tmp) or log files that will be accessed frequently. The kernel has specific support for this mapping of memory to file system, called *tmpfs*. Create a RAM disk of 50MB size as follows:

Listing 9.13.1: Create a RAM disk   *Bash*

```
1    sudo mkdir /mnt/ramdisk
2    sudo mount -t tmpfs -o size=50M newdisk /mnt/ramdisk
```

Note files in the directory /mnt/ramdisk are not persistent. This directory is lost when the system is powered down. RAM disks are particularly useful for embedded devices like the Raspberry Pi, for which repeated high frequency writes to disk can cause SD card corruption.

9.14 Fixing up broken file systems

Persistent storage media may be unreliable. Bad blocks should be detected and avoided. File systems have mechanisms for recording bad blocks to ensure data is not allocated to these blocks. For instance, FAT has a bad block marker.

Sometimes, file systems are in an inconsistent state if the system is powered down unexpectedly, or devices are removed without unmounting. Some data may have been cached in RAM, but not written back to disk before the shutdown or removal.

Fixup utilities like fsck can check and repair file system glitches. They check for directory integrity and make alterations (e.g., to inode reference counts) as appropriate. File System journals may be used to replay incomplete actions on file systems.

These general-purpose tools can handle many common file system problems. For more serious issues, expert cyber forensic tools are available. These facilitate partial data recovery from damaged devices.

9.15 Advanced topics

Some storage media are read-only, such as optical disks. On Linux, any file system may be mounted for read-only access. This implies that only certain operations are permitted, and no metadata updates (even access timestamps) are possible. Generally, read-only media have specialized file system formats such as the universal disk format (UDF) for DVDs.

Specialized Raspberry Pi Linux distributions may mount the root file system as read-only, with any file writes directed to transient RAM disk storage. This is an attempt to guarantee system integrity, e.g., for public display terminals in museums.

Network file systems are commonplace, particularly given widespread internet connectivity. In addition to the issues outlined above for local file systems, network file system protocols must also handle:

1. Distributed access control: global user identities are managed and authenticated in the system.

2. High and variable latency: underlying data may be stored in remote locations over a wide area network, with clients experiencing occasional lack of connectivity.

3. Consistency: multiple users may concurrently access and modify a shared, possibly replicated, resource.

A union file system, also known as an overlay file system, is a transparent composition of two distinct file systems. The base layer, often a read-only system like a live boot CD, is composed with an upper layer, often a writeable USB stick. Overlays are also extensively used for containerization, in systems like Docker. From user space, the union appears to be a single file system. The listing below shows how you can set up a sample union file system on your Raspberry Pi. If you inspect the lower layer, it is not affected by modifications in the merged layer. The upper layer acts like a 'file system diff' applied to the lower layer.

```Bash
Listing 9.15.1: A sample union file system

1   cd /tmp
2   # set up directories
3   mkdir lower
4   echo "hello" > a.txt
5   touch b.txt
6   mkdir upper
7   mkdir work
8   mkdir merged
9   sudo mount -t overlay overlay -olowerdir=/tmp/lower,\
10      upperdir=/tmp/upper,workdir=/tmp/work /tmp/merged
11  cd merged
12  echo "hello again" >> b.txt
13  touch c.txt
14  ls
15  ls ../upper
16  ls ../lower
```

Standard, concrete file system implementations are built into the kernel, or loaded as kernel modules. The goal of the FUSE project is to enable file systems in user space. FUSE consists of:

1. A small kernel module that mediates with VFS on behalf of non-privileged code.

2. An API that can be accessed from user space.

FUSE enables more flexibility for development and deployment of experimental file systems. Multiple high-level language bindings available, allowing developers to create file systems in languages as diverse as Python and Haskell.

9.16 Further reading

The ext4 file system is introduced, motivated, and empirically evaluated in a paper [1] by some of its development team. There are a number of helpful illustrations in this paper. It also includes details on high-level design decisions that underpin ext4.

The wiki page at http://ext4.wiki.kernel.org features a comprehensive collection of online resources about ext4.

The detailed coverage of VFS and legacy ext2/ext3 file systems in the O'Reilly textbook on Understanding the Linux Kernel [2] is well worth reading. The authors provide much more detail, including relevant commentary on kernel source code data structures and algorithms.

9.17 Exercises and questions

9.17.1 Hybrid Contiguous and linked file system
Consider a block-structured file system where the first N blocks of a file are arranged contiguously, and then subsequent blocks are linked together in a linked list data structure (like FAT). What are the advantages of this file system organization? What are the potential disadvantages?

9.17.2 Extra FAT file pointers
Consider a linked file system, like FAT. The directory entry for each file has a single pointer to the first block of the file. Why might it be a good idea to keep a second pointer, to the final block of the file? Which operations would have their efficiency improved?

Imagine a FAT style system with doubly linked lists, i.e., each FAT entry has pointers to both the next and previous blocks. Would this improve file seek times, in general? Do you think the space overhead is acceptable?

9.17.3 Expected file size
Inspect your ext4 root file system. See how much space is available on it with df -h. Then see how many inodes are free with df -i. Use these results to calculate the expected space to be occupied by each future file, assuming a single inode per file (i.e., no multiple links).

9.17.4 Ext4 extents
This question concerns the relative merits of ext4 style extents in comparison to traditional block map indexing. Consider creating and writing data to an N-block file, where the data blocks are laid out contiguously on disk. How many bytes would need to be written for extent-based location metadata? How many bytes would need to be written for a block map index? When might a block map index be more efficient than extent-based metadata?

9.17.5 Access times
Create a RAM disk, using the commands outlined above. Now plug in a USB drive. Compare the write latencies for both devices, by writing a 100MB file of random data to them. Use the dd command with source data from /dev/urandom. Which device has lower latency, and why? You might also compare these times with writing 100MB to your Pi SD card.

9.17.6 Database decisions

Imagine you have to architect a big data storage system to run on the Linux platform. You can choose between:

1. A massive single monolithic data dump file

2. A set of small files, each of which stores a single data record

Discuss the implementation trade-offs involved in this decision. Which alternative would you select, and why?

References

[1] A. Mathur, M. Cao, S. Bhattacharya, A. Dilger, A. Tomas, and L. Vivier, "The new ext4 file system: current status and future plans," in *Proceedings of the Linux Symposium*, vol. 2, 2007, pp. 21–33.

[2] D. P. Bovet and M. Cesati, *Understanding the Linux Kernel*, 3rd ed. O'Reilly, 2005.

Chapter 10

Networking

10.1 Overview

This chapter will introduce networking from an operating systems perspective. We discuss why networking is treated differently from other types of I/O and what the operating system requirements are to support networking. We introduce POSIX socket programming both in terms of the role the OS plays (e.g., socket buffers, file abstraction, supporting multiple clients,.) as well as from a practical perspective.

The focus of this book is not on networking *per se*; we refer the reader to the standard textbooks by Peterson and Davies [1] or Tanenbaum [2] or the open source book [3] by Bonaventure[1].

What you will learn
After you have studied the material in this chapter, you will be able to:

1. Explain the role of the Linux kernel in networking.

2. Discuss the relationship between and structure of the Linux networking stack and the kernel networking architecture.

3. Use the POSIX API for programming networking applications: data types, common API and utility functions.

4. Build TCP and UDP client/server applications and handle multiple clients.

10.2 What is networking

When we say "networking," we refer to the interaction of a computer system with other computer systems using an intermediate communication infrastructure. In particular, our focus will be on the TCP/IP protocol and protocols implemented on top of TCP/IP such as HTTP; and to a lesser extent on the wired (802.3) and wireless (802.11) Ethernet media access control (MAC) protocols.

10.3 Why is networking part of the kernel?

The network interface controller (NIC, aka network adapter) is a peripheral I/O device . Therefore, as with all peripherals, access to this device is controlled via a device driver which must be part of the kernel. However, why does the kernel also implement the TCP/IP protocol suite? Why does it not leave this to user space and simply deliver the data as received by the NIC straight to the user application?

And indeed, there are a number of user space TCP/IP implementations [4, 5, 6, 7]. Some of these claim to outperform the Linux kernel TCP/IP implementation, but the performance of the Linux kernel network stack has improved considerably, and version 4.16 (the current kernel at the time of writing) contained a lot of networking changes.

---

[1] Available at http://cnp3book.info.ucl.ac.be/

However, there are two main reasons to put networking in the kernel:

- If we would not do this, only a single process at a time could have access to the network card. By using the kernel network stack, we have the ability to run multiple network applications, servers as well as clients. Achieve the same result efficiently in user space is impossible because a process cannot preempt another process like the OS scheduler can.

- Furthermore, there is the issue of control over the incoming packets. Unlike other peripherals, which are typically an integral part of the system and entirely under control of the user, the NIC delivers data from unknown sources. If we would delegate the networking functionality to user space, then the kernel couldn't act as the controller of the incoming (and outgoing) data.

10.4 The OSI layer model

Communication networks have traditionally been represented as layered models. In particular, the OSI (Open Systems Interconnection) reference model [8], officially the ITU standard X.200, is very widely known. A shown in Table 10.1), this model consists of seven layers. The *protocol data unit* (PDU) is information that is transmitted as a single unit among peer entities of a computer network.

Layer		Protocol data unit	Function
Host layers	7. Application	Data	The sole means for the application process to access the OSI environment, i.e., all OSI services directly usable by the application process.
	6. Presentation		Representation of information communicated between computer systems. This could, for example, include encoding, compression, and encryption.
	5. Session		Control of the connections between computer systems. Responsible for session management, including checkpointing and recovery.
	4. Transport	Segment, Datagram	Transparent transfer of data, including reliability, flow control, and error control.
Media layers	3. Network	Packet	Functionality to transfer packets between computer systems. In practice, this means the routing protocol and the packet format.
	2. Data link	Frame	Functionality to manage data link (i.e. node-to-node) connections between computer systems.
	1. Physical	Symbol	Actual hardware enabling the communication between computer systems as raw bitstreams.

Table 10.1: OSI layer model.

The upper four layers, Application, Presentation, Session, and Transport, are known as the "Host layers." They are responsible for accurate and reliable data delivery between applications in computer systems. They are called "host" layers because their functionality is implemented—at least in principle—solely by the host systems, and the intermediate systems in the network don't need to implement these layers. The lower three layers, Network, Data Link and Physical, are known as "Media layers" (short for communications media layer). The media layers are responsible for delivering the information to the destination for which it was intended. The functionality of these layers is typically implemented in the network adapter.

10.5 The Linux networking stack

In practice, the Session and Presentation layers are not present as distinct layers in the typical TCP/IP based networking stack. A practical layer model for the TCP/IP protocol suite is shown in Figure 10.1.

Network stack	Example
User space	
User/Application	Web browser, email client
Application layer	HTTP, SMTP, SSL protocols
Kernel space	
Transport layer	TCP, UDP protocol
Network layer	IP, IPv6 protocols
Link layer	Ethernet driver
Hardware layer	Ethernet

Figure 10.1: Layer model for the TCP/IP protocol suite.

The Linux kernel provides the link layer, network layer, and transport layer. The link layer is implemented through POSIX-compliant device drivers; the network and transport layers (TCP/IP) are implemented in the kernel code. In the next sections, we provide an overview of the Linux kernel networking architecture (Figure 10.2).

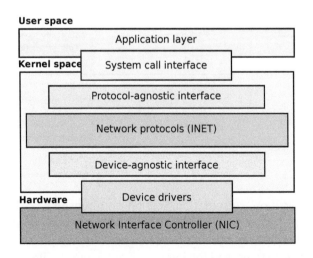

Figure 10.2: Linux kernel networking architecture.

10.5.1 Device drivers
The physical network devices (NIC) are managed by device drivers. For what follows, we assume the NIC is an Ethernet device. The device driver is a software interface between the kernel and the device hardware. On the kernel side, it uses a low-level but standardized API so that any driver for a different NIC can be used in the same way. In other words, the device driver abstracts away as much as possible the specific hardware.

The normal file operations (read, write, ...) do not make sense when applied to the interaction between a driver and a NIC, so they do not follow the "everything is a file" philosophy. The main difference is that a file, and by extension a file storage device is passive, whereas a network device actively wants to push incoming packets toward the kernel. So NIC interrupts are not a result of a previous kernel action (as is the case with, e.g. file operations), but of the arrival of a packet. Consequently, network interfaces exist in their own namespace with a different API.

10.5.2 Device-agnostic interface
The network protocol implementation code interfaces with the driver code through an agnostic interface layer which allows us to connects various protocols to a variety of hardware device drivers. To achieve this, the calls work on a packet-by-packet basis so that it is not necessary to inspect the packet content or keep protocol-specific state information at this level. The interface API is defined in linux/net/core/dev.c. The actual interface is a struct of function pointers called net_- device_ops, defined in include/linux/netdevice.h. In the driver code, the applicable fields are populated using driver-specific functions.

10.5.3 Network protocols
Packets get handed over the actual network protocol functionality in the kernel. For our purpose, we focus on the TCP/IP protocol, known in the Linux kernel as *inet*. This is a whole suite of protocols, the best-known of which are IP, TCP, and UDP. The code for this can be found in net/ipv4 for IP v4 and in net/ipv6 for IP v6.

In particular, IPv4 protocols are initialized in a *inet_init()* (defined in linux/net/ipv4/af_inet.c). This function registers each of the built-in protocols using the *proto_register()* function (defined in linux/net/core/sock.c). It adds the protocol to the active protocol list and also optionally allocates one or more slab caches. The Linux kernel implements a caching memory allocator to hold caches (called slabs) of identical objects. A slab is a set of one or more contiguous pages of memory set aside by the slab allocator for an individual cache.

10.5.4 Protocol-agnostic interface
The network protocols interface with a protocol-agnostic layer that provides a set of common functions to support a variety of different protocols. This layer is called the sockets layer, and it supports not only the common TCP and UDP transport protocols but also the IP routing protocol, various Ethernet protocols, and others, e.g., Stream Control Transmission Protocol (SCTP). We will discuss the POSIX socket interface in more detail in section 10.6.

The *socket* interface is an abstraction for the network connection. The socket datastructure contains all of the required state of a particular socket, including the particular protocol used by the socket and the operations that may be performed on it. The networking subsystem knows about the available protocols through a special structure that defines its capabilities. Each protocol maintains a (large) structure called *proto* (defined in include/net/sock.h). This struct defines the particular socket operations that can be performed from the sockets layer to the transport layer (for example, how to create a socket, how to establish a connection with a socket, how to close a socket, etc.).

10.5.5 System call interface

We have covered the Linux system call interface in Chapter 5. Essentially, this is the interface between user space and kernel space. Recall that Linux system calls are identified by a unique number and take a variable number of arguments. When a networking call is made by the user, the system call interface of the kernel maps it to a call to sys_socketcall (defined as `SYSCALL_`‐`DEFINE2(socketcall,...)` in net/socket.c), which then further demultiplexes the call to its intended target, e.g., `SYS_SOCKET, SYS_BIND`, etc.

It is also possible to use the file abstraction for networking I/O. For example, typical read and write operations may be performed on a networking socket (which is represented by a file descriptor, just as a normal file). Therefore, while there exist a number of operations that are specific to networking (creating a socket with the socket call, connecting it to a destination with the connect call, and so on), there are also a number of standard file operations that apply to networking objects just as they do to regular files.

10.5.6 Socket buffers

A consequence of having many layers of network protocols, each one using the services of another, is that each protocol needs to add protocol headers (and/or footers) to the data as it is transmitted and to remove them as packets are received. This could make passing data buffers between the protocol layers difficult as each layer would need to find where its particular protocol headers and footers are located within the buffer. Copying buffers between layers would, of course, work, but it would be very inefficient. Instead, the Linux kernel uses *socket buffers* (a.k.a. *sk_buffs*) (struct sk_buff) to pass data between the protocol layers and the network device drivers. Socket buffers contain pointer and length fields that allow each protocol layer to manipulate the application data via standard functions.

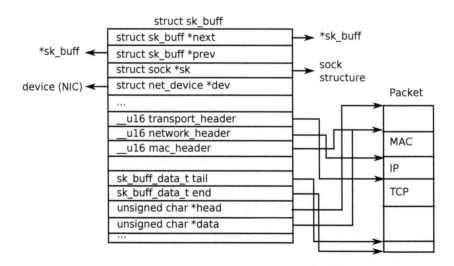

Figure 10.3: Socket buffer structure.

Essentially, an sk_buff combines a control structure with a block of memory. Two main sets of functions are provided in the sk_buff library: the first set consists of routines to manipulate doubly linked lists of sk_buffs; the second set of functions for controlling the attached memory. The buffers are stored in linked lists optimized for the common network operations of append to end and remove from start. In practice, the structure is quite complicated (the complete struct comprises 66 fields). Figure 10.3 shows a simplified diagram of the sk_buff struct.

10.6 The POSIX standard socket interface library

In this section, we present some of the most useful POSIX standard socket interface library functions and the related internet data types and constants. The selection focuses on IPv4 TCP stream sockets.

10.6.1 Stream socket (TCP) communications flow

The Transmission Control Protocol is a core protocol in the TCP/IP stack and implements one of the two transport layer (OSI layer 4) protocols (the other being UDP, the User Datagram Protocol). All incoming IP network layer packets marked with the relevant TCP identifier in the IP protocol ID header field are passed upwards to TCP, and all outgoing TCP packets are passed down to the IP layer for sending. In turn, TCP is responsible for identifying the (16-bit) port number from the TCP packet header and forwarding the TCP packet payload to any active socket associated with the specified port number.

TCP is reliable and connection-oriented and as such employs various handshaking activities in the background between the TCP layers in the communicating nodes to handle the setup, reliability control and shutdown of the TCP connection. The socket API provides a simplified programming model for the TCP to application interface, and the connected stream sockets can be considered as the communication endpoints of a virtual data circuit between two processes.

To establish a socket connection, one of the communicating processes (the *server*) needs to be actively waiting for a connection on an active socket and the other process (the *client*) can then request a connection and if successful the connection is made. The timeline of the various socket library function calls required in a typical (simple) stream socket connection is shown below:

Server timeline	Client timeline	Description
1. Socket(. . .)		Server creates a socket file descriptor
2. Setsockopt(. . .)		Configure server socket protocol options (1 call per option)
3. Bind(. . .)		Associate the server socket with a predefined local port number
4. Listen(. . .)		Allow client connections on the server socket
5. Accept(. . .)		Wait for client connection request
	1. Socket(. . .)	Client creates a socket file descriptor
	2. Connect(. . .)	Client requests connection to the server socket
6. Recv(. . .)/send(. . .)	3. Recv(. . .)/send(. . .)	Client/Server data communications
7. Close(. . .)	4. Close(. . .)	Either process can close the stream socket connection first

Treating stream sockets as standard system devices: read()/write()

The read() and write() low level I/O library functions are not part of the standard socket library; however stream sockets behave in much the same manner as any other operating system device (standard input/output, file, etc) and low-level system device I/O operations are therefore compatible with stream socket I/O. The use of these functions in place of the standard socket library functions send(), and recv() (used for stream sockets only) is a common programming nicety that will allow the simple redirection of process communications from network to any other available I/O device in the host OS. In comparison; the standard socket library functions sendto() and recvfrom() used for datagram sockets (UDP) are not compatible with the low-level stream I/O due to their unreliable and connectionless characteristics and therefore cannot be treated in the same way.

Note

A read from a stream socket (using the read() or recv() functions) may not return all of the expected bytes in the first go, and the read operation may need to be repeated an unspecified number of times with the read results concatenated until the full number of expected bytes has been received. If the expected number of bytes is not known in advance, the stream should be read a small block of bytes (possible 1 byte) at a time until the receive count is identified using a data size field within the received data or a predefined data terminator sequence. It is up to the individual internet application to define any data size field syntax and/or data terminators used. Attempting to read more data that has been sent will block the read() or recv() function call which will hang waiting for new data.

10.6.2 Common Internet data types

As mentioned previously – only the stream socket related library functions and associated data types and constants are listed here. Due to target differences in the fundamental integer data types utilised between various implementations of the standard socket interface – the POSIX defined types '*u_char*' (8-bit), '*u_short*' (16-bit) and '*u_long*' (32-bit) (normally declared in '*sys/types.h*' for UNIX systems) are used here to signify fixed word length integer data types and may be utilized in any required programming type casts.

The following sections discuss some reference material for useful standard socket interface library functions and internet data types.

Socket address data type: struct sockaddr

The socket address data structure used in various socket library function calls is defined in sys/socket.h as:

```
Listing 10.6.1: socket address struct                                          C

1    struct sockaddr {
2        u_char sa_family; /* address family */
3        char sa_data[14]; /* value of address */
4    };
```

Internet socket address data type: struct sockaddr_in

The members of the socket address data structure do not seem to relate much to what we would expect for an internet address (and port number). This is due to the fact that the socket interface is not restricted to internet communications and many alternative underlying host to host transport mechanisms are available (specified by the value of the *'sa_family'* socket address structure member), and these have different address schemes that have to be supported. The 14-byte address data is formatted in different ways depending on the underlying transport. For simplicity; a specific internet socket address structure has also been defined which is used as an overlay to the more generic socket address structure. This makes programming the address information much more convenient as a template for the specific internet address value format is provided:

Listing 10.6.2: internet socket address struct   C

```
1   #include <netinet/in.h>
2   struct sockaddr_in {
3     sa_family_t sin_family; /* address family: AF_INET */
4       in_port_t     sin_port;  /* port in network byte order */
5       struct in_addr sin_addr; /* internet address */
6   };
```

The internet socket address structure has the member type *struct in_addr*:

Listing 10.6.3: internet address struct (IPv4)   C

```
1   #include <netinet/in.h>
2
3   struct in_addr {
4     uint32_t      s_addr;        /* address in network byte order */
5   };
```

When using a variable of internet socket address type, it is good practice to zero-fill the overlay padding *sin_zero*.

Network byte order versus host byte order

The network byte order for TCP/IP is defined as big-endian; this is reflected in the data types used in the standard socket interface library. As such it is essential that the host byte order is correctly mapped to the network byte order when setting values of the standard socket data type variables used and vice versa when interpreting these values. The *htons()* and *htonl()* functions are used to convert host byte order 16-bit and 32-bit data types to their respective network byte order and *ntohs()* and *ntohl()* functions are used to convert network byte order 16-bit and 32-bit data types to their respective host byte order. This feature of standard socket programming is a minor but essential aspect to ensure the portability of internet application code.

Arm platforms can be configured to run in little-endian or big-endian mode at boot time, so it is essential to use the above conversion functions to ensure correctness of the code.

10.6.3 Common POSIX socket API functions

Create a socket descriptor: *socket()*

A socket (socket(2)) is opened, and its descriptor created using:

```
Listing 10.6.4: socket() API call                                                    C

1    #include <sys/types.h>              /* See NOTES */
2    #include <sys/socket.h>
3
4    int socket(int domain, int type, int protocol);
```

Return value: the returned socket descriptor is a standard I/O system file descriptor and can also be used with the I/O functions: *close()* and in the case of stream type sockets with *read()'* and *'write().'* On error, the value **-1** is returned.

Input parameters: The address family parameter **domain** should be set to AF_INET for internet socket communications. The socket type parameter **type** should be selected from SOCK_STREAM or SOCK _DGRAM for stream (TCP) and datagram (UDP) sockets respectively. The protocol **family** parameter family can be set to 0 to allow the socket function to select the associated protocol family automatically.

Bind a server socket address to a socket descriptor: *bind()*

For 'server' type applications (i.e., those that listen for incoming connections on an opened socket) the server socket address is bound to a socket descriptor using bind(2):

```
Listing 10.6.5: bind() API call                                                       C

1    #include <sys/types.h>              /* See NOTES */
2    #include <sys/socket.h>
3    int bind(int sockfd, const struct sockaddr *addr,
4    socklen_t addrlen);
```

Return value: the function returns **0** on success or **-1** if the socket is invalid, the specified socket address is invalid or in use or the specified socket descriptor is already bound.

Input parameters: typically for internet server type applications an internet socket address is used for convenience when specifying the local socket address; however since the internet socket address structure is designed as an overly to the generic socket address structure — variables of **type struct sockaddr_in** can be passed as the **addr** parameter using a suitable type cast. Before calling the **bind()** function it is necessary to populate the internet socket address (shown as **myaddr** below) with the local system IP address and the required server port number:

Listing 10.6.6: populating the internet socket address for bind()　　　　　　　　　　　C

```c
1   mysd = socket(AF_INET, SOCK_STREAM, 0);
2   memset((char *) &myaddr, 0, sizeof(struct sockaddr_in)); /* zero socket address */
3   myaddr.sin_len = (u_char) sizeof(struct sockaddr_in);    /* address length */
4   myaddr.sin_family = AF_INET;                    /* internet family */
5   myaddr.sin_addr.s_addr = inet_addr("192.168.0.10");      /* local IP address */
6   myaddr.sin_port = htons(3490);                 /* local server port */
7   bind(mysd, (struct sockaddr_in *) &myaddr, sizeof(struct sockaddr) );
```

Note the use of '*memset()*' from the ANSI string library to first zero the internet socket address bytes and the internet address manipulation function ***inet_addr()*** to produce the (network byte order) 4 byte IP address. Using the specific port number 0 tells ***bind()*** to choose a suitable unused port — if that is desired rather than having a fixed server port allocation (the selected port gets written to the supplied socket address before return). Writing the specific local IP address is not very convenient, and the code can ultimately be made more portable using the INADDR_ANY predefined IP address (declared for use with ***struct sockaddr_in***) which tells ***bind()*** to use the local system IP address automatically (which is also written to the supplied socket address before return). Therefore, the server local IP address is more typically set using:

```c
myaddr.sin_addr.s_addr = htonl(INADDR_-
ANY);      /* auto local IP address */
```

Enable server socket connection requests: *listen()*

Once a server socket descriptor has been bound to a socket address it is then necessary to enable connection requests to this socket and create an incoming connection request queue using listen(2):

Listing 10.6.7: listen() API call　　　　　　　　　　　C

```c
1   #include <sys/types.h>           /* See NOTES */
2   #include <sys/socket.h>
3
4   int listen(int sockfd, int backlog);
```

Return value: the function returns **0** if okay or **-1** if the socket is invalid or unable to listen.

Input parameters: incoming connection requests are queued until accepted by the server. The parameter ***backlog*** is used to specify the maximum length of this queue and should have a value of at least **1**.

Accept a server socket connection request: *accept()*

Server socket connection requests are accepted using accept(2):

Listing 10.6.8: accept() API call　　　　　　　　　　　C

```c
1   #include <sys/types.h>           /* See NOTES */
2   #include <sys/socket.h>
3
4   int accept(int sockfd, struct sockaddr *addr, socklen_t *addrlen);
```

Return value: the function returns the newly created socket descriptor associated with the client socket address on success or **-1** on error.

Input parameters: a socket address structure variable (more likely of type **struct sockaddr_in** with a suitable type cast) is provided as parameter **addr** and is used to record the socket address associated with the socket descriptor of the accepted incoming connection request which is returned on success. A pointer to an integer containing the socket address structure length is provided as parameter **addrlen**, and this integer variable should contain the length of the socket address structure on input and is modified to the actual address bytes used on return.

On success, the returned client socket descriptor can be used by the server to send and receive data to the client.

If no pending connections are present on the queue, and the socket is not marked as nonblocking, *accept()* blocks until a connection is present. If the socket is marked nonblocking and no pending connections are present on the queue, *accept()* fails with the error EAGAIN or EWOULDBLOCK.

Linux kernel implementation of accept()
If the *accept()* is blocking, the kernel will take care of sleeping the caller until the call returns. The process will be added to a wait queue and then suspended until a TCP connection request is received. Once a connection request has been received, the *sock* data structure is returned to the socket layer. The file descriptor number of the new socket is returned to the process as the return value of the *accept()* call.

Client connection request: 'connect()'
For 'client' type applications (i.e., those that connect to an active server socket) a connection request to a specified server socket address is made using connect(2):

Listing 10.6.9: connect() API call

```c
1    #include <sys/types.h>          /* See NOTES */
2    #include <sys/socket.h>
3
4    int connect(int sockfd, const struct sockaddr *addr,
5                     socklen_t addrlen);
```

Return value: the function returns 0 on success or -1 on error.

Input parameters: typically for internet client type applications an internet socket address is used for convenience when specifying the remote server socket address; however since the internet socket address structure is designed as an overly to the generic socket address structure — variables of type **struct sockaddr_in** can be passed as the **addr** parameter using a suitable type cast. Before calling the **connect()** function, it is necessary to populate the internet socket address (shown as **srvaddr** below) with the remote server system IP address and the required server port number:

Listing 10.6.10: populating the internet socket address for connect()   *C*

```
1    srvsd = socket(AF_INET, SOCK_STREAM, 0);
2    memset((char *) &srvaddr,0, sizeof(struct sockaddr_in)); /* zero socket address */
3    srvaddr.sin_len = (u_char) sizeof(struct sockaddr_in);   /* address length */
4    srvaddr.sin_family = AF_INET;                 /* internet family */
5    srvaddr.sin_addr.s_addr = inet_addr("192.168.0.10");     /* server IP address */
6    srvaddr.sin_port = htons(3490);               /* server port */
7    connect(srvsd, (struct sockaddr_in *) &srvaddr, sizeof(struct sockaddr) );
```

On success, the socket descriptor used in the connection request can be used by the client to send and receive data to the server.

Write data to a stream socket: *send()*
Data is written to a stream socket using send(2):

Listing 10.6.11: send() API call   *C*

```
1    #include <sys/types.h>
2    #include <sys/socket.h>
3
4    ssize_t send(int sockfd, const void *buf, size_t len, int flags);
5    ssize_t sendto(int sockfd, const void *buf, size_t len, int flags,
6                       const struct sockaddr *dest_addr, socklen_t addrlen);
7    ssize_t sendmsg(int sockfd, const struct msghdr *msg, int flags);
```

Return value: the function returns the actual number of bytes sent or -1 on error.

Input parameters: in-stream sockets the socket transport protocol bitwise flags of MSG_OOB (send as urgent) and MSG_DONTROUTE (send without using routing tables) can be used (multiple bitwise flags can be set concurrently by OR'ing the selection). For standard data sending the value **0** is used for parameter *flags*.

Because of the stream socket operation compatibility with system I/O device operation, the *send()* socket-specific function is sometimes replaced with the generic *write()* system I/O function. This means that data sending can be easily redirected to other system devices (such as an opened file or standard output).

Read data from a stream socket: *recv()*
Data is written to a stream socket using recv(2):

Listing 10.6.12: recv() API call   *C*

```
1    #include <sys/types.h>
2    #include <sys/socket.h>
3
4    ssize_t recv(int sockfd, void *buf, size_t len, int flags);
5    ssize_t recvfrom(int sockfd, void *buf, size_t len, int flags,
6                       struct sockaddr *src_addr, socklen_t *addrlen);
7    ssize_t recvmsg(int sockfd, struct msghdr *msg, int flags);
```

Return value: the function returns the actual number of bytes read into the receive buffer; or 0 on end of file (socket disconnection); or -1 on error.

Input parameters: in-stream sockets the socket transport protocol bitwise flags of MSG_OOB (receive urgent data) and MSG_PEEK (copy data without removing it from the socket) can be used (multiple bitwise flags can be set concurrently by OR-ing the selection). For standard data reception, the value **0** is used for parameter *flags*.

Because of the stream socket operation compatibility with system I/O device operation, the *recv()* socket specific function is sometimes replaced with the generic *read()* system I/O function. This means that data reception can be easily redirected to other system devices (such as an opened file or standard input). Care should be taken when reading an expected number of bytes; the socket transport does not guarantee when to receive bytes will be available, and blocks may be split into smaller receive sections which may confound a simple socket read approach.

If no messages are available at the socket, the *recv()* call waits for a message to arrive, unless the socket is nonblocking (see fcntl(2)), in which case the value -1 is returned and the external variable errno is set to EAGAIN or EWOULDBLOCK. The *recv()* call normally returns any data available, up to the requested amount, rather than waiting for receipt of the full amount requested. Therefore in practice, *recv()* is usually called in a loop until the required number of bytes has been received.

Setting server socket options: *setsockopt()*
It is possible to set important underlying protocol options for a server socket using setsockopt(2):

```c
1   #include <sys/types.h>          /* See NOTES */
2   #include <sys/socket.h>
3   int getsockopt(int sockfd, int level, int optname,
4                     void *optval, socklen_t *optlen);
5   int setsockopt(int sockfd, int level, int optname,
6                     const void *optval, socklen_t optlen);
```

Listing 10.6.13: setsockopt() API call

Return value: the function returns 0 on success or -1 if the socket is invalid, or the option is unknown, or the function is unable to set the option.

Input parameters:

Socket Option	Used For
SO_KEEPALIVE	Detecting dead connections (connection is dropped if dead)
SO_LINGER	Graceful socket closure (does not close until all pending transactions complete)
TCP_NODELAY	Allowing immediate transmission of small packets (no congestion avoidance)
SO_DEBUG	Invoking debug recording in the underlying protocol software module
SO_REUSEADDR	Allows socket reuse of port numbers associated with "zombie" control blocks
SO_SNDBUF	Adjusting the maximum size of the send buffer
SO_RCVBUF	Adjusting the maximum size of the receive buffer
SO_RCVBUF	Enabling the use of the TCP expedited data transmission.

The most commonly applied socket option for internet server applications is the socket reuse address option which is required to allow the server to bind a socket to a specific port that has not yet been entirely freed by a previous session. Without this setting, any call to **bind()** may be prevented by a "zombie" session. In order to set this option, the defined SOL_SOCKET (socket protocol level) is used for parameter **level**; the SO_REUSEADDR (the predefined name of socket reuse address option) is used for parameter **optname** and for this option the value is an integer which is set to 0 (OFF) or 1 (ON). A simple example of this for the **myfd** server socket descriptor is shown below:

Listing 10.6.14: Example setsockopt() API call

```
1   sra_val = 1;
2   setsockopt(myfd, SOL_SOCKET, SO_REUSEADDR, (char *) &sra_val, sizeof(int))
```

Many other protocol options are available, see the man page for more details.

10.6.4 Common utility functions

Internet address manipulation functions
The following internet address manipulation functions are available:

Listing 10.6.15: Internet address manipulation functions

```
1   #include <arpa/inet.h>
2   /* converts dotted decimal IP address string */
3   /* to network byte order 4 byte value */
4   u_long inet_addr(char * addr);
5   /* converts network byte order 4 byte IP addr*/
6   /* to dotted decimal IP address string */
7   char *inet_ntoa(struct in_addr addr);
```

Internet network/host byte order manipulation functions
The following network/host byte order manipulation functions are available and should be consistently applied:

Listing 10.6.16: Network/host byte order manipulation functions

```
1   #include <netinet/in.h>
2   u_short htons(u_short x);    /* 16-bit host to network byte order convert */
3   u_short ntohs(u_short x);     /* 16-bit network to host byte order convert */
4   u_long htonl(u_long x);    /* 32-bit host to network byte order convert */
5   u_long ntohl(u_long x);     /* 32-bit network to host byte order convert */
```

Host table access functions

The local host name can be read from the host table using:

```c
1   #include <unistd.h>
2   int gethostname (
3     char *name,      /* name string buffer */
4     int namelen      /* length of name string buffer */
5   );
```

Listing 10.6.17: Host table access functions

Return value: the function returns 0 on success or -1 on error.

10.6.5 Building applications with TCP

The TCP protocol provides a reliable, bi-directional stream service over an IP-based network between pairs of processes.

One process is known as the server; when it comes to life, it binds itself to a particular TCP port number on the host upon which it executes and at which it will provide its particular service.

The other process is known as the client; when it comes to life, it connects to a server on a particular host that is bound to a particular TCP port number. Upon completion of the connection, either party can begin sending bytes to the other party over the stream.

Request/response communication using TCP

The TCP protocol is designed to maximize the reliable delivery of data end-to-end; to enable both the reliable delivery and to maximize the amount of data so delivered, the protocol is allowed to ship the data supplied by the sender into as many packets as it likes (within reason). In particular, TCP does **not** guarantee that:

- A sender's data is sent as soon as the send() or write() system call completes — i.e., your system can choose to buffer the data from several send()/write() system calls before actually sending the data over the network to the server.

- A receiver receives the data in the same sized chunks that were specified in the sender's send()/write() system calls — i.e., it does not maintain "message" boundaries.

If you are trying to implement a request/response application protocol over TCP, then you need to program around these features. In the following sections, it is assumed that your client and server must maintain message boundaries.

Force the sending side to send your data over the network immediately

```
1    int s;      /* your socket that has been created and connected */
2    int len;
3    FILE *sockout;
4    sockout = fdopen(s, "w");      /* FILE stream corresponding to file descriptor */
5    len = strlen("your message\n");   /* calculate length of message */
6    write(s, "your message\n", len);   /* send the message */
7    fflush(sockout);         /* force the message over the network */
```

Maintaining message boundaries

- If your messages consist only of characters, use a sentinel character sequence at the end of each message — e.g., <cr><lf>

- If you have binary messages, then the actual message sent consists of a 2-byte length, in network order, followed by that many bytes.

TCP server

As described in Section 10.6.1 above, a TCP server must execute the socket functions according to the following pseudocode:

```
1    s = socket();        /* create an endpoint for communication */
2    bind(s);         /* bind the socket to a particular TCP port number */
3    listen(s);          /* listen for connection requests */
4    while(1) {          /* loop forever */
5       news = accept(s);      /* accept first waiting connection */
6       send()/recv() over news   /* interact with connected process */
7       close(news);      /* disconnect from connected process */
8    }
9    close(s);
```

You may need to perform one or more setsockopt() calls before invoking bind(). Below is an example of a skeleton TCP server that reads all data from the connection and writes it to stdout.

```
1    #include <stdio.h>
2    #include <sys/types.h>
3    #include <sys/socket.h>
4    #include <netinet/in.h>
5
6    #define MYPORT 3490     /* the port users will be connecting to */
7
8    int main(int argc, char *argv[]) {
9      int sfd, cfd;                    /* listen on sfd, new connections on cfd */
10     struct sockaddr_in my_addr;          /* my address information */
11     struct sockaddr_in their_addr;       /* client address information */
12     int sin_size, c;
13     int yes=1;
```

```
14
15    /**** open the server (TCP) socket */
16      if ((sfd = socket(AF_INET, SOCK_STREAM, 0)) == -1) {
17        perror("socket");
18        return(-1);
19      }
20
21    /**** set the Reuse-Socket-Address option */
22      if (setsockopt(sfd, SOL_SOCKET, SO_REUSEADDR, (char*)&yes, sizeof(int))==-1) {
23        perror("setsockopt");
24        close(sfd);
25        return(-1);
26      }
27
28    /**** build server socket address */
29      bzero((char*) &my_addr, sizeof(struct sockaddr_in));
30      my_addr.sin_family = AF_INET;
31      my_addr.sin_addr.s_addr = htonl(INADDR_ANY);
32      my_addr.sin_port = htons(MYPORT);
33
34    /**** bind server socket to the local address */
35      if (bind(sfd, (struct sockaddr *)&my_addr, sizeof(struct sockaddr)) == -1) {
36      perror("bind");
37      close(sfd);
38      return(-1);
39      }
40
41    /**** create queue (1 only) for client connection requests */
42      if (listen(sfd, 1) == -1) {
43        perror("listen");
44        close(sfd);
45        return(-1);
46      }
47
48    /**** accept connection and read data until EOF, copying to standard output */
49      sin_size = sizeof(struct sockaddr_in);
50      if ((cfd = accept(sfd, (struct sockaddr *)&their_addr, &sin_size)) == -1) {
51        perror("accept");
52        close(sfd);
53        return(-1);
54      }
55      while (read(cfd, &c, 1) == 1)
56        putc(c, stdout);
57      close(cfd);
58      close(sfd);
59
60      return 0;
61    }
```

TCP client

As described above, a TCP client must execute the socket functions according to the following pseudocode:

```
Listing 10.6.21: TCP client pseudocode                                               C

1    s = socket();      /* create an endpoint for communication */
2    connect(s);        /* connect the socket to a particular host and TCP port number */
3    send()/recv() over s   /* interact with server process */
4    close(s);          /* disconnect from connected process */
```

You can see from the above code that a server needs to know the port to which they will bind, and from the pseudocode that the client needs to know the port to which the server is bound. A stream in TCP is identified by a 4-tuple of the form [source host, source port, destination host, destination port]. The connect() socket call actually assigns a random TCP port to the client. Since it is not a server, the fact that the port is randomly chosen from the legal port space is immaterial. The following TCP client connects to the above server and sends all data obtained from standard input to the server.

Listing 10.6.22: Example skeleton TCP client

```c
/*
** TCPclient.c -- a TCP socket client
**        connects to 127.0.0.1:3490, sends contents of standard input
**
*/

#include <stdio.h>
#include <sys/types.h>
#include <sys/socket.h>
#include <netinet/in.h>

#define MYPORT 3490     /* the port users will be connecting to */

int main(int argc, char* argv[]) {
  int sfd;                       /* connect on sfd */
  struct sockaddr_in s_addr;         /* server address information */
  char buf[1024];
  int len;

/**** open the server (TCP) socket */
  if ((sfd = socket(AF_INET, SOCK_STREAM, 0)) == -1) {
  perror("socket");
  return(-1);
}

/**** build server socket address */
  bzero((char*) &s_addr, sizeof(struct sockaddr_in));
  s_addr.sin_family = AF_INET;
  s_addr.sin_addr.s_addr = inet_addr("127.0.0.1");
  s_addr.sin_port = htons(MYPORT);

/**** connect to server */
  if (connect(sfd, (struct sockaddr *)&s_addr, sizeof(struct sockaddr)) == -1) {
    perror("connect");
    close(sfd);
    return(-1);
  }

  while (fgets(buf, sizeof(buf), stdin) != NULL) {
    len = strlen(buf);
    if (send(sfd, buf, len, 0) != len) {
      perror("send");
      close(sfd);
      return(-1);
    }
  }
  close(sfd);

  return 0;
}
```

10.6.6 Building applications with UDP
The UDP protocol provides an unreliable, bi-directional datagram service over an IP-based network between pairs of processes. Unlike TCP, there are no "connections" in UDP. A process that wishes to interact with other processes via UDP simply has to bind itself to a UDP port on its host. As long as it knows of at least one other process's host/port pair, it can begin to communicate with that process. When a process receives a UDP message, it can be informed of the host/port pair for the process that sent the message.

If you think about servers in the TCP realm, they advertise on well-known ports . We can think of long-lived processes that bind themselves to well-known UDP ports as servers.

Processes that bind themselves to random UDP ports, and that initiate communications with other processes, can be considered to be UDP clients.

The timeline of the various socket library function calls required in a typical (simple) datagram socket interaction is shown below:

Server Process	Client Process	Alternative Client	Description
1. socket(. . .)	1. socket(. . .)	1. socket(. . .)	Creates a socket file descriptor
2. bind(. . .)	2. bind(. . .)	2. bind(. . .)	Associate the socket with a UDP port number (server's is predefined)
3. connect(. . .)	3. recvfrom(. . .)/ sendto(. . .)	3. sendto(. . .)/ recvfrom(. . .)	Client binds server info to socket
4. send(. . .)/recv(. . .)	4. Close(. . .)	4. Close(. . .)	Client/Server data communications
5. Close(. . .)			Stop using the socket

Note that UDP communication is unreliable. UDP primarily provides the ability to put application-level data directly into IP packets, with the UDP header providing the port information necessary to direct the data, if received, to the correct process. UDP also provides a data integrity checksum of the application data so that a receiver knows that if it receives the data, it has received the correct data — i.e. the data in the packet has not been corrupted.

Since the application data is placed in an IP packet, this implies that the size of the application message, plus the UDP and IP headers, cannot exceed the size of an IP packet. Hosts negotiate the maximum IP packet size for communications between them; most networks support packets containing 1536-byte UDP packets, but some are limited to 512 bytes UDP packets. If you have larger messages to send, then you must fragment your message into multiple UDP packets, and reassemble them at the receiver. For this reason, most uses of UDP are for short messages, such as measurements from distributed sensors.

The following program listings are for UDP versions of the service provided in Section 10.6.5.

UDP server

Listing 10.6.23: Example skeleton UDP server   C

```
1   / *
2    * UDPserver.c -- a UDP socket server
3    *
4    */
5
6   #include <sys/socket.h>
7   #include <sys/types.h>
8   #include <netinet/in.h>
9   #include <arpa/inet.h>
10  #include <stdio.h>
11
12  #define MYPORT 3490      /* the port to which the server is bound */
13
14  int main(int argc, char *argv[]) {
15    int sfd;          /* the socket for communication */
16    int len, n;
17    struct sockaddr_in s_addr;  /* my s(erver) address data */
18    struct sockaddr_in c_addr;  /* c(lient) address data */
19    char buf[1024];
20
21    memset(&s_addr, 0, sizeof(s_addr));  /* my address info */
22    s_addr.sin_family = AF_INET;
23    s_addr.sin_port = htons(MYPORT);
24    s_addr.sin_addr.s_addr = htonl(INADDR_ANY);
25
26  /**** open the UDP socket */
27    if ((sfd = socket(AF_INET, SOCK_DGRAM, 0)) < 0) {
28      perror("socket");
29      return(-1);
30    }
31
32  /**** bind to my local port number */
33    if ((bind(sfd, (struct sockaddr *)&s_addr, sizeof(s_addr)) < 0)) {
34      perror("bind");
35      return(-1);
36  }
37
38  /**** receive each message on the socket, printing on stdout */
39    while (1) {
40    memset(&c_addr, 0, sizeof(s_addr));
41    len = sizeof (c_addr);
42    n = recvfrom(sfd, buf, sizeof(buf), 0, (struct sockaddr *)&c_addr, &len);
43    if (n < 0) {
44      perror("recvfrom");
45      return(-1);
46    }
47    fputs(buf, stdout);
48    fflush(stdout);
49    }
50  }
```

UDP client

Listing 10.6.24: Example skeleton UDP client   C

```c
1    /*
2     * UDPclient.c -- a UDP socket client
3     *
4     */
5
6    #include <sys/types.h>
7    #include <sys/socket.h>
8    #include <netinet/in.h>
9    #include <arpa/inet.h>
10   #include <stdio.h>
11
12   #define MYPORT 3490      /* the port to which the server is bound */
13
14   int main(int argc, char *argv[]) {
15     int sfd;         /* the socket for communication */
16     struct sockaddr_in s_addr, m_addr;  /* s(erver) and m(y) addr data */
17     char buf[1024];
18     int n;
19
20     memset(&m_addr, 0, sizeof(m_addr));  /* my address information */
21     m_addr.sin_family = AF_INET;
22     m_addr.sin_port = 0;         /* 0 ==> assign me a port */
23     m_addr.sin_addr.s_addr = htonl(INADDR_ANY);
24
25     memset(&s_addr, 0, sizeof(s_addr));  /* server addr info */
26     s_addr.sin_family = AF_INET;
27     s_addr.sin_port = htons(MYPORT);
28     s_addr.sin_addr.s_addr = inet_addr("127.0.0.1");
29
30   /**** open the UDP socket */
31     if ((sfd = socket(AF_INET, SOCK_DGRAM, 0)) < 0) {
32       perror("socket");
33       return(-1);
34     }
35
36   /**** bind to local UDP port (randomly assigned) */
37     if (bind(sfd, (struct sockaddr *)&m_addr, sizeof(m_addr)) < 0) {
38       perror("bind");
39       return(-1);
40     }
41
42   /**** send each line from stdin as a separate message to server */
43     while (fgets(buf, sizeof(buf), stdin) != NULL) {
44       n = strlen(buf) + 1;  /* include the EOS! */
45       sendto(sfd, buf, n, 0, (struct sockaddr *)&s_addr, sizeof(s_addr));
46     }
47
48   /**** close the socket */
49     close(sfd);
50
51   }
```

UDP client using connect()

Instead of the using sendto()/recvfrom(), the UDP client could first make a call to connect(), and then use send()/recv():

```
1    /* After call to bind() */
2    /**** connect to remote host and UDP port */
3      if (connect(sfd, (struct sockaddr *)&s_addr, sizeof(s_addr)) < 0) {
4        perror("connect");
5        return(-1);
6      }
```

10.6.7 Handling multiple clients

The skeleton TCP server code from Section 10.6.5 will block on the accept() and read() calls for the connection to a single client. That means that it can only serve this client. Typically, serves should be able to handle many client requests. In this section, we discuss the mechanisms that can be used to build multi-client servers.

The select() system call

The select(2) call enables one to monitor several sockets at the same time. It indicates which sockets are ready for reading, which are ready for writing, and which sockets have raised exceptions. While select() is primarily used for networking applications, it works for file descriptors bound to any type of I/O device. The synopsis is:

```
1    /* According to POSIX.1-2001, POSIX.1-2008 */
2    #include <sys/select.h>
3    /* According to earlier standards */
4    #include <sys/time.h>
5    #include <sys/types.h>
6    #include <unistd.h>
7
8    int select(int nfds, fd_set *readfds, fd_set *writefds,
9               fd_set *exceptfds, struct timeval *timeout);
```

Return value: the return value is the number of file descriptors that have been set in the fd_- sets; if a timeout occurred, then the return value is 0. On error, the value -1 is returned.

Input parameters: For the *nfds* parameter, see below. Each *fd_set* parameter should have bits set corresponding to file descriptors of interest for reading/writing/exceptions; upon return, the *fd_set* parameter will only have bits set for those file descriptors that are ready for reading/writing or those that have generated exceptions. The *timeout* parameter should contain the time to wait before returning; if the parameter has a value of 0, then select() simply checks the current state of the file descriptors in the *fd_set* parameters and returns immediately; if *timeout* is NULL, then select() waits until there is some activity on one of the file descriptors specified.

The function monitors sets of file descriptors; in particular readfds, *writefds*, and *exceptfds*. Each of these is a simple bitset. If you want to see if you can read from standard input and some socket descriptor, *sockfd*, just add the file descriptors 0 (for stdin) and *sockfd* to the set *readfds*.

The parameter *numfds* should be set to the values of the highest file descriptor plus one. In this example, it should be set to *sockfd*+1, since it is assuredly higher than standard input (0).

The select call will block until either:

◼ a file descriptor becomes ready;

◼ the call is interrupted by a signal handler; or

◼ the timeout expires.

When *select()* returns, *readfds* will be modified to reflect which of the file descriptors you selected which is ready for reading. You can test this with the macro FD_ISSET(). The following macros are provided to manipulate sets of type *fd_set*:

`void FD_ZERO(fd_set *set)`: clears a file descriptor set

`void FD_SET(int fd, fd_set *set)`: adds fd to the set

`void FD_CLR(int fd, fd_set *set)`: removes fd from the set

`void FD_ISSET(int fd, fd_set *set)`: tests to see if fd is in the set

The struct timeval allows you to specify a timeout period. If the time is exceeded and select() still hasn't found any ready file descriptors; it will return so you can continue processing.

The struct timeval has the following fields:

```
Listing 10.6.27: timeval struct                                                  C

1    struct timeval {
2       int tv_sec;          /* seconds to wait */
3       int tv_usec;         /* microseconds to wait */
4    };
```

When select() returns, *timeout* might be updated to show the time still remaining. You should not depend upon this, but this does imply that you must reset *timeout* before each call.

Despite the provision for microseconds, the usual timer interval is around 10 milliseconds, so you will probably wait that long no matter how small you set your struct timeval. It is advisable to set your timers to be multiples of 10 milliseconds.

Linux kernel implementation of *select()*

The *select()* call works by looping over the list of file descriptors. For every file descriptor, it calls the *poll()* method, which will add the caller to that file descriptor's wait queue, and return which events (readable, writeable, exception) currently apply to that file descriptor.

The implementation of the poll() method depends on the corresponding device driver, but all implementations have the following prototype:

Listing 10.6.28: Linux kernel poll() method prototype   C

```
1    unsigned int (*poll) (struct file *, poll_table *);
```

The driver's method will be called whenever the *select()* system call is performed. It is responsible for two actions:

- Call *poll_wait()* on one or more wait queues that could indicate a change in the poll status.

- Return a bitmask describing operations that could be immediately performed without blocking.

The *poll_table* struct (the second argument to the *poll()* method), is used within the kernel to implement the *poll()* and *select()* calls; it is defined in linux/poll.h as a struct which contains a method to operate on a poll queue and a bitmask.

Listing 10.6.29: Linux kernel poll table struct   C

```
1    typedef struct poll_table_struct {
2      poll_queue_proc _qproc;
3      __poll_t _key;
4    } poll_table;
```

An event queue that could wake up the process and change the status of the poll operation can be added to the *poll_table* structure by calling the function *poll_wait()*:

Listing 10.6.30: Linux kernel poll_wait() call   C

```
1    static inline void poll_wait(struct file * filp,
2      wait_queue_head_t * wait_address, poll_table *p){
3      if (p && p->_qproc && wait_address)
4        p->_qproc(filp, wait_address, p);
5    }
```

Below is an example TCP server skeleton that uses *select()*. It simply prints the message received from the client on STDOUT.

Listing 10.6.31: Code skeleton for server with select() (1): setup, bind and listen　　　　　　　　　C

```c
1    #include <stdlib.h>
2    #include <string.h>
3    #include <stdio.h>
4    #include <sys/types.h>
5    #include <sys/socket.h>
6    #include <netinet/in.h>
7
8    #include <sys/time.h>
9    #include <sys/select.h>
10
11   #define MYPORT 3490     /* the port users will be connecting to */
12   #define MAX_NCLIENTS 5
13   #define MAX_NCHARS 128 /* max number of characters to be read/written at once */
14   #define FALSE 0
15   /* =================================================================== */
16
17   int main(int argc, char * argv[]) {
18       fd_set master; /* master set of file descriptors */
19       fd_set read_fds; /* set of file descriptors to read from */
20       int fdmax; /* highest fd in the set */
21       int s_fd;
22
23       FD_ZERO(&read_fds);
24       FD_ZERO(&master);
25       /* get the current size of file descriptors table */
26       fdmax = getdtablesize();
27
28       struct sockaddr_in my_addr;          /* my address information */
29       struct sockaddr_in their_addr;       /* client address information */
30
31       /**** open the server (TCP) socket */
32       if ((s_fd = socket(AF_INET, SOCK_STREAM, 0)) == -1) {
33          perror("socket");
34          return(-1);
35       }
36
37       /**** set the Reuse-Socket-Address option */
38       const int yes=1;
39       if (setsockopt(s_fd, SOL_SOCKET, SO_REUSEADDR, (char*)&yes, sizeof(int))==-1) {
40          perror("setsockopt");
41          close(s_fd);
42          return(-1);
43       }
44
45       /**** build server socket address */
46       bzero((char*) &my_addr, sizeof(struct sockaddr_in));
47       my_addr.sin_family = AF_INET;
48       my_addr.sin_addr.s_addr = htonl(INADDR_ANY);
49       my_addr.sin_port = htons(MYPORT);
50
51       /**** bind server socket to the local address */
52       if (bind(s_fd, (struct sockaddr *)&my_addr, sizeof(struct sockaddr)) == -1) {
53          perror("bind");
54          close(s_fd);
55          return(-1);
56       }
57
58       listen(s_fd, MAX_NCLIENTS);
```

Listing 10.6.32: Code skeleton for server with select() (2): select, accept and read   C

```c
1      FD_SET(s_fd, &master); // add s_fd to the master set
2
3      fdmax = s_fd;
4
5      while (1) {
6          read_fds=master;
7          select(fdmax+1, &read_fds, NULL, NULL, (struct timeval *)NULL); // never time out
8          /* run through the existing connections looking for data to read */
9          for(int i = 0; i <= fdmax; i++) {
10             if (FD_ISSET(i, &read_fds)) { // if i belongs to the set read_fds
11                 if (i == s_fd) { // fd of server socket
12                     // accept on new client socket newfd
13                     int sin_size = sizeof(struct sockaddr_in);
14                     int newfd = accept(s_fd, (struct sockaddr *)&their_addr, &sin_size);
15                     if (newfd == -1) {
16                         perror("accept");
17                     }
18                     FD_SET(newfd, &master); // add newfd to the master set
19                     if (newfd > fdmax) {
20                         fdmax = newfd;
21                     }
22                 } else { // i is a client socket
23                     printf("Hi, client\n");
24                     /* handle client request */
25                     char clientline[MAX_NCHARS]="";
26                     char tmpchar;
27                     char newline = '\n';
28                     int eob = 0;
29                     while(eob==0 && strlen(clientline)<MAX_NCHARS) {
30                         read(i,&tmpchar,1);
31                         eob=(tmpchar==newline) ? 1 : 0;
32                         strncat(clientline,&tmpchar,1);
33                     }
34                     printf("%s",clientline);
35
36                     /* clean up: close fd, remove from master set, decrement fdmax */
37                     close(i);
38                     FD_CLR(i, &master);
39                     if (i == fdmax) {
40                         while (FD_ISSET(fdmax, &master) == FALSE) {
41                             fdmax -= 1;
42                         }
43                     }
44                 } // i?=s_fd
45             } // FD_ISSET
46         } // for i
47     } // while()
48     return 0;
49 }
```

Multiple server processes: fork() and exec()

Handling multiple clients using select() can be a good option on a single-core system. However, on a system with multiple cores, we would like to take advantage of the available parallelism to increase the server performance. One way to do this is by forking a child process (as discussed in Chapter 4) to handle each client request. Even on a single-threaded system, this approach has an advantage: if a fatal error would occur in the process handling the client request, the main server process would not die. If we handle the client request in the same code as the main server activity (as is the case if we use select()) then an exception in the client code would kill the entire server process.

Although *fork()/exec()* based code is conceptually simple, the TCP server skeleton below is a bit more complicated because of the need of dealing with the zombie child processes. We do this using an asynchronous signal handler *sigchld_handler()* which gets called whenever a child process exits. For a discussion on signals, see Chapter 4; for details on signals and handlers, see sigaction(2). Essentially, what the server does is fork a client handler whenever a request is accepted. The handler reads the client message until a newline is encountered, then it prints the message, closes the connection, and exits.

Multithreaded servers using pthreads

A final mechanism to handle multiple clients is to use POSIX threads. The approach is quite similar to the fork-based server: the server spawns a client handler thread whenever a request is accepted. The handler reads the client message until a newline is encountered, then it prints the message, closes the connection, and exits.

```c
1    #include <unistd.h>
2    #include <string.h>
3    #include <stdio.h>
4    #include <sys/types.h>
5    #include <sys/socket.h>
6    #include <netinet/in.h>
7    #include <pthread.h>
8
9    #define MYPORT 3490        /* the port users will be connecting to */
10   #define MAX_NCLIENTS 5
11   #define MAX_NCHARS 128     /* max number of characters to be read/written at once */
12   #define FALSE 0
13   /* ================================================================= */
14
15   void *client_handler(void *);
16
17   int main(int argc, char * argv[]) {
18
19       struct sockaddr_in my_addr;        /* my address information */
20       struct sockaddr_in their_addr;     /* client address information */
21
22       pthread_t tid;
23       pthread_attr_t attr;
24       pthread_attr_init(&attr);
25       pthread_attr_setdetachstate(&attr,PTHREAD_CREATE_DETACHED);
26
27       /**** open the server (TCP) socket */
28       int s_fd = socket(AF_INET, SOCK_STREAM, 0);
29       if (s_fd == -1) {
30           perror("socket");
31           return(-1);
32       }
33
34       /**** set the Reuse-Socket-Address option */
35       const int yes=1;
36       if (setsockopt(s_fd, SOL_SOCKET, SO_REUSEADDR, (char*)&yes, sizeof(int))==-1) {
37           perror("setsockopt");
38           close(s_fd);
```

Listing 10.6.35: Code skeleton for server with pthreads (1): setup, bind and listen

```
39        return(-1);
40    }
41
42    /**** build server socket address */
43    bzero((char*) &my_addr, sizeof(struct sockaddr_in));
44    my_addr.sin_family = AF_INET;
45    my_addr.sin_addr.s_addr = htonl(INADDR_ANY);
46    my_addr.sin_port = htons(MYPORT);
47
48    /**** bind server socket to the local address */
49    if (bind(s_fd, (struct sockaddr *)&my_addr, sizeof(struct sockaddr)) == -1) {
50        perror("bind");
51        close(s_fd);
52        return(-1);
53    }
54
55    listen(s_fd, MAX_NCLIENTS);
```

Listing 10.6.36: Code skeleton for server with pthreads (2): accept, create thread and read

```
1    unsigned int sin_size = sizeof(struct sockaddr_in);
2
3    while (1) {
4        // accept on new client socket newfd
5        int newfd = accept(s_fd, (struct sockaddr *)&their_addr, &sin_size);
6        if (newfd == -1) {
7            perror("accept");
8        } else {
9            // Create new thread
10            pthread_create(&tid, &attr, client_handler, (void*)newfd);
11        }
12    } // while()
13    return 0;
14  }
15
16  void * client_handler(void* fdp) {
17    /* handle client request */
18    int c_fd = (int) fdp;
19    char clientline[MAX_NCHARS]="";
20    char tmpchar;
21    char newline = '\n';
22    int eob = 0;
23
24    while(eob==0 && strlen(clientline)<MAX_NCHARS) {
25        read(c_fd,&tmpchar,1);
26        eob=(tmpchar==newline) ? 1 : 0;
27        strncat(clientline,&tmpchar,1);
28    }
29    printf("%s",clientline);
30
31    close(c_fd);
32    pthread_exit(0);
33  }
```

10.7 Summary

In this chapter, we have discussed why and how networking is implemented in the Linux kernel and provided an overview of the POSIX API for socket programming. We have provided examples of the most typical client and server functionality and discussed the different mechanisms a server can use to handle multiple clients.

10.8 Exercises and questions

10.8.1 Simple social networking

1. Implement a minimal Twitter-like TCP/IP client-server system.

- The client can send messages of 140 characters to one other client via a server.

- Each client has an 8-character name.

- Implement the server using select(), fork/exec, and pthreads.

2. Add additional features:
a) client discovery;
b) ability to send to multiple clients.

10.8.2 The Linux networking stack

1. Discuss the structure of the Linux networking stack and the structure and role of the socket buffer datastructure.
2. How does the Linux model differ from the OSI model?

10.8.3 The POSIX socket API

1. Why does Linux use a separate socket API for networking, instead of using the file API?
2. Sketch in pseudocode the timeline of the various socket library function calls required in a typical (simple) stream socket connection.
3. Which POSIX socket API calls are blocking and why?

References

[1] L. L. Peterson and B. S. Davie, *Computer networks: a systems approach*. Elsevier, 2007.

[2] A. S. Tanenbaum et al., "*Computer networks*, 4th edition," Prentice Hall, 2003.

[3] O. Bonaventure, *Computer Networking: Principles, Protocols, and Practice*. The Saylor Foundation, 2011.

[4] E. Jeong, S. Woo, M. A. Jamshed, H. Jeong, S. Ihm, D. Han, and K. Park, "mTCP: a highly scalable user-level TCP stack for multicore systems." in *NSDI*, vol. 14, 2014, pp. 489–502.

[5] S. Thongprasit, V. Visoottiviseth, and R. Takano, "Toward fast and scalable key-value stores based on user space TCP/IP stack," in *Proceedings of the Asian Internet Engineering Conference*. ACM, 2015, pp. 40–47.

[6] T. Barbette, C. Soldani, and L. Mathy, "Fast userspace packet processing," in *Proceedings of the Eleventh ACM/IEEE* Symposium on Architectures for networking and communications systems. IEEE Computer Society, 2015, pp. 5–16.

[7] K. Zheng, "Enabling 'protocol routing': Revisiting transport layer protocol design in internet communications," *IEEE Internet Computing*, vol. 21, no. 6, pp. 52–57, November 2017.

[8] H. Zimmermann, "OSI reference model–the ISO model of architecture for open systems interconnection," *IEEE Transactions on communications*, vol. 28, no. 4, pp. 425–432, 1980.

Chapter 11

Advanced topics

11.1 Overview

So far in this textbook, we have presented standard concepts for current mainstream OS distributions, with particular reference to Linux. This final chapter will outline more advanced trends and features: many of these are not yet reflected in contemporary OS code bases; however, they may be integrated within the next decade. Rather than presenting concrete details, this chapter will provide pointers and search keywords to facilitate further investigation.

What you will learn
After you have studied the material in this chapter, you will be able to:

1. Give examples of different classes of systems on which Linux is deployed.

2. Explain how the characteristics of diverse systems lead to various trade-offs in OS construction and configuration.

3. Justify the requirement for lightweight, rapid deployments of specialized systems, particularly in the cloud.

4. Illustrate security vulnerabilities and mitigations in modern manycore systems, particularly with respect to speculative execution.

5. Assess the need for formal verification of OS components in various target scenarios.

6. Appreciate the community-based approach to developing new features in the Linux kernel.

11.2 Scaling down

The computer on which Torvalds initially developed Linux in 1991 was a 32-bit 386 processor clocked at 33MHz, with 4MB of RAM. Thanks to Moore's law, present-day smartphones and wearable devices are much more powerful than this original Linux machine. Many such small-scale consumer devices run variants of Linux such as Android, Tizen, or Chrome OS, see Figure 11.1. The compelling advantage of Linux is that it provides a highly customizable, off-the-shelf, core OS platform, enabling rapid time-to-market for consumer electronics. These modern Linux variants are specialized to enable fast boot times on specialized, proprietary hardware. They often restrict execution to a controlled set of trusted vendor-supplied apps.

The motivation is radically different for Raspberry Pi and other single board computers, which are intended to be as flexible and general-purpose as possible. These devices will support the broad flexibility of Linux kernel configurations, with a vast range of optional hardware device support. Generally, single board computers track smartphone hardware in terms of features and capabilities, since they are often based around similar chipsets and peripherals.

Smaller, less capable, embedded devices include internet-of-things (IoT) sensors or network edge devices. These nodes have minimal RAM and persistent storage, and may only have access to low bandwidth, intermittent network connections. Generally, such devices are targeted with specialized

Linux distributions. One example is Alpine Linux, which has a minimal installation footprint of around 100MB. Reduced runtime memory requirements are supported by a specialized C library, such as musl, and monolithic executables that provide a range of Unix utilities, e.g., busybox.

Figure 11.1: Chromebook running a Linux variant on an Arm chipset. Photo by author.

There is a logical progression in this trend to consolidate OS kernel, libraries, and application into a single monolithic image. If the user knows ahead-of-time the precise system use-cases, then it is feasible to eliminate large portions of the OS and libraries from the build, since they will never be required. This is the *unikernel* concept, exemplified by MirageOS, which performs aggressive specialization and dead code elimination to produce slim binaries for deployment.

11.3 Scaling up

Linux is the default OS for supercomputers. Since 2017, all machines in the TOP500 list of most powerful supercomputers in the world run Linux.

Generally, high-performance computing tasks are handled via a parallel framework such as MPI (see Section 7.6.3). Work is divided into small units to execute on the various nodes. Each shared-memory node runs Linux individually, so a supercomputer may have tens of thousands of Linux kernels running concurrently. The Archer facility at the Edinburgh Parallel Computing Centre, see Figure 11.2, incorporates 4920 nodes.

Similarly, large-scale cloud datacenters may have hundreds of thousands of nodes, each running a Linux image with higher-level control software, such as OpenStack, to enable effective resource management. This is warehouse-scale computing, a phrase appropriately coined by Google engineers [1].

Figure 11.2: Archer high-performance computing facility. Photo by Edinburgh Parallel Computing Centre.

Rack-scale systems feature tens of nodes, with hundreds of cores. Large data processing tasks are scheduled on such systems and may require inter-node cooperation, e.g., for distributed garbage collection. This inter-node synchronization of activities is effectively a meta-level OS [2].

As system architectures become larger and more complex, and the distinction between on-node and off-node memory is increasingly blurred, there is a trend towards multi-node, distributed OS designs.

The Barrelfish experimental OS is a multikernel system. Each CPU core runs a small, single-core kernel, and the OS is organized as a distributed system of message-passing processes on top of these kernels. Processes are location agnostic, since inter-process communication may be with local or remote cores. From a programmer perspective, there is no distinction.

A related project is Plan 9 from Bell Labs, a distributed operating system that maintains the 'everything is a file' abstraction. Its developers include some of the original designers of Unix. The key novelties are a per-process namespace (individual view of the shared network file system) and a message-based file system protocol for all communication. Eric Raymond summarizes the elegance of Plan 9 and the reasons for its minimal adoption [3]. Note there is a Plan 9 OS image available for installation on the Raspberry Pi.

The growth of heterogeneous computing means many machines have special-purpose accelerators such as GPUs, encryption units, or dedicated machine learning processors. These resources should be under the control of the OS, which mediates access by users and processes. This is particularly important for utility computing contexts, where many tenants are sharing an underlying physical resource.

In addition to supporting scaled up computing on large machines, the next-generation OS also needs to handle scaled-up storage. Traditional Linux file systems like ext4 do not scale well to massive and distributed contexts, due to the metadata updates and consistency that are required. Parallel frameworks often layer custom distributed file systems on top of per-node file systems, for instance, HDFS for Hadoop.

Global-scale distributed data systems are often key-value stores, such as etcd or mongodb, which feature replication and eventual consistency to mitigate latencies in wide area networks. Object stores, such as Minio and Ceph, allow binary blobs to be stored at known locations (perhaps web addresses) with associated access controls and other metadata.

11.4 Virtualization and containerization

Utility computing implies general compute resource is situated in the cloud. Users simply rent CPU time on virtual servers they can provision on-demand.

Virtualization enables multiple virtual machines (VMs) to be hosted and isolated from each other on a single physical node. The hypervisor layer multiplexes guest VMs on top of the host machine. Figure 11.3 presents the concepts of virtualization as a schematic diagram. This approach is crucial for infrastructure service providers to support flexible deployment and resource overprovisioning. It is possible to migrate a VM to another physical node if service levels are not sufficient. Modern processors have extensions to support virtualization natively. These include extra privilege levels and an additional layer of indirection in memory management. Linux supports hardware virtualization with the Kernel-based Virtual Machine (KVM), which acts as a hypervisor layer. Virtual machine software that runs on top of KVM includes the QEMU full system emulator. This allows a distinct guest OS, possibly compiled for a different processor architecture, to execute on top of the Linux host OS.

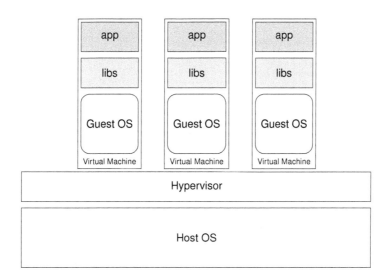

Figure 11.3: Schematic diagram for virtualization, showing that an app actually runs on top of two kernels (in guest and host OS respectively).

There is an alternative approach: unlike fully-fledged virtualization where each VM runs a distinct guest OS, Linux containers enable lightweight isolation of processes that share a common host OS kernel. While containers lack the flexibility of heavyweight virtualization, they are potentially much more efficient. For this reason, containerization is popular for use cases requiring rapid deployment times such as DevOps, cloud systems, and serverless computing. A user wants to spin up a relevant application service with minimal latency. Tools like Docker enable services to be specified and composed declaratively as scripts, then prebuilt images can match these scripts. This avoids lengthy configuration and build times, enabling services to come up quickly.

Linux kernel facilities such as control groups (cgroups) enable containerization. Key concepts are namespace isolation and resource limiting. Sets of processes can be collected together into a cgroup and controlled as a unit. The bash listing below illustrates how to exercise this control, and Figure 11.4 shows the outcome on a typical quad-core Raspberry Pi node.

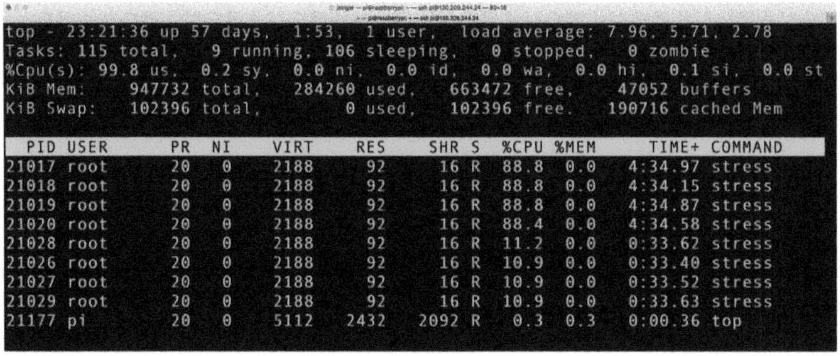

Figure 11.4: CPU usage from top command, showing how Linux distributes CPU resource based on cgroups configuration.

```
Listing 11.4.1: Using cgroups to limit CPU resource                                    Bash

1    sudo apt-get install stress       # tool for CPU stress-testing
2    sudo apt-get install cgroup-tools # utils for cgroups
3    sudo cgcreate -g cpu:morecpu
4    sudo cgcreate -g cpu:lesscpu
5    cgget -r cpu.shares morecpu        # default is 1024
6    sudo cgset -r cpu.shares=128 lesscpu  # limit CPU usage
7    # now run some stress code in different control groups
8    sudo cgexec -g cpu:lesscpu stress --cpu 4 &
9    sudo cgexec -g cpu:morecpu stress --cpu 4 &
10   top # to see the CPU usage
11   sudo killall stress # to stop the stress jobs
```

Process sandboxes support throw-away execution. Processes may be run once; then, their side-effects may be isolated and discarded. In this sense, Linux containers are a progression of earlier Unix chroot and BSD jail concepts. User-friendly configuration tools like Docker have massively popularized containerization.

The growth in the utility computing market requires greater levels of resource awareness in the underlying system. In particular, the OS needs to support three key activities:

1. **Predicting**: The OS must estimate ahead-of-time how long user tasks will take to complete and which resources they will need. This is useful for efficient scheduling.

2. **Accounting**: The OS must keep track of precisely which resources are used by each application. This depends on low-level tools like perf, alongside higher-level application-specific metrics such as a number of database queries. This is essential for billing users accurately for their workloads.

3. **Constraining**: The OS must allow certain sets of actions for each application. Similar to sandboxing, there are constraints on the application behavior. Often the constraints are expressed as a blacklist of disallowed actions; this is generally how smartphone apps are executed. On the other hand, the constraints could be expressed as a whitelist of allowable actions; this might be supported by a capability-based system. CPU usage constraints, as outlined above, rely on quantitative thresholds that must be enforced by the kernel.

11.5 Security

In this section, we discuss two recently discovered types of exploits that make use of flaws in the hardware to compromise the system. Appreciating these exploits requires knowledge of hardware architecture (DRAM, cache, TLB, MMU, DMA), the memory subsystem, memory organization (paging), and memory protection. Therefore studying these exploits is a very good way to assess your understanding of concepts covered in the book.

Figure 11.5: Logos for the Rampage exploit and Guardion mitigation.

11.5.1 Rowhammer, Rampage, Throwhammer, and Nethammer

The original Rowhammer exploit makes use of a vulnerability in modern DRAM, in particular, DDR3 and DDR4 SDRAM. Essentially, in such DRAMs, there is a non-zero probability of flipping a bit in a given row by alternated accesses to the adjacent rows [4]. The actual exploit uses this flaw by causing permission bits to be flipped in a page table entry (PTE) that causes the PTE to point to a physical page containing a page table of the attacking process. That process thereby gets read-write access to one of its own page tables, and hence to the entire physical memory. A very good explanation is given in the original blog post by Mark Seaborn. You can also test if your own computer is vulnerable.

Several variants of this exploit have been developed: Rowhammer.js which uses https://github.com/IAIK/rowhammerjs [5], Rampage, which uses the Android DMA buffer management API to induce the bit flips [6], and building on this https://vusec.net/projects/throwhammer, which exploits remote direct memory access (RDMA) [7] and Nethammer [8], which uses only a specially crafted packet stream. Neither of these exploits requires the attacker to run code on the target machine. All of the cited papers also discuss mitigation strategies against the exploits.

The DRAM on the Raspberry Pi board is DDR2, which is generally not vulnerable to Rowhammer-type exploits.

11.5.2 Spectre, Meltdown, Foreshadow

A modern OS has memory protection mechanisms which stop a process from accessing data belonging to another user, and also stop user processes from accessing kernel memory. Speculative execution attacks exploit the fact that a CPU will already start accessing data before it knows if it is allowed to, i.e., while the memory protection check is in progress. In theory, this is permissible because the results of this speculative execution should be protected at the hardware level. If a process does not have the right privilege, it is not allowed to access this data, and the data is discarded.

However, the protected data is stored in the cache regardless of the privilege of the process. Cache memory can be accessed more quickly than regular memory. The attacker process can try to access memory locations to test if the data there has been cached, by timing the access. This is known as a side-channel attack. Both Spectre and Meltdown, and also the more recent Foreshadow exploit, work by combining speculative execution and a cache side-channel attack.

Meltdown [9] gives a user process read access to kernel memory. The mitigation in Linux is a fundamental change to how memory is managed: as explained in Chapter 6, Linux normally maps kernel memory into a portion of the user address space for each process. On systems vulnerable to the Meltdown exploit, this allows the attacker process to read from the kernel memory. The solution is called kernel page-table isolation (KPTI).

Spectre [10] is a more complex exploit, harder to execute, but also harder to mitigate against. There are two variants: one ("bounds-check bypass", CVE-2017-5753) depends on the existence of a vulnerable code sequence that is conveniently accessible from user space; the other ("branch target injection", CVE-2017-5715) depends on poisoning the processor's branch-prediction mechanism so that indirect jumps will under speculative execution be redirected to an attacker-chosen location. The mitigation strategies are discussed in a post on LWN.

Finally, Foreshadow [11] (or L1 Terminal Fault) is the name for three speculative execution vulnerabilities that affect Intel processors. Foreshadow exploits a vulnerability in Intel's SGX (Software Guard Extensions) technology. SGX creates a 'secure enclave' in which users can provide secure software code that will run without being observed by even the operating system. SGX protects Meltdown and Spectre; however, Foreshadow manages to circumvent this protection. A good explanation of the exploit is given by Jon Masters, chief ARM architect at Red Hat.

The Arm processor on the Raspberry Pi board is not susceptible to these speculative execution attacks as it does not perform speculative execution.

Figure 11.6: Logos for the Meltdown and Spectre exploits—it seems that eye-catching graphics are compulsory for OS security violations.

11.6 Verification and certification

Formal verification techniques use mathematical models and proofs to provide guarantees about the properties and behavior of systems. This is essential as software grows in size and complexity, and as it becomes the essential foundation of our everyday societal interactions. Many industrial sectors are establishing certified requirements for software to be verified formally, e.g., ISO 26262 for automotive vehicles and DO-178C for aerospace. Since the OS is a critical part of the software stack, it will become increasingly necessary to apply verification techniques to sets of OS components.

Microsoft pioneered verified components for the Windows OS with its device driver verification program. Poor quality, third-party device drivers running in privileged mode can compromise kernel data structures and invariants, often resulting in the 'blue screen of death,' see Figure 11.7. This is the Windows equivalent of the Unix kernel panic. At one point, bugs in device drivers caused 85% of system crashes in Windows XP. [12]

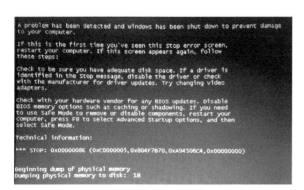

Figure 11.7: Blue screen of death in Windows XP (left) and Windows 10 (right) — since the driver verification program, such blue screens are much less common. Photo by author.

The SLAM project blends ideas from static analysis, model checking, and theorem proving [13]. The key tool is the Static Driver Verifier (SDV) which analyzes C source code, typically a device driver implementation comprising thousands of lines of code, to check it respects a set of hard-coded rules that encapsulate legal interactions with the Windows kernel.

The SDV simplifies input C code by converting it to an abstract boolean program, retaining the original control flow but encoding all relevant program state as boolean variables. This abstract program is executed symbolically to identify and report kernel API rule violations. An example rule specifies that locks should be acquired then subsequently released in strict sequence. The collection of pre-packaged API rules is harvested from previously identified error reports and Windows driver documentation. Empirical evidence shows the SDV approach has significantly reduced bugs in Windows device drivers.

When modern OS software is built-in high-level languages such as C# and Rust, it is feasible to perform static analysis directly on the source code, to provide guarantees about memory safety and data race freedom, for instance. Such guarantees may be composed to generate high-level OS safety properties.

The seL4 project is a fully verified microkernel system [14]. The OS consists of small independent components with clearly defined communication channels. Minimal functionality is provided in verified microkernel, which is implemented in 10K lines of code, mostly C with some assembler. Properties include access control guarantees, memory safety, and system call termination. Generally, there is proof that the C source code matches the high-level abstract specification of the system. These kinds of proofs are extremely expensive, in terms of expert human effort, to construct.

Certification involves mechanisms to guarantee the integrity of executable code. Cryptographic hashes, such as MD5 and SHA1, are used to check a file has not been modified. For instance, when you download a Raspbian SD card image from the Raspberry Pi website or a mirror, it is possible to check the published SHA-256 hash of the file to guarantee its authenticity, see Figure 11.8.

Figure 11.8: OS image hash is published alongside the download link to ensure authenticity.

A signed executable ensures provenance as well as integrity. Using public key infrastructure, a code distributor can sign the executable file or a hash of the file with their private key. A potential user can check the signature and the hash, to be sure the code is from an appropriate source and has not been modified. Linux utilities like elfsign or the Integrity Measurement Architecture support digital signatures for executable files. Hardware support, such as Arm TrustZone, is required for secure code certification. In particular, it is necessary to check the firmware and boot loader to ensure that only certified code is able to run on the system.

Reproducibility is a key goal in modern systems. This is important for scientific experiments, for debugging, for ensuring compatibility in a highly eclectic system of software components. Declarative scripting languages, like those provided by Nix or Puppet, enable systems to be configured easily to a common standard. This is ideal for DevOps scenarios. The Nix package manager keeps track of all data and code dependencies required to build each executable, via a cryptographic hash. This is encoded directly in the path for the executable, e.g. `/nix/store/a9i0a06gcs8w9fj9nghsl0b6vvqpzpi4-bash-4.4-p23` which means multiple versions of an application can co-exist in the same system, and be managed easily with configurable profiles. System administrators never need to 'overwrite' an old application or library when they upgrade to a new version, which makes compatibility and rollback much easier.

Listing 11.6.1: Example nix docker session *Bash*

```
1   # check out https://nixos.org/nix/manual/
2   # for more details
3   docker pull nixos/nix
4   docker run -it nixos/nix
5   nix-env -qa
6   nix-build '<nixpkgs>' -A hello
7   nix-shell '<nixpkgs>' -A hello
8   ./result/bin/hello
9   ls -l ./result
```

11.7 Reconfigurability

As computing platforms become more flexible, incorporating technology such as FPGA accelerators, the OS must support on-the-fly reconfiguration. Similarly, in cloud computing contexts, the resources available to a VM may change as the guest OS is migrated to different virtual servers with a range of hardware options. Even a commodity CPU on a laptop can be configured to operate at different clock frequencies, trading off compute performance and power consumption.

Presently, Linux supports dynamic reconfiguration with a range of heuristic policies for particular resources. For instance, there is a CPU frequency governor that controls processor clock frequency depending on current resource usage. Various research projects have explored the potential for machine learning to enable automatic runtime tuning of OS parameters. To date, there is no machine learning component embedded in a mainstream OS kernel. Self-tuning systems based on machine learning may arrive soon, although they would not be compliant with current domain-specific certification, e.g., in the automotive or aerospace sectors.

There is an accelerating trend to move OS components into user space. We introduced the notion of a file system in user space (FUSE) in Chapter 9. Networking in user space is also supported, with frameworks like the Data Plane Development Kit (DPDK) that support accelerated, customized packet processing in user application code. This flexibility enables techniques like software-defined networking and network function virtualization. Effectively, the network stack can be reconfigured at runtime in software.

In theory, as the Linux kernel transfers these traditional OS responsibilities to user space code, its architecture increasingly resembles a micro-kernel OS. The historical criticism of Linux was that it was too monolithic to scale and survive, see Figure 11.9. Torvalds addressed these criticisms directly at the time, and reflected on his design principles at a later date [15].

Subject: LINUX is obsolete
MINIX is a microkernel-based system.
The file system and memory management
are separate processes, running outside
the kernel. The I/O drivers are also
separate processes (in the kernel, but
only because the brain-dead nature of
the Intel CPUs makes that difficult to
do otherwise). LINUX is a monolithic
style system. This is a giant step back
into the 1970s. That is like taking an
existing, working C program and rewriting
it in BASIC. To me, writing a monolithic
system in 1991 is a truly poor idea.
Tanenbaum's criticism of the Linux architecture on Usenet (29 Jan 1992)

Andrew Tanenbaum

>1. MICROKERNEL VS MONOLITHIC SYSTEM
True, linux is monolithic, and I agree
that microkernels are nicer. With a less
argumentative subject, I'd probably have
agreed with most of what you said. From
a theoretical (and aesthetical) standpoint
linux loses [sic].
>MINIX is a microkernel-based system.
>[deleted, but not so that
>you miss the point]
>LINUX is a monolithic style system.
If this was the only criterion for
the "goodness" of a kernel, you'd be
right...
Excerpt of Torvalds' response on Usenet (29 Jan 1992)

Linus Torvalds

Figure 11.9: Part of the famous 'Linux is obsolete' debate focused on its non-microkernel architecture. Cartoons by Lovisa Sundin.

11.8 Linux development roadmap

There is no formal roadmap for Linux kernel development. There are a number of release candidates with experimental features, some of which will be incorporated in future stable releases.

Check https://kernel.org for the latest details. The Linux Weekly News service keeps track of ongoing changes to the kernel, see https://lwn.net/Kernel/

11.9 Further reading

Throughout this chapter, we have given a flavor of contemporary trends in OS development and deployment. Some of these issues have an immediate impact on Linux; others may affect the platform over the next decade.

The annual workshop on Hot Topics in Operating Systems (HotOS) is an excellent venue for OS future studies and speculation. If you are interested in OS research and development, consult recent years' proceedings of this event, which should be available online.

11.10 Exercises and questions

11.10.1 Make a minimal kernel
Configure and build a custom Linux kernel for your Raspberry Pi. How small a kernel image can you create?

11.10.2 Verify important properties
Verified software systems provide formal guarantees about their properties and behavior. Suggest some properties you might want to prove about components of an OS.

11.10.3 Commercial comparison
Much of the popularity of Linux could be attributed to the fact it is free, open-source, software (FOSS). Compare Linux with a mainstream OS that is not FOSS. Can you identify differences, and explain why they might occur? Is there a different emphasis on developing new features?

11.10.4 For or against certification
Software certification has a number of advantages and disadvantages, which must be carefully assessed. Draw up a debate card, listing the pros and cons of OS certification. This could form the basis for a group discussion with your peers.

11.10.5 Devolved decisions
The modern Linux kernel abdicates responsibility for certain policies to user space, e.g., for file systems (with FUSE) and networking (with DPDK). Discuss other services that might be transferred from the kernel to user space. System logging is one candidate.

11.10.6 Underclock, overclock
It is possible to modify the configuration of your Raspberry Pi board to change the CPU clock frequency. Find the line specifying arm_freq = 1200 in your /boot/config.txt and modify this. The frequency is specified as an integer, denoting MHz. There are other frequencies you can change, such as those for GPU and memory. Check online documentation for details, and note that some settings may void your warranty.

You can investigate how frequency and power trade-off, by monitoring your Raspberry Pi power consumption when you run CPU-intensive applications (perhaps the stress utility). You will need to use an external USB digital multimeter or power monitor. Produce a graph to show the relationship between frequency in MHz and power in W.

References

[1] L. A. Barroso, U. Hölzle, and P. Ranganathan, *The Datacenter as a Computer: Designing Warehouse-Scale Machines*, 3rd ed. Morgan Claypool, 2018.

[2] M. Maas, K. Asanovic′, T. Harris, and J. Kubiatowicz, "Taurus: A holistic language runtime system for coordinating distributed managed-language applications," in *Proceedings of the Twenty-First International Conference on Architectural Support for Programming Languages and Operating Systems*, 2016, pp. 457–471.

[3] E. S. Raymond, *Plan 9: The Way the Future Was*. Addison Wesley, 2003, http://catb.org/~esr/writings/taoup/html/plan9.html

[4] Y. Kim, R. Daly, J. Kim, C. Fallin, J. H. Lee, D. Lee, C. Wilkerson, K. Lai, and O. Mutlu, "Flipping bits in memory without accessing them: An experimental study of DRAM disturbance errors," in *ACM SIGARCH Computer Architecture News*, vol. 42, no. 3, 2014, pp. 361–372.

[5] D. Gruss, C. Maurice, and S. Mangard, "Rowhammer.js: A remote software-induced fault attack in Javascript," in *International Conference on Detection of Intrusions and Malware, and Vulnerability Assessment*. Springer, 2016, pp. 300–321.

[6] V. Van Der Veen, Y. Fratantonio, M. Lindorfer, D. Gruss, C. Maurice, G. Vigna, H. Bos, K. Razavi, and C. Giuffrida, "Drammer: Deterministic Rowhammer attacks on mobile platforms," in *Proceedings of the 2016 ACM SIGSAC conference on computer and communications security*, 2016, pp. 1675–1689.

[7] A. Tatar, R. Krishnan, E. Athanasopoulos, C. Giuffrida, H. Bos, and K. Razavi, "Throwhammer: Rowhammer attacks over the network and defenses," in *2018 USENIX Annual Technical Conference*, 2018.

[8] M. Lipp, M. T. Aga, M. Schwarz, D. Gruss, C. Maurice, L. Raab, and L. Lamster, "Nethammer: Inducing Rowhammer faults through network requests," *arXiv preprint arXiv:1805.04956*, 2018.

[9] M. Lipp, M. Schwarz, D. Gruss, T. Prescher, W. Haas, A. Fogh, J. Horn, S. Mangard, P. Kocher, D. Genkin et al., "Meltdown: Reading kernel memory from user space," in *27th USENIX Security Symposium*, 2018, pp. 973–990.

[10] P.Kocher, D.Genkin, D.Gruss, W.Haas, M.Hamburg, M.Lipp, S.Mangard, T.Prescher, M.Schwarz, and Y. Yarom, "Spectre attacks: Exploiting speculative execution," *arXiv preprint arXiv:1801.01203*, 2018.

[11] J.VanBulck, M.Minkin, O.Weisse, D.Genkin, B.Kasikci, F.Piessens, M.Silberstein, T.F.Wenisch, Y. Yarom, and R. Strackx, "Foreshadow: Extracting the keys to the Intel SGX kingdom with transient out-of-order execution," in *27th USENIX Security Symposium*, 2018, pp. 991–1008.

[12] T.Ball, E.Bounimova, B.Cook, V.Levin, J.Lichtenberg, C.McGarvey, B.Ondrusek, S.K.Rajamani, and A. Ustuner, "Thorough static analysis of device drivers," *ACM SIGOPS Operating Systems Review*, vol. 40, no. 4, pp. 73–85, 2006.

[13] T.Ball, B.Cook, V.Levin, and S.K.Rajamani, "SLAM and Static Driver Verifier: Technology transfer of formal methods inside Microsoft," Tech. Rep. MSR-TR-2004-08, 2004, https://www.microsoft.com/en-us/research/wp-content/uploads/2016/02/tr-2004-08.pdf

[14] G.Klein, J.Andronick, K.Elphinstone, G.Heiser, D.Cock, P.Derrin, D.Elkaduwe, K.Engelhardt, R.Kolanski, M. Norrish, T. Sewell, H. Tuch, and S. Winwood, "seL4: Formal verification of an operating-system kernel," *Communications of the ACM*, vol. 53, no. 6, pp. 107–115, Jun. 2010.

[15] L. Torvalds, *The Linux Edge*. O'Reilly, 1999, http://www.oreilly.com/openbook/opensources/book/linus.html

Glossary of terms

Address space	A set of discrete *memory addresses*. The physical address space is the set of all of the memory in a computer system, including the system memory (*DRAM*) as well as the I/O devices and other *peripherals* such as disks.
Application binary interface (ABI)	The specifications to which an executable must conform in order to execute in a specific execution environment.
Arithmetic logic unit (ALU)	The part of a processor that performs computations.
Assembly language	A low-level programming language with a very strong correspondence between the program's statements and the architecture's machine code instructions, used as a target by compilers for higher-level languages.
Atomic operation	An operation which is guaranteed to be isolated from interrupts, signals, concurrent processes, and threads.
Booting	The process of starting up a computer system and putting it in a state so that it can be used.
Cache	A small but fast memory used to limit the time spent by the CPU in waiting for main memory access. For every memory read operation, first the processor checks if the data is present in the cache, and if so (*cache hit*) it uses that data rather than accessing the DRAM. Otherwise (*cache miss*) it will fetch the data from memory and store it in the cache.
Cache coherency	In a multicore computer system with multiple caches, cache coherency (or cache coherence or) is the mechanism that ensures that changes in data are propagated throughout the memory system in a timely fashion so that all the caches of a resource have the same data.
Clock tick	Informal synonym for _clock cycle_, the time between two consecutive rising (positive) edges of the system clock signal.
Complex instruction set computing (CISC)	A CPU with a large set of complex and specialized instructions rather a small set of simple and general instructions. The typical example is the x86 architecture.
Concurrency	The fact that more than one task is running concurrently (at the same time) on the system. In other words, concurrency is a property of the workload rather than the system, provided that the system has support for running more than one task at the same time. In practice, one of the key reasons to have an OS is to support concurrency through scheduling of tasks on a single shared CPU.

Critical section	A section of a program which cannot be executed by more than one process or thread at the same time. Critical sections typically access a shared resource and require synchronization primitives such as mutual exclusion locks to function correctly.
Deadlock	The state in which each process in a group of communicating process is waiting for a message from the other process in order to proceed with an action. Alternatively, in a group of processes with shared resources, there will be deadlock if each process is waiting for another process to release the resource that it needs to proceed with the action.
Direct memory access (DMA)	A mechanism that allows peripherals to transfer data directly into the main memory without going through the processor registers. In Arm systems, the DMA controller unit is typically a *peripheral*.
DRAM	Dynamic random-access memory, high-density memory, slower than SRAM. It is typically used as the main memory in a computer system. A DRAM cell is typically a small capacitor. As the charge leaks, it needs to be periodically refreshed.
Endianness	The sequential order in which bytes are arranged into words when stored in memory or when transmitted over digital links. There are two incompatible formats in common use, called *big-endian* and *little-endian*. In big-endian format, the most significant byte (the byte containing the most significant bit) is stored at the lowest address. Little-endian format reverses this order.
Everything is a file	A key concept in Linux and other UNIX-like operating systems. It does not mean that all objects in Linux are files as defined above, but rather that Linux prefers to treat all objects from which the OS can read data or to which it can write data using a consistent interface. So it might be more accurate to say, "everything is a stream of bytes." Linux uses the concept of a file descriptor, an abstract handle used to access an input/output resource (of which a file is just one type). So one can also say that in Linux, "everything is a file descriptor."
File	A named set of related data that is presented to the user as a single, contiguous block of information, and that is kept in persistent storage.
File system	A system for the logical organization of data. The purpose of most file systems is to provide the file and directory (folder) abstractions. A file system not only allows to store information in the form of files organized in directories but also information about the permissions of usages for files and directories, as well as timestamp information. The information in a file system is typically organized as a hierarchical tree of directories, and the directory at the root of the tree is called the root directory.

Hypervisor	A program, firmware, or hardware system that creates and runs virtual machines.
Instruction	A computer program consists of a series of *instructions*. Each instruction determines how the processor interacts with the system through the address space.
Interrupt	A signal sent to the processor by hardware (*peripherals*) or software indicating an event that needs immediate attention. The action of sending the signal is called an *interrupt request* (IRQ).
Kernel	The program that is the core of an operating system, with complete control over everything in the system. It is usually one of the first programs loaded when booting the system (after the bootloader). It handles the rest of startup and initialization as well as requests for system services from other processes.
Memory	The hardware that stores information for immediate use in a computer, typically SRAM or DRAM.
Memory management unit (MMU)	A computer system hardware component which manages memory access control and memory address translation, in particular, the translation of virtual memory addresses to physical addresses.
Memory address	An unsigned integer value used as the identifier for a *word* of data stored in *memory*.
MIPS for the masses	The slogan of the original Arm design team, which aimed to create a cheap but powerful processor that would provide lots of processing power ("MIPS" means Millions of Instructions Per Second) for a price that everybody could afford.
Mnemonic	An abbreviation for an operation. Assembly language uses mnemonics to represent each low-level machine instruction or opcode, typically also each architectural register, flag, etc. Also the surname of the eponymous character in William Gibson's novella "Johnny Mnemonic" (1981).
MPI (Message passing interface)	An API specification designed for high-performance computing. It provides a distributed memory model for parallel programming. Its main targets have been clusters and multiprocessor machines, but recently also manycore system. The message passing model means that tasks do not share any memory. Instead, every task has its own private memory, and any communication between tasks is via the exchange of messages.

Mounting	The operation performed by the kernel to provide access to a file system. Mounting a file system attaches that file system to a directory (mount point) and makes it available to the system. The root file system is always mounted. Any other file system can be connected or disconnected from the root file system at any point in the directory tree.
Multitasking	The *concurrent* execution of multiple tasks (also known as processes) over a certain period of time.
Network interface controller (NIC)	Also known as a network interface card or network adapter, is a computer hardware component that connects a computer to a computer network.
Networking	The interaction of a computer system with other computer systems using an intermediate communication infrastructure.
Opcode	An opcode or *operation code* is the part of a machine language instruction that specifies the operation to be performed. Most instructions also specify the data to be processed in the form of operands.
OpenCL	An open standard for parallel computing on heterogeneous architectures.
OpenMP	A standard for shared-memory parallel programming. It is based on a set of compiler directives or pragmas, combined with a programming API to specify parallel regions, data scope, synchronization, etc.. OpenMP is a portable parallel programming approach, and the specification supports C, C++, and Fortran.
Operating system	An operating system (OS) is a dedicated program that manages the hardware and software resources of a computer system and provides common services for computer programs running on the system. Modern operating systems keep track of resource usage of tasks and use time-sharing to schedule tasks for efficient use of the system.
Parallelism	Parallel processing is a capability of a computer system.
Partition	A disk can be divided into partitions, which means that instead of presenting as a single blob of data, it presents as several different blobs. Partitions a are logical rather than physical, and the information about how the disk is partitioned is stored in a partition table.
Peripheral	A device connected to a computer, used to put information into and get information out of the computer. "The Peripheral" is also the name of a science fiction novel by William Gibson (2014).

Persistent storage	Also known as non-volatile storage is a type of storage that retains its data even if the device is powered off. Examples are solid-state drives (SSD), hard disks, and magnetic tapes.
Polling	The action of periodically checking the state of a peripheral.
POSIX	The *Portable Operating System Interface* (POSIX) is a family of IEEE standards aimed at maintaining compatibility between operating systems. POSIX defines the application programming interface (API) used by programs to interact with the operating system.
Preemption	The act of temporarily interrupting a task being carried out by a computer system (and in particular a process running on a CPU), without requiring the cooperation of that task, and with the intention of resuming the task at a later time. Preemption is a key feature of *preemptive multitasking*. The alternative approach where the cooperation of a task is needed is called *cooperative multitasking*.
Process	A process is a running program, i.e., the code for the program and all system resources it uses. The concept of a process is used for the separation of code and resources. With this definition, a process can consist of multiple *threads*.
Process control block (PCB)	Also called Task Control Block (TCB). The operating system kernel data structure, which contains the information needed to manage the scheduling of a particular process.
RAM	Random-access memory. Data stored in RAM can be read or written in almost the same amount of time irrespective of the physical location of data inside the memory. This as opposed to other direct-access data storage media such as hard disks, CDs, DVDs, and magnetic tapes.
Reduced instruction set computing (RISC)	A CPU with a small set of simple and general instructions, rather than a large set of complex and specialized instructions. Arm processors have a RISC architecture.
Register file	An array of words called *registers*, typically implemented as SRAM memory and part of the CPU.
Root user	In Linux and other Unix-like computer OSes, *root* is the conventional name of the user who has all rights or permissions (to all files and programs) in all modes (single- or multi-user). Alternative names include superuser and administrator. In Linux, the actual name of the account is not the determining factor.
Scheduling	The mechanism used by the operating system kernel to allocate CPU time to tasks.

SIMD (Single instruction multiple data)	A type of parallel computation where multiple processing elements perform the same operation on multiple data points simultaneously.
SRAM	Static random-access memory, lower-density memory, faster than DRAM. It is typically used for cache memory in a computer system. An SRAM cell is a latch, so it retains its value as long as the device is powered on, without the need for refreshing.
Symmetric multiprocessing (SMP)	An operational model for multicore computer systems where two or more identical cores are connected to a single, shared main memory, have full access to all input and output devices, and are controlled by a single operating system instance that treats all processors equally, reserving none for special purposes. Most modern multicore systems use an SMP architecture.
System clock	A counter of the time elapsed since some arbitrary starting date called the epoch. Linux and other POSIX-compliant systems encode system time as the number of seconds elapsed since the start of the Unix epoch at 1 January 1970 00.00.00 UT, with exceptions for leap seconds.
System state	The set of all information in a system that the system remembers between events or user interactions.
System-on-chip (SoC)	Also called system-on-a-chip, an IC (integrated circuit) that integrates all components of a computer system. These components typically include a CPU, memory, I/O ports, and secondary storage, combined on a single chip.
Task	A unit of execution or a unit of work on a computer system. The term is somewhat less strictly defined and usually relates to scheduling.
Thread	Multiple concurrent tasks executing within a single process are called threads of execution. The threads of a process share its resources. For a process with a single thread of execution, the terms task and process are often used interchangeably.
Timer	A specialized type of clock used for measuring specific time intervals.
Translation look-aside buffer (TLB)	A special type of cache which stores recent translations of virtual memory to physical memory. It is part of the *MMU*.
User	In general, a user is a person who utilizes a computer system. However, in the context of an operating system, the term *user* is used more broadly to identify the ownership of processes and resources. Therefore a user does not need to be a person.

Virtual machine   A program which emulates a computer system. Virtual machines are based on computer architectures and provide the functionality of a physical computer. Modern computer systems provide hardware support for deployment of Virtual Machines (virtualization) through *hypervisors*.

Word   A fixed-size, contiguous array of bits used by a given processor design. A word is a fixed-sized piece of data handled as a unit by the instruction set or the hardware of the processor. The number of bits in a word (also called word size, word width, or word length) is a key characteristic for any specific processor architecture. Typically, a word consists of a number of bytes (a sequence of 8 bits), which are stored either in *little-endian* or *big-endian* format (see *endianness*). The most common word sizes for modern processors are 64 and 32 bits, but processors with 8 or 16-bit word size are still used for embedded systems.

Index

Arm Education Media
Online Courses

Our online courses have been developed to help students learn about state-of-the-art technologies from the Arm partner ecosystem. Each online course contains 10-14 modules, and each module comprises lecture slides with notes, interactive quizzes, hands-on labs and lab solutions. The courses will give your students an understanding of Arm architecture and the principles of software and hardware system design on Arm-based platforms, skills essential for today's computer engineering workplace.

Available now:

 Efficient Embedded Systems Design and Programming

 Rapid Embedded Systems Design and Programming

 Digital Signal Processing

 Internet of Things

 Graphics and Mobile Gaming

 System-on-Chip Design

 Real-Time Operating Systems Design and Programming

 Advanced System-on-Chip Design

 Embedded Linux

 Mechatronics and Robotics

Contact: edumedia@arm.com

Introduction to System-on-Chip Design
Online Courses

The Internet of Things promises devices endowed with processing, memory, and communication capabilities. These processing nodes will be, in effect, simple Systems-on-Chips (SoCs). They will need to be inexpensive, and able to operate under stringent performance, power and area constraints.

The Introduction to System-on-Chip Design Online Course focuses on building SoCs around Arm Cortex-M0 processors, which are perfectly suited for IoT needs. Using FPGAs as prototyping platforms, this course explores a typical SoC development process: from creating high-level functional specifications to design, implementation, and testing on real FPGA hardware using standard hardware description and software programming languages.

Learning outcomes:

Knowledge and understanding of
- Arm Cortex-M processor architectures and Arm Cortex-M based SoCs
- Design of Arm Cortex-M based SoCs in a standard hardware description language
- Low-level software design for Arm Cortex-M based SoCs and high-level application development

Intellectual
- Ability to use and choose between different techniques for digital system design and capture
- Ability to evaluate implementation results (e.g., speed, area, power) and correlate them with the corresponding high-level design and capture

Practical
- Ability to use commercial tools to develop Arm Cortex-M based SoCs

Course Syllabus:

Prerequisites: Basics of hardware description language (Verilog or VHDL), Basic C, and assembly programming.

Modules
1. Introduction to Arm-based System-on-Chip Design
2. The Arm Cortex-M0 Processor Architecture: Part 1
3. The Arm Cortex-M0 Processor Architecture: Part 2
4. AMBA3 AHB-Lite Bus Architecture
5. AHB SRAM Memory Controller
6. AHB VGA Peripheral
7. AHB UART Peripheral
8. Timer, GPIO, and 7-Segment Peripherals
9. Interrupt Mechanisms
10. Programming an SoC Using C Language
11. Arm CMSIS and Software Drivers
12. Application Programming Interface and Final Application

Discover more at www.armedumedia.com

Arm Education Media
Books

The Arm Education books program aims to take learners from foundational knowledge and skills covered by its textbooks to expert-level mastery of Arm-based technologies through its reference books. Textbooks are suitable for classroom adoption in Electrical Engineering, Computer Engineering, and related areas. Reference books are suitable for graduate students, researchers, aspiring and practicing engineers.

Available now:

 Embedded Systems Fundamentals with Arm Cortex-M based Microcontrollers: A Practical Approach
By Dr. Alexander G. Dean
ISBN 978-1-911531-03-6

 Digital Signal Processing using Arm Cortex-M based Microcontrollers: Theory and Practice
By Cem Ünsalan, M. Erkin Yücel, H. Deniz Gürhan
ISBN 978-1-911531-16-6

 System-on-Chip Design with Arm® Cortex®-M Processors: Reference Book
By Joseph Yiu
ISBN 978-1-911531-18-0

Contact: edumedia@arm.com

CPSIA information can be obtained
at www.ICGtesting.com
Printed in the USA
LVHW061151201221
706707LV00001B/5